GRAMMAR for Writing

Building Writing and Grammar Skills for School and Life!

Grammar for Writing **helps students:**

- Meet national English language arts standards.
- Learn core skills and effective strategies through abundant guided practice.
- Apply conventions of writing to real-world tasks.
- Prepare for success on assessments and in life.

6th Grade

7th Grade

8th Grade

Sadlier

A Complete Writing and Grammar Program

Grammar for Writing is . . .

- research-based
- flexible
- standards-aligned
- practice-driven
- balanced
- focused on six writing traits

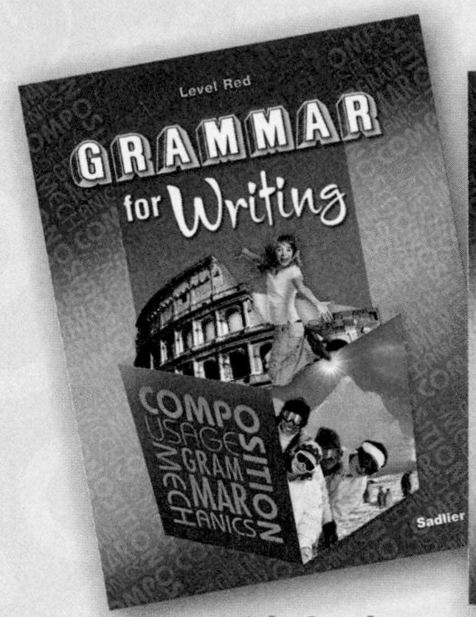

6th Grade

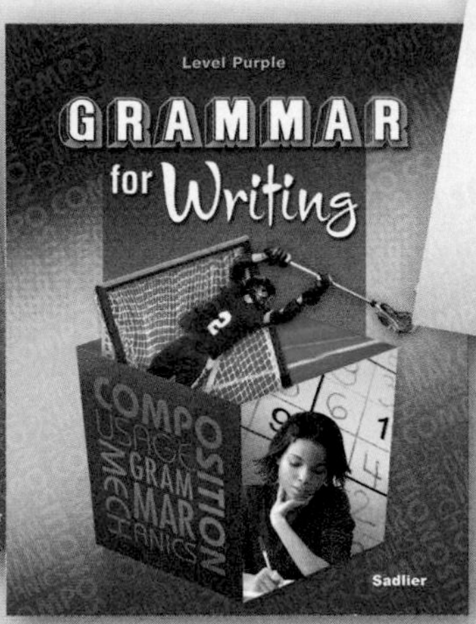

7th Grade

8th Grade

***Grammar for Writing* 6–8** includes everything middle school students need for a complete language arts curriculum.

The middle school levels of ***Grammar for Writing*** have been developed under the direction of Beverly Ann Chin, professor of English at the University of Montana and past president of the National Council of Teachers of English (NCTE). The series helps students write effectively in school, on standardized tests, and in everyday situations.

Grammar for Writing Grows with Students

The ***Grammar for Writing*** program increases in difficulty and sophistication from one grade to the next. Distinguishing features include the following:

6th Grade (Level Red)

- 60 lessons
- 272 pages
- Emphasis on descriptive and narrative writing
- Building blocks of grammar

7th Grade (Level Purple)

- 72 lessons
- 304 pages
- Emphasis on persuasive writing
- Additional grammar content

8th Grade (Level Yellow)

- 84 lessons
- 336 pages
- Emphasis on expository and persuasive writing and also literary analysis
- Advanced grammar content

- Longer and more challenging practice exercises and writing workshops as the grade levels progress
- More rigorous content and grammar conventions from grade to grade
- Increasing focus on persuasive writing from grade to grade
- Content-area connections in each grade, such as World History and Earth Science topics in Grade 6, U.S. History and Life Science topics in Grade 7, and U.S. History and Physical Science topics in Grade 8
- Consistent focus on the six writing traits
- Grade-appropriate literary models and an increasing number of nonfiction selections in the higher grades
- Available in softcover (consumable) and hardcover editions

Research says. . .

"Writing skill is a predictor of academic success and a basic requirement for participation in civic life and in the global economy."
Writing Next (October 2006)

"Eleven Elements of Effective Adolescent Writing Instruction

1. Writing strategies
2. Summarization
3. Collaborative writing
4. Specific writing goals
5. Word processing tips
6. Sentence combining
7. Prewriting
8. Inquiry activities
9. Process writing approach
10. Study of models
11. Writing for content learning"

Writing Next (October 2006)

"The National Commission on Writing (2003) has called for a National Writing Agenda that includes the recommendation that 'assessments of student writing must go beyond multiple-choice, machine-scorable items. Assessment should provide students with adequate time to write and should require students to actually create a piece of prose'" (p. 4).
***Research Notes (December 2007)* by The College Board (SAT publisher)**

"The ACT Writing Test is a 30-minute essay test. Students are given one writing prompt that defines an issue and describes two points of view on that issue. The student produces a direct writing sample that responds to the question about the student's position on the issue. The ACT Writing Test measures a student's ability to express judgments, maintain a focus, develop a position on a topic, organize ideas in a logical way, and use language clearly and effectively according to the rules of standard written English."
ACT National Curriculum Survey (2005–06)

"In 2002, 31% of eighth graders were at or above the proficient level."
***The Nation's Report Card: Writing 2007 (April 2007)* by the National Assessment of Educational Progress (NAEP)**

Grammar for Writing delivers. . .

- In the first half of the book, lessons dedicated to core writing topics and the Writing Process.
- Integrated writing workshops and applications that cover a variety of purposes, modes, and forms, including real-world writing.

- Chapters dedicated to writing strategies.
- Writing applications on summarizing and lessons on sentence combining.
- Working Together writing exercises and peer review activities.
- Writing workshops and applications with detailed writing goals.
- Tips for writing with computers.
- Chapters on the Writing Process and workshops that guide students through each stage of the writing process.
- Professional literary models with Reading as a Writer questions.
- Writing exercises on content-area topics.

- Writing applications on responding to writing prompts.
- "Write What You Think" exercises that encourage students to write a paragraph or essay.
- Chapter Reviews and *Test Book* assessments that require students to write short answer responses, such as short essays.

- Writing applications on taking essay tests.
- Writing workshops on persuasive writing.
- Chapters on writing effective essays.
- Lessons on developing and supporting a thesis statement.
- Chapter Reviews that alternate between the ACT and SAT test formats.

- Lessons on taking a position, developing arguments, organizing information, making transitions between ideas, and focusing on word choice—all the attributes of "skillful" responses in National Assessment of Educational Progress (NAEP) writing.

Aligns with Standards

Grammar for Writing teaches a core of the most widely taught standards. Lessons in the student edition derive from a detailed analysis of the language arts standards across the country, focusing on the core standards.

Chapter 1 The Writing Process

Lesson	Core Standards
1.1 Prewriting	✔ **Writing:** Uses a variety of prewriting strategies (e.g., makes outlines, uses published pieces as writing models, constructs critical standards, brainstorms, builds background)
1.2 Drafting	✔ **Writing:** Uses a variety of strategies to draft (e.g., uses an organizational scheme, uses sensory words and figurative language, thinks and writes for different audiences and purposes) ✔ **Writing:** Uses content, style, and structure (e.g., formal or informal language, genre, organization) appropriate for specific audiences (e.g., public, private) and purposes (e.g., to entertain, to persuade, to inform)
1.3 Revising	✔ **Writing:** Uses a variety of strategies to revise written work (e.g., analyzes and clarifies meaning, makes structural and syntactical changes, uses an organizational scheme, uses sensory words and figurative language, rethinks and rewrites for different audiences and purposes, checks for a consistent point of view and for transitions between paragraphs) ✔ **Writing:** Evaluates own and others' writing ✔ **Listening & Speaking:** Asks questions to seek elaboration and clarification of ideas
1.4 Editing and Proofreading	✔ **Writing:** Uses a variety of strategies to edit written work (e.g., eliminates slang; edits for grammar, punctuation, capitalization, and spelling at a developmentally appropriate level; proofreads using reference materials, word processor, and other resources; edits for clarity, word choice, and language usage) ✔ **GUMS:** Uses grammatical and mechanical conventions in written compositions

Source of Standards: Marzano, Robert & Kendall, John (2008). Content Knowledge: A Compendium of Standards and Benchmarks for K-12 Education, 4th ed. Denver, CO: McREL.
Online: www.mcrel.org/standards-benchmarks/

Chapter 1 The Writing Process

Lesson	Core Standards
1.5 Publishing and Presenting	✔ **Writing:** Uses a variety of strategies to publish written work (uses a word processor or other technology to publish written work) ✔ **Listening & Speaking:** Makes oral presentations to the class
Writer's Workshop: Description	✔ **Writing:** Uses the general skills and strategies of the writing process ✔ **Writing:** Uses descriptive language that clarifies and enhances ideas (e.g., establishes tone and mood, uses figurative language, uses sensory images and comparisons) ✔ **Reading:** Understands specific devices an author uses to accomplish his or her purpose (e.g., persuasive techniques, style, word choice, language structure) ✔ **GUMS:** Uses conventions of punctuation in written compositions (e.g., uses commas in a series)
Chapter Review	✔ **Test-taking:** Uses a variety of test-taking strategies

Chapter 7 Nouns and Pronouns

7.1 Nouns	✔ **GUMS:** Uses nouns in written compositions (e.g., forms possessives of nouns; forms irregular plural nouns)
7.2 Pronouns	✔ **GUMS:** Uses pronouns in written compositions (e.g., uses personal [i.e., possessive] pronouns)
7.3 Subject and Object Pronouns	✔ **GUMS:** Uses pronouns in written compositions (e.g., uses personal [i.e., subject, object] pronouns)
7.4 Pronoun Agreement	✔ **GUMS:** Uses pronouns in written compositions (e.g., uses pronouns that agree with their antecedents)
Writer's Workshop: How-to Essay	✔ **Writing:** Writes expository compositions (e.g., states a thesis or purpose; presents information that reflects knowledge about the topic of the report; organizes and presents information in a logical manner, including an introduction and conclusion; uses own words to develop ideas; uses common expository structures and features, such as compare–contrast or problem–solution) ✔ **Writing:** Uses the general skills and strategies of the writing process ✔ **Writing:** Uses explicit transitional devices ✔ **GUMS:** Uses pronouns in written compositions (e.g., uses pronouns that agree with their antecedents)
Chapter Review	✔ **Test-Taking:** Uses a variety of test-taking strategies

Examples from Grade 6 standards correlation charts

Ensures Mastery of Content

Skills are taught, assessed, and reinforced to ensure that students grasp and master the concepts introduced.

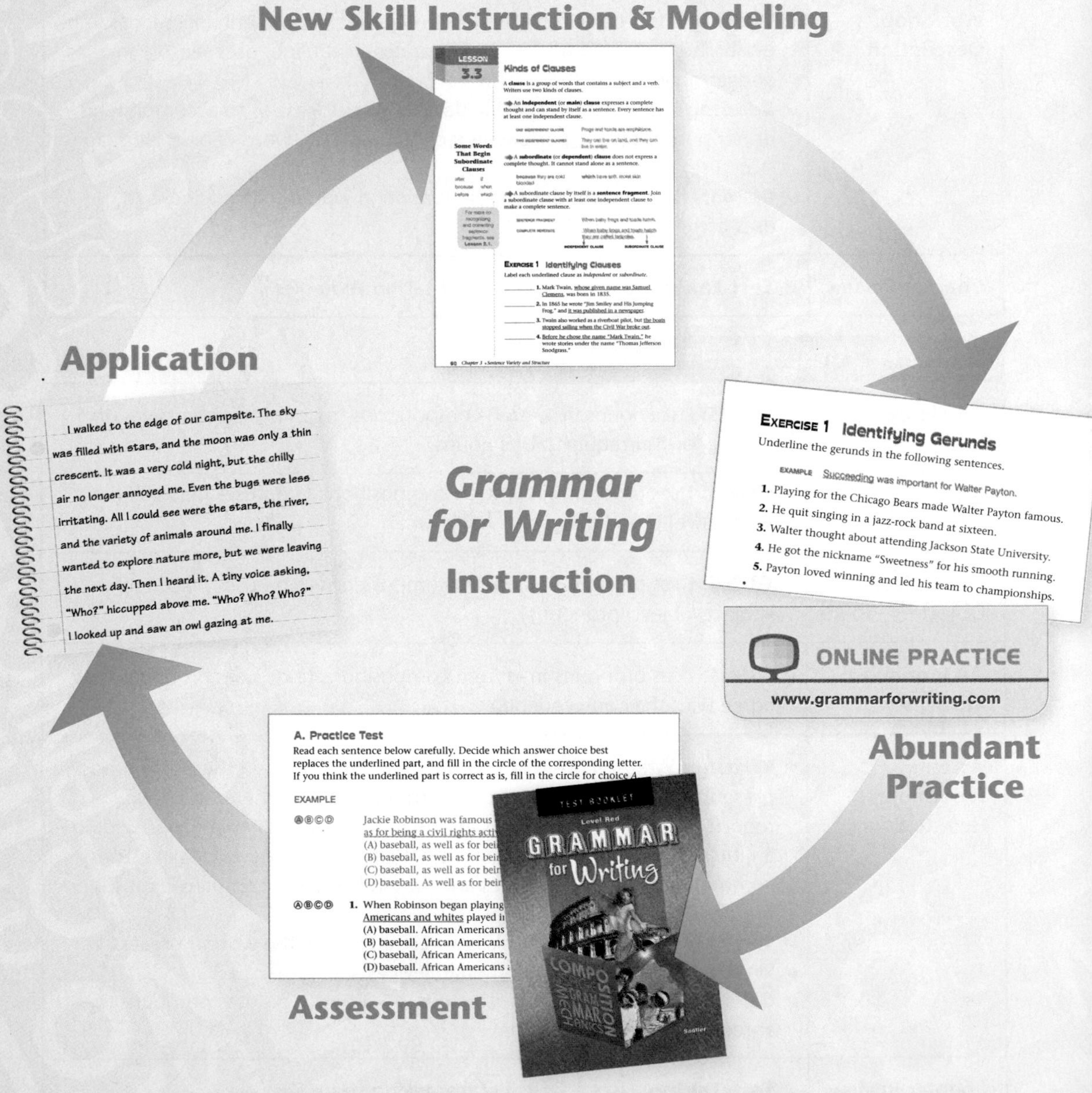

* The Test Booklet is available as an optional purchase.

Provides Flexible Curriculum Options

Grammar for Writing complements any language arts curriculum with succinct instruction that works in tandem with anthologies, reading programs, or class-assigned novels.

LESSON 10.2

Phrases Between Subject and Verb

In many sentences, **prepositional phrases** (P) come between, or interrupt, the subject (S) and verb (V).

S P V
The plants **in the garden** need water.

The subject of a sentence is never in a prepositional phrase. Make sure the verb agrees with the subject and not with the object of the preposition.

INCORRECT The **road** to the mountains **are** bumpy.

CORRECT The **road** to the mountains **is** bumpy. [The subject is *road*, not *mountains*, which is the object of the preposition *to*. *Road* is singular and needs a singular verb.]

INCORRECT The **classes** at the school **begins** at noon.

CORRECT The **classes** at the school **begin** at noon. [The subject is *classes*, not *school*, which is the object of the preposition *at*. *Classes* is plural and needs a plural verb.]

Remember

A prepositional phrase is a group of words that begins with a preposition. It ends with the object of the preposition, which is a noun or a pronoun.

PREPOSITION OBJECT
inside the **park**
near the **sand**

For more on prepositional phrases, see **Lesson 9.4**.

Exercise 1 Explaining Agreement

In each sentence below, cross out the prepositional phrase that comes between the subject and the verb. Then write a sentence that identifies the subject and explains the agreement.

EXAMPLE The wings ~~of a monarch butterfly~~ are orange and black.

The verb, <u>are</u>, is plural because the subject, <u>wings</u>, is plural.

1. The stages in a butterfly's life cycle look different.
2. The four stages of the cycle are egg, larva, pupa, and adult.
3. The eggs of a butterfly are round or oval.
4. A butterfly in the early stages is called a caterpillar.
5. The colors of a monarch butterfly are orange and black.
6. An adult of some species lives only about a month.
7. Insect lovers around the world collect moths and butterflies.

Chapter 10 • Subject-Verb Agreement **203**

From Grade 6 Student Edition, Chapter 10, page 203

Important terms are highlighted, defined, and applied in examples.

Differentiated Instruction

Grammar for Writing also provides lesson-by-lesson teacher support for English Learners and Striving Learners (see pages T42–T53).

Grammar for Writing meets individual classroom needs with flexible pacing, modeling, and plentiful exercises to fit whole-class instruction, focused minilessons, and reteaching opportunities.

Includes Abundant Practice

Each teaching lesson includes multiple exercises to build mastery of the skills. Exercises combine analysis and identification of key terms along with creative, authentic applications of the lesson concepts.

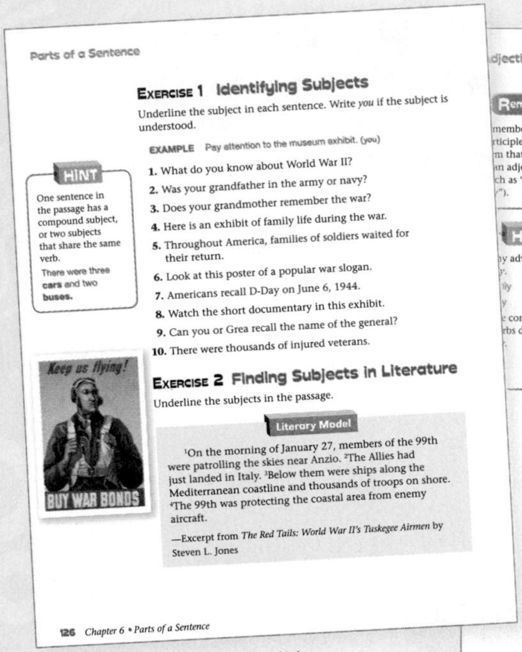

Parts of a Sentence

Exercise 1 Identifying Subjects

Underline the subject in each sentence. Write *you* if the subject is understood.

EXAMPLE Pay attention to the museum exhibit. (you)

1. What do you know about World War II?
2. Was your grandfather in the army or navy?
3. Does your grandmother remember the war?
4. Here is an exhibit of family life during the war.
5. Throughout America, families of soldiers waited for their return.
6. Look at this poster of a popular war slogan.
7. Americans recall D-Day on June 6, 1944.
8. Watch the short documentary in this exhibit.
9. Can you or Grea recall the name of the general?
10. There were thousands of injured veterans.

HINT
One sentence in the passage has a compound subject, or two subjects that share the same verb.
There were three **cars** and two **buses.**

Exercise 2 Finding Subjects in Literature

Underline the subjects in the passage.

Literary Model

[1]On the morning of January 27, members of the 99th were patrolling the skies near Anzio. [2]The Allies had just landed in Italy. [3]Below them were ships along the Mediterranean coastline and thousands of troops on shore. [4]The 99th was protecting the coastal area from enemy aircraft.

—Excerpt from *The Red Tails: World War II's Tuskegee Airmen* by Steven L. Jones

126 *Chapter 6 • Parts of a Sentence*

From Grade 6 Student Edition, Chapter 6, page 126

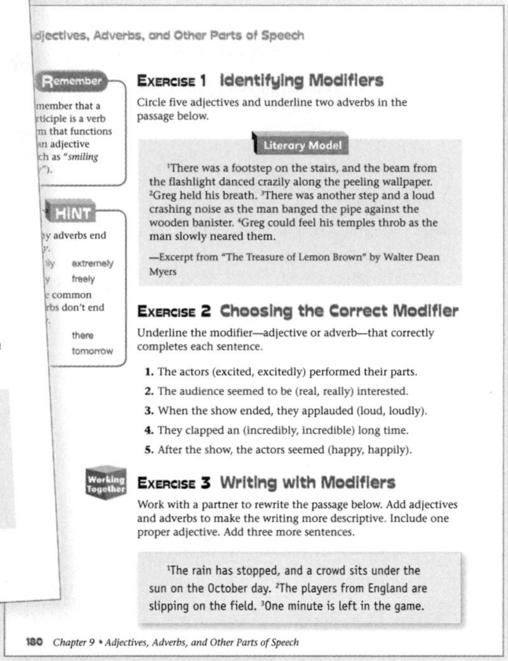

djectives, Adverbs, and Other Parts of Speech

Remember
member that a rticiple is a verb m that functions an adjective ch as "*smiling*").

Exercise 1 Identifying Modifiers

Circle five adjectives and underline two adverbs in the passage below.

Literary Model

[1]There was a footstep on the stairs, and the beam from the flashlight danced crazily along the peeling wallpaper. [2]Greg held his breath. [3]There was another step and a loud crashing noise as the man banged the pipe against the wooden banister. [4]Greg could feel his temples throb as the man slowly neared them.

—Excerpt from "The Treasure of Lemon Brown" by Walter Dean Myers

HINT
y adverbs end
extremely
freely
common rbs don't end
there
tomorrow

Exercise 2 Choosing the Correct Modifier

Underline the modifier—adjective or adverb—that correctly completes each sentence.

1. The actors (excited, excitedly) performed their parts.
2. The audience seemed to be (real, really) interested.
3. When the show ended, they applauded (loud, loudly).
4. They clapped an (incredibly, incredible) long time.
5. After the show, the actors seemed (happy, happily).

Working Together

Exercise 3 Writing with Modifiers

Work with a partner to rewrite the passage below. Add adjectives and adverbs to make the writing more descriptive. Include one proper adjective. Add three more sentences.

[1]The rain has stopped, and a crowd sits under the sun on the October day. [2]The players from England are slipping on the field. [3]One minute is left in the game.

180 *Chapter 9 • Adjectives, Adverbs, and Other Parts of Speech*

From Grade 6 Student Edition, Chapter 9, page 180

Technology

At ***www.grammarforwriting.com***, students have access to additional practice for every grammar lesson, as well as step-by-step workshop models to guide them through the writing process.

ONLINE PRACTICE
www.grammarforwriting.com

Online teacher resources at ***www.grammarforwriting.com*** include professional development materials, writing rubrics, and answer keys.

Provides Assessment and National and State Test Preparation

Through a variety of chapter tests, ***Grammar for Writing*** prepares students for high-stakes standardized tests.

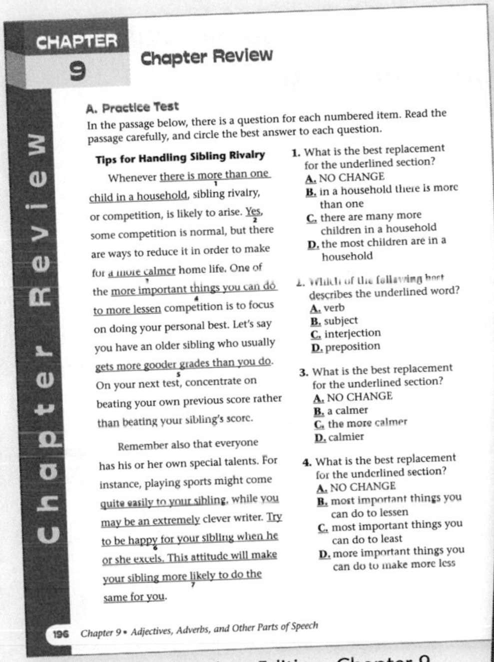

CHAPTER 9

Chapter Review

A. Practice Test

In the passage below, there is a question for each numbered item. Read the passage carefully, and circle the best answer to each question.

Tips for Handling Sibling Rivalry

Whenever there is more than one child in a household, sibling rivalry, or competition, is likely to arise. Yes, some competition is normal, but there are ways to reduce it in order to make for a more calmer home life. One of the more important things you can do to more lessen competition is to focus on doing your personal best. Let's say you have an older sibling who usually gets more gooder grades than you do. On your next test, concentrate on beating your own previous score rather than beating your sibling's score.

Remember also that everyone has his or her own special talents. For instance, playing sports might come quite easily to your sibling, while you may be an extremely clever writer. Try to be happy for your sibling when he or she excels. This attitude will make your sibling more likely to do the same for you.

1. What is the best replacement for the underlined section?
   A. NO CHANGE
   B. in a household there is more than one
   C. there are many more children in a household
   D. the most children are in a household
2. Which of the following best describes the underlined word?
   A. verb
   B. subject
   C. interjection
   D. preposition
3. What is the best replacement for the underlined section?
   A. NO CHANGE
   B. a calmer
   C. the more calmer
   D. calmier
4. What is the best replacement for the underlined section?
   A. NO CHANGE
   B. most important things you can do to lessen
   C. most important things you can do to least
   D. more important things you can do to make more less

Chapter Review

196 *Chapter 9 • Adjectives, Adverbs, and Other Parts of Speech*

From Grade 6 Student Edition, Chapter 9, pages 196 and 198

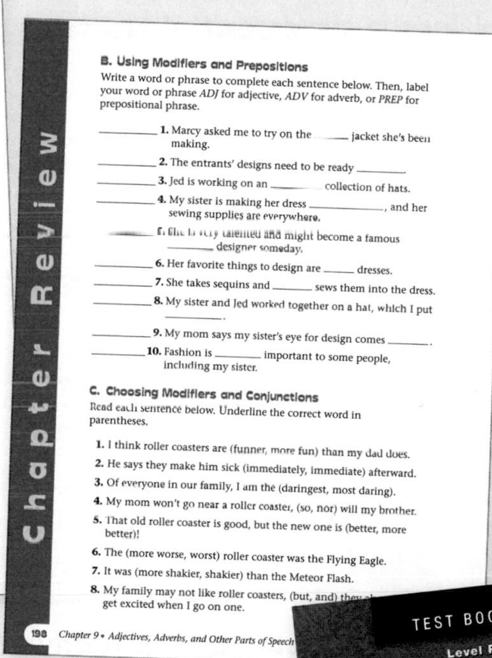

B. Using Modifiers and Prepositions

Write a word or phrase to complete each sentence below. Then, label your word or phrase *ADJ* for adjective, *ADV* for adverb, or *PREP* for prepositional phrase.

_____ 1. Marcy asked me to try on the _____ jacket she's been making.
_____ 2. The entrants' designs need to be ready _____.
_____ 3. Jed is working on an _____ collection of hats.
_____ 4. My sister is making her dress _____, and her sewing supplies are everywhere.
_____ 5. She is very talented and might become a famous _____ designer someday.
_____ 6. Her favorite things to design are _____ dresses.
_____ 7. She takes sequins and _____ sews them into the dress.
_____ 8. My sister and Jed worked together on a hat, which I put _____.
_____ 9. My mom says my sister's eye for design comes _____.
_____ 10. Fashion is _____ important to some people, including my sister.

C. Choosing Modifiers and Conjunctions

Read each sentence below. Underline the correct word in parentheses.

1. I think roller coasters are (funner, more fun) than my dad does.
2. He says they make him sick (immediately, immediate) afterward.
3. Of everyone in our family, I am the (daringest, most daring).
4. My mom won't go near a roller coaster, (so, nor) will my brother.
5. That old roller coaster is good, but the new one is (better, more better)!
6. The (more worse, worst) roller coaster was the Flying Eagle.
7. It was (more shakier, shakier) than the Meteor Flash.
8. My family may not like roller coasters, (but, and) they ... get excited when I go on one.

Chapter Review

198 *Chapter 9 • Adjectives, Adverbs, and Other Parts of Speech*

Chapter tests cover the instruction emphasized in state and national standards and reinforce all of the standards taught in the chapter.

A variety of testing formats, including multiple choice, matching, fill-in-the-blank, writing prompt, and revising exercises, familiarize students with traditional testing formats and questions.

The Test Booklet* provides additional assessment in standardized test formats.

* additional purchase

Integration of Writing and Grammar

Balances Writing and Grammar

Grammar for Writing offers the perfect combination of grammar and writing instruction. Lessons on grammar, usage, and mechanics are integrated with writing workshops and writing applications throughout the student edition.

The composition section of ***Grammar for Writing*** also highlights and explains the **six essential traits of good writing**.

Integrated. Each chapter includes a writing workshop or application that applies grammar, usage, and mechanics to students' own writing.

Part I: Composition

From Grade 6 Student Edition, Table of Contents

Grammar for Writing emphasizes the application of grammar, usage, and mechanics within students' own writing. Students not only learn grammar but also practice applying it while working on their own writing. Each chapter includes a Writing Workshop or Application that weaves grammar principles into engaging writing activities.

Grammar, usage, and mechanics are reinforced through a variety of features infused throughout the student edition. Features include "Connecting Grammar and Writing," which emphasizes important links between the two areas.

Part II: Grammar, Usage, and Mechanics

From Grade 6 Student Edition, Table of Contents

Complete Scope and Sequence Provides Consistency

The ***Grammar for Writing*** series starts in middle school and extends into high school.

Category	Topic	Grade 6	Grade 7	Grade 8	Grade 9	Grade 10	Grade 11	Grade 12
Writing Process	The Writing Process	■■■■■	■■■■■	■■■■■	■■■■	■■■■	■■■■	■■■■
Sentences and Word Choice	Improving Sentences		■■	■■	■	■■	■■	■■
	Combining Sentences	■	■■	■■■	■■■■	■■■	■■■	■■■
	Sentence Variety and Structure	■■	■■■	■■■	■■	■■	■■	■■
	Phrases and Clauses	■	■	■■	■■■■■	■■■■■	■■■■■	■■■■■
	Wordiness and Word Choice	■	■■■	■■■■	■			
Paragraphs	Structure/ Details	■■	■	■■	■	■	■	■
	Unity/ Coherence	■■■	■■■	■■■	■■	■■	■■	■■
	Paragraph Types/ Purposes		■	■■	■	■	■	■
	Paragraph in Essays	■■■■	■■■■■	■■■■■	■	■	■	■
Writing Workshops	Descriptive Writing/ Narrative Writing	■■■	■■■	■■■	■	■	■	■■
	Expository Writing	■■	■■■	■■■	■	■	■	■■■
	Persuasive Writing	■■	■■	■■	■	■	■■	■
	Writing About Literature	■	■	■	■	■	■	■
	Research Paper	■	■	■	■	■	■	■
	Workplace/ Real-World Writing	■■	■	■		■		■
	Timed Essay			■	■	■	■	
	Writing for Assessment	■	■	■	■	■	■	■
Sentence Parts	Complete Sentences/ Kinds of Sentences	■	■	■	■■	■■	■■	■■
	Subjects/ Predicates	■■■■	■■■	■■■	■■	■■	■■	■■
	Sentence Fragments/ Run-ons	■■	■■■	■■	■■■	■■	■■■	■■■
	Objects/ Subject Complements	■■	■■	■■	■■■	■■■	■■■	■■■
Nouns and Pronouns	Using Nouns	■	■■	■■	■	■	■	■
	Using Pronouns	■	■	■	■	■	■	■
	Subject/ Object	■	■	■■	■■■	■■■	■■■	■■■
	Agreement with Antecedent	■	■	■	■	■	■	■
	Other Pronoun Usage	■	■	■■	■	■■	■■	■■

KEY ■ = Lesson(s) dedicated to listed topic

Category	Topic	Grade 6	Grade 7	Grade 8	Grade 9	Grade 10	Grade 11	Grade 12
Verbs	Using Verbs	■	■	■	■	■	■	■
	Regular/ Irregular Verbs	■■	■■	■■	■■■	■■■	■■■	■■■
	Verb Tense	■	■	■■	■	■	■	■
	Active Voice/ Usage		■	■	■■	■	■	■
	Verbals	■	■	■■■	■■■	■■■	■■■	■■■
Adjectives and Adverbs	Using Adjectives and Adverbs	■■	■■	■	■■	■■	■■	■■
	Comparisons	■■	■	■■	■■	■■	■■	■■
	Double Negatives/ Other Modifier Usage		■	■	■	■	■	■
	Misplaced/ Dangling Modifiers		■	■	■	■■	■■	■■
Prepositions, Conjunctions, and Interjections	Using Prepositions and Prepositional Phrases	■	■	■	■■	■■	■■	■■
	Using Conjunctions and Interjections	■	■	■	■	■	■	■
Subject-Verb Agreement	Number/ Compound Subjects	■■	■■	■	■■	■■	■■	■
	Other Agreement Problems	■■	■■■	■■■■	■■	■■■	■■■	■■■■
Punctuation	End Marks/ Abbreviations	■	■■	■	■	■	■	■
	Commas	■■	■■	■■■	■■■■	■■■■	■■■■	■■■■
	Colons/ Semicolons	■	■	■	■■	■■	■■	■■
	Quotation Marks/ Italics	■	■	■■	■■	■■	■■	■■
	Apostrophes	■	■	■	■	■	■	■
	Other Marks	■	■	■		■	■	■
Capitalization and Spelling	Capitalization	■■	■■■	■■■	■■■■	■■■■	■■■■	■■■■
	Spelling Rules/ Using a Dictionary	■	■	■	■■	■■	■■	■■
	Prefixes and Suffixes			■	■	■	■	■
	Plural Nouns	■	■	■	■	■	■	■
Skills and Question Types	Strategies and Types of Objective Questions	■	■	■				
	Writing a Timed Essay	■	■	■	■	■■	■■	■■
Test Practice	Grammar and Usage Questions (SAT Format)	■	■	■	■	■	■	■
	ACT Format				■	■	■	■
	Chapter Test	■	■	■	■	■	■	■
	Online Practice	■	■	■	■	■	■	■

Also Available for Grades 9-12

Nationally recognized English professor Beverly Ann Chin designed ***Grammar for Writing*** for middle school and high school students. Dr. Chin is Senior Project Consultant for the 2011 Writing Framework for National Assessment of Educational Progress (NAEP). Using best practices and active pedagogy, Dr. Chin conducts writing workshops that align curriculum and instruction with assessments.

***Grammar for Writing* Grades 9–12** builds upon the solid foundation of language arts started in middle school and prepares high school students for the ACT and SAT tests, the world of work, and the demands of college writing. Available in softcover (consumable) and hardcover editions.

9th Grade

10th Grade

11th Grade

12th Grade

Sadlier®

TEACHER'S EDITION

Level Red
Grade 6

GRAMMAR for Writing

Senior Series Consultant
Beverly Ann Chin
Professor of English
University of Montana
Missoula, MT

Series Consultant
Frederick J. Panzer, Sr.
English Dept. Chair, Emeritus
Christopher Columbus High School
Miami, FL

Series Consultant
Anthony Bucco
Language Arts Literacy Teacher
Pierrepont Middle School
Rutherford, NJ

Series Editor
Phyllis Goldenberg

Sadlier

Reviewers

Maria Davis Baisier
English Teacher
Holy Cross School
New Orleans, LA

Joan Borrasso
English Teacher
Aquinas Academy
Gibsonia, PA

Melissa Churchwell
Language Arts Teacher
Brooklawn Middle School
Parsippany, NJ

Jay Falls
Language Arts Teacher
Solon Middle School
Solon, OH

Stephanie Jones
Sixth Grade Teacher
Saint Francis of Assisi
Cordova, TN

Sister Rita Ann Keller, IHM
Language Arts Teacher
St. Gregory the Great
Virginia Beach, VA

Cheryl Kordes
Language Arts Teacher
St. Peter in Chains
Hamilton, OH

John T. Ludwig
Language Arts Teacher
Our Lady of Lourdes
Melbourne, FL

Darbie Dallman Safford
Language Arts Teacher
St. Monica School
Dallas, TX

Joan Sieja
Language Arts/Reading Teacher
Mary Queen of Heaven
Brooklyn, NY

Sister June Clare Tracy, O.P., Ed.D.
District Superintendent
Manhattan Catholic Schools
New York, NY

Mollie Mumau Williams
Language Arts Teacher
James W. Parker Middle School
Edinboro, PA

Acknowledgments

T6-T7 Marzano, Robert & Kendall John (2008). Content Knowledge: A Compendium of Standards and Benchmarks for K-12 Education, 4th ed. Denver, CO: McREL. Online www.mcrel.org/standards-benchmarks/ <http://www.mcrel.org/standards-benchmarks/>

Every good faith effort has been made to locate the owners of copyrighted material to arrange permission to reprint selections. In several cases this has proved impossible. Thanks to the following for permission to reprint copyrighted material.

Excerpt from *Becoming Naomi León* by Pamela Muñoz Ryan. Copyright © 2004 by Pam Muñoz Ryan. Published by Scholastic Press, an imprint of Scholastic Inc.

Excerpt from *Blizzard*. Copyright © 2000 by Jim Murphy. Published by Scholastic Press, an imprint of Scholastic Inc.

Excerpt from *BREAKING THROUGH* by Francisco Jiménez. Copyright © 2001 by Francisco Jiménez. Reprinted by permission of Houghton Mifflin Harcourt Publishing Company. All rights reserved.

Reprinted with the permission of Simon & Schuster Books for Young Readers, an imprint of Simon & Schuster Children's Publishing Division from *THE HOUSE OF DIES DREAR* by Virginia Hamilton. Copyright © 1968 Virginia Hamilton.

Excerpt from *A Friendship for Today*. Copyright © 2007 by Patricia McKissack. Published by Scholastic Press, an imprint of Scholastic Inc.

Excerpt from "The Jacket" from *The Effects of Knut Hamsun on a Fresno Boy: Recollections and Short Essays* by Gary Soto. Copyright © 1983, 2001. Reprinted by permission of Persea Books, Inc. (New York)

Excerpt from *LINCOLN: A Photobiography* by Russell Freedman. Copyright © 1987 by Russell Freedman. Reprinted by permission of Clarion Books, an imprint of Houghton Mifflin Harcourt Publishing Company. All rights reserved.

From *MANIAC MAGEE* by Jerry Spinelli. Copyright © 1990 by Jerry Spinelli. By permission of LITTLE, BROWN & COMPANY.

Our Poisoned Waters by Edward Dolan. Copyright © 1997 by Edward Dolan. Published by Cobblehill Books.

Excerpt from *SILENT SPRING* by Rachel Carson. Copyright © 1952 by Rachel L. Carson, renewed by Roger Christie. Reprinted by permission of Houghton Mifflin Harcourt Publishing Company. All rights reserved.

Excerpt from *Surviving the Applewhites*. Copyright © 2002 by Stephanie S. Tolan. Published by Harper Collins Children's Books, a division of Harper Collins *Publishers*. All rights reserved.

Excerpt from "Taste of Snow" from *Beyond Manzanar* (Capra Press), by Jeanne Wakatsuki Houston. Copyright © 1985 by Jeanne Wakatsuki Houston.

Excerpt from *Ties That Bind, Ties That Break*. Copyright © 1999 by Leslie Namioka. Published by Delacorte Press, a division of Random House, Inc.

Excerpt from *The Treasure of Lemon Brown*. Reprinted by permission of Miriam Altshuler Literary Agency, on behalf of Walter Dean Myers. Copyright © 1983, by Walter Dean Myers.

Excerpt from *World War II's Tuskegee Airman*, © 2001 Perfection Learning Corporation.

Excerpt from *Yao Ming: Gentle Giant*. Used by permission of Avisson Press, Inc.

Credits

Cover Art and Design
William H. Sadlier, Inc. and Studio Montage

Cover Photos
Getty Images/Minden Pictures/Tui de Roy: penguins in Antarctica; Punchstock/Corbis: Colosseum; Punchstock/PhotoAlto: bottom three teenagers in winter clothing; Punchstock/Rubberball: girl jumping; Punchstock/Purestock: top teenager in winter clothing

Chapter Opener Photos
Alamy/Glow Images: 120 background; ImageGap: 30 background; Gunter Marx: 200 background; Robert Harding Picture Library Ltd/Adina Tovy: 54 background; Robert Harding Picture Library Ltd/RH Productions: 140 background; Rubberball: 200. Getty Images/Digital Vision/Roger Weber: 140; Minden Pictures/Tui de Roy: 78 background; Photodisc/SW Productions: 100; Photographic Choice RR/Geri Lavrov: 242; Photonica/Vincent Ricardel: 216. Jupiter Images/PhotoAlto Agency/Laurence Mouton: 160. Punchstock/BananaStock: 178; Corbis: 8 background; MIXA: 178 background; PhotoAlto: 78; Photodisc: 54, 216 background; Photosindia.com: 30; Rubberball: 8; Punchstock/Purestock: 78 inset top. Used under license from Shutterstock.com/Thomas Barrat: 100 background; David Hughes: 160 background; Graca Victoria: 242 background

Interior Photos
Getty Images/Tim Boyle: 16; Marc Carter: 226; ColorBlind Images: 10; Getty Images: 126, 142, 224; Dario Mitidieri: 243; Arnold Newman: 122; Erin Patrice O'Brien: 89; Purestock: 188; Tui De Roy: 234; Stringer/Joe Patronite: 170; Stockbyte: 59; Time & Life Pictures: 222; David Young-Wolff: 128; Norbert Wu: 22; istock International Inc/Anna Chelnokova: 104; Robert Churchill: 186; Matt Craven: 162; Christa Brunt: 92; Karen Hogan: 82; istock International Inc.: 42; Bonnie Jacobs: 149, 182; Paul Kline: 189; Evgeniya Lazareva: 219; Rich Legg: 231; Jakob Leitner: 62; MyShotz.com: 252; Jane Norton: 67; Shelly Perry: 148; Ray Roper: 230; Beth Skwarecki: 109; Nancy Catherine Walker: 21; Jan Will: 248; Monika Wisniewska: 103; Jupiterimages Corporation/AbleStock.com: 39, 45; Brand X Pictures: 133; Comstock Images: 20, 38, 79, 171; Creatas Images: 146; Liquidlibrary: 36, 164; Photos.com: 57, 168, 174, 228; Thinkstock Images: 64, 69; Library of Congress: 41; 86; NASA: 34; Shutterstock Images/John Bell: 204; Carlos Caetano: 68; Markus Gann: 87; Salvador Garcia Gil: 179; Vladislav Gurfinkel: 246; Andrew Kua Seng How: 130; Kostyantyn Ivanyshen: 203; Brandon Jennings: 31; Karl Keller: 81; Le Loft: 250; William J. Mahnken: 90; Mikhail Nekrasov: 65; Plastique: 106; Sasha Radosavljevich: 110; Franziska Richter: 202; Gina Sanders: 55; Vnlit: 85; Lisa F. Young: 61; SuperStock/ZSSD: 35

Printed in the United States of America
Teacher's Edition: ISBN: 978-0-8215-0226-6
Student Edition (s/c): ISBN: 978-0-8215-0216-7
Student Edition (h/c): ISBN: 978-0-8215-0206-8
1 2 3 4 5 6 7 8 9 / 13 12 11 10 09 08

CONTENTS

ONLINE PRACTICE

www.grammarforwriting.com

Available at www.grammarforwriting.com:

For Teachers

- ✔ password-protected supplemental Answer Keys
- ✔ full-length research-based article by Beverly Ann Chin, Ph.D.
- ✔ writing rubrics

For Students

- ✔ additional practice for grammar lessons
- ✔ work-in-progress writing models for each step of the writing process
- ✔ full-length writing models for each writing workshop
- ✔ step-by-step writing models

For more information about ***Grammar for Writing*** Online Components, see page T54.

Five Ways to Use *Grammar for Writing*

Flexible and versatile, ***Grammar for Writing*** can facilitate a variety of instructional purposes. Teachers may opt to use the program as the core vehicle for delivering language arts instruction, or they may choose to use it as a supplement to meet specific curricular goals and students' needs.

1. **As a Complete Course**

   The Student Edition, Teacher's Edition, Test Booklet, and Online Resources give teachers everything they need to meet the grammar and writing standards of English Language Arts. Research-proven approaches support instruction. Practice is thorough, and assessments measure students' progress.

2. **As a Reference Tool**

   The organization of program materials makes locating topics easy. Explanations are clear. Examples are abundant. With the Student Edition at the ready, students can easily access the information they need to answer their grammar questions and to solve the problems they encounter as they write. They can review sample Writing Models online.

3. **As a Tool to Guide Independent and Small Group Learning**

   Whether working alone or with a group of peers, step-by-step features guide their study, and a wealth of hints and tips helps them along their way.

4. **As a Source of Review and Practice Material**

   Every lesson includes engaging and effective practice exercises. After teaching a topic, teachers can send students to their Student Editions to work on meaningful, student-centered activities that develop skills.

5. **For Test Preparation**

   Every Chapter Review in the Student Edition includes a Practice Test in standardized test format. The Test Booklet provides additional tests for assessment purposes. Together, these tools give students much-needed practice and success with high-stakes tests.

Program Features Support 5 Ways of Using *Grammar for Writing*

Instructional Use	Key Features and Support
Complete Course	• Comprehensive coverage of core language arts standards • Research-based instructional approaches • Instruction, practice, assessment, and reteaching • Full array of components
Reference Tool	• Easy two-part organization, numbered chapters and lessons • Complete index • Clear explanations • Abundant examples • List of Frequently Misspelled Words • List of Commonly Confused Words • Online reference tools
Guide for Independent and Small Group Learning	• Straightforward explanations of lesson topics • Explanatory charts and graphic organizers • Annotated Literary Models and sample Writing Models • Exercises for Working Together • Strategically placed hints, tips, and reminders
Source of Review and Extra Practice	• Exercises with every lesson • Additional practice online • Writing Workshops • Writing Applications • Chapter Review activities
Test Preparation	• Test-taking Tips • Practice Test in every Chapter Review • Additional tests in Test Booklet • Tests in standardized test formats • Writing Applications for practice taking writing tests

Engaging Middle School Students in Writing and Grammar Instruction

By Beverly Ann Chin, Ph.D.

As teachers seek to balance instruction in the development and organization of ideas with choices in language fluency and correctness, they often ask, "What is the relationship between writing instruction and grammar?" Teachers also wonder, "What strategies help students in their understanding and command of conventions of standard written English? How can teachers make grammar instruction meaningful and enjoyable?" A review of the research provides answers to these important questions.

What is the relationship between writing instruction and grammar?

Based on its own review of the research in writing and grammar instruction, the National Council of Teachers of English (NCTE) asserts: "Language skills and conventions (grammar, punctuation, spelling) are most successfully learned with a combination of carefully targeted lessons applied within the context of meaningful writing" (*<http://www.ncte.org/prog/writing/research/113177.htm>*).

As middle school students read more diverse and sophisticated texts, teachers can help students observe how writers make choices in ideas, organization, language, and conventions to create an effect on readers. Teachers can also encourage students to reflect on how their writing choices affect their communication purpose and audience. By analyzing the conventions used by published authors as well as classmates, middle school students discover how grammar, usage, and mechanics are tools that clarify meaning.

What strategies help students in their understanding and command of standard written English?

Based on an extensive review of the research on instructional methods, Graham and Perin (2007) identified eleven instructional practices that improve secondary students' writing skills. Their findings are published in *Writing Next: Effective strategies to improve writing of adolescents in middle and high school.* Among the recommended instructional practices are the following:

- **Writing Strategies:** Teaching students strategies for planning, revising, and editing their compositions
- **Collaborative Writing:** Instructional arrangements in which students work together to plan, draft, revise, and edit their compositions
- **Sentence Combining:** Teaching students to construct more complex, sophisticated sentences
- **Study of Models:** Providing students with opportunities to read, analyze, and emulate models of good writing

Teachers who integrate grammar into their writing instruction during the revising and editing stages enable students to learn the conventions of standard written English in meaningful ways. Keeping in mind the recommendations of *Writing Next*, let's look at two strategies that help students understand and apply the rules of grammar, usage, and mechanics in their own writing.

Sentence Combining

Sentence combining is a strategy in which students combine short, choppy sentences into longer, more fluent ones. As students experiment with different ways to combine their sentences, they discover how sentence beginnings, lengths, and complexities relate to the meaning and overall effect of the message. Through oral and written sentence combining activities, students learn to experiment with language and to make choices about language fluency.

Sentence combining is most effective when it is presented to students during the revising and editing stages of the writing process. Because sentence combining is based on students' own drafts, students do not need to focus on generating or organizing ideas. Teachers can use examples of sentences from students' writing to create sentence-combining activities. During the editing stage, teachers can use sentence combining to discuss punctuation rules—especially those related to commas, apostrophes, and semicolons. By using students' new sentence combinations, teachers can also provide instruction in grammar concepts, such as independent and dependent clauses, phrases, subject-verb agreement, antecedents, active and passive voice, and parallel structure.

Study of Models

Sentence imitation is a strategy that uses the study of good models. When students imitate sentences, they replicate the syntax of a model text, but use their own words and ideas. Teachers usually begin by showing a well-crafted sentence or paragraph, often from a published author. The teacher helps the students analyze how the author used specific parts of speech to create the text. Then, using their own topics, ideas, and words, students create their own sentences as they imitate the syntax of the model text.

Through sentence imitation, students can also learn to identify important grammar concepts, such as independent and dependent clauses, phrases, and modifiers, and punctuation rules, such as commas, dashes, parentheses, and colons. Students can discuss how the author's use of grammar, usage, and mechanics affects their understanding of the text.

Teachers usually introduce sentence-imitation activities during the revising stage as students work on their sentence fluency and voice. When students imitate sentences with complex punctuation, parallel syntax, or sophisticated modification, they enter the editing stage of the writing process.

Example of Modeling

Original Model

Unusual rock formations appear in the cliffs by the river and provide valuable specimens for geologists from scientific organizations and universities.

Sentence Imitations

Healthy young people exercise in many ways throughout the week and eat balanced meals with varieties of green vegetables and fruits.

Majestic bald eagles soar in the sky above the mountains and cast dark shadows over lakes of deep blue and aquamarine.

How can teachers make grammar instruction meaningful and enjoyable?

When middle school students value their writing purpose and audience, they discover how conventions affect the clarity and impact of their message. Here are four teaching suggestions that can help students enjoy learning grammar.

1. **Emphasize the positive.** Look for what students are doing effectively in their writing. By pointing out students' correct use of conventions, you reinforce the importance of grammar, usage, and mechanics as tools that help readers understand the written message.
2. **Keep the grammar lesson focused.** Prioritize and select the one or two important concepts to address in each lesson. Introducing too many concepts at the same time overwhelms many students.
3. **Show examples of grammar concepts in different texts and genres.** Create a bulletin board that displays the ways in which grammar, usage, and mechanics are used in various publications, such as magazines, poetry, and graphic novels. Cartoons and newspaper headlines offer creative opportunities to examine punctuation and word choice. Encourage students to contribute to the display.
4. **Make grammar lively.** Show examples from print and non-print media that use language in creative and unusual ways. Have students look for examples of humor and ambiguity in written language. Jokes, puns, and misplaced modifiers offer opportunities to discuss grammar.

During the middle school years, students are discovering the power of their voices in written communication. They are learning how purpose and audience influence the selection and organization of ideas. Students are also learning how word choice and sentence variety contribute to the written message. Furthermore, they are learning how the conventions of standard written English—grammar, usage, and mechanics—help their readers focus on the content and intent of this message.

A more comprehensive discussion of current research in grammar and writing instruction, as well as suggestions for classroom practices that reflect that research, can be found in the Sadlier-Oxford Professional Development paper "Effective Strategies for Engaging Middle School Students in Writing and Grammar Instruction," by Beverly Ann Chin, Ph.D. For more information, visit www.grammarforwriting.com.

Pacing Instruction

Depending on how a teacher plans to use the ***Grammar for Writing*** program, there can be many different ways to pace instruction. Teachers can dedicate three weeks to each chapter. For teachers who use the program as a complete course in Language Arts, the following chart suggests pacing.

Pacing Calendar: 36 Weeks

Week 1 *Chapter 1* *Lesson 1.1* *Lesson 1.2* *Lesson 1.3* *Lesson 1.4*	**Week 2** *Chapter 1* *Lesson 1.5* *Writer's Workshop: Description*	**Week 3** *Chapter 1* *Review and reteaching as needed*	**Week 4** *Chapter 2* *Lesson 2.1* *Lesson 2.2* *Lesson 2.3* *Lesson 2.4*	**Week 5** *Chapter 2* *Lesson 2.5* *Writing Application: Friendly Letter*
Week 6 *Chapter 2* *Review and reteaching as needed*	**Week 7** *Chapter 3* *Lesson 3.1* *Lesson 3.2* *Lesson 3.3* *Lesson 3.4*	**Week 8** *Chapter 3* *Lesson 3.5* *Writer's Workshop: Autobiographical Incident*	**Week 9** *Chapter 3* *Review and reteaching as needed*	**Week 10** *Chapter 4* *Lesson 4.1* *Lesson 4.2* *Lesson 4.3* *Lesson 4.4*
Week 11 *Chapter 4* *Lesson 4.5* *Writing Application: Opinion Paragraph*	**Week 12** *Chapter 4* *Review and reteaching as needed*	**Week 13** *Chapter 5* *Lesson 5.1* *Lesson 5.2* *Lesson 5.3* *Lesson 5.4*	**Week 14** *Writer's Workshop: Persuasive Essay*	**Week 15** *Chapter 5* *Review and reteaching as needed*
Week 16 *Chapter 6* *Lesson 6.1* *Lesson 6.2* *Lesson 6.3* *Lesson 6.4*	**Week 17** *Chapter 6* *Lesson 6.5* *Lesson 6.6* *Writing Application: Story*	**Week 18** *Chapter 6* *Review and reteaching as needed*	**Week 19** *Chapter 7* *Lesson 7.1* *Lesson 7.2* *Lesson 7.3* *Lesson 7.4*	**Week 20** *Chapter 7* *Writer's Workshop: How-to Essay*

Pacing Calendar: 36 Weeks *(Continued)*

Week 21	**Week 22**	**Week 23**	**Week 24**
Chapter 7 Review and reteaching as needed	*Chapter 8* *Lesson 8.1* *Lesson 8.2* *Lesson 8.3* *Lesson 8.4*	*Chapter 8* *Lesson 8.5* *Writing Application: Summary*	*Chapter 8 Review and reteaching as needed*
Week 25	**Week 26**	**Week 27**	**Week 28**
Chapter 9 *Lesson 9.1* *Lesson 9.2* *Lesson 9.3* *Lesson 9.4*	*Chapter 9* *Lesson 9.5* *Writer's Workshop: Personal Response to Literature*	*Chapter 9 Review and reteaching as needed*	*Chapter 10* *Lesson 10.1* *Lesson 10.2* *Lesson 10.3* *Lesson 10.4*
Week 29	**Week 30**	**Week 31**	**Week 32**
Chapter 10 *Writing Application: Business E-mail* *Chapter 10 Review and reteaching as needed*	*Chapter 11* *Lesson 11.1* *Lesson 11.2* *Lesson 11.3* *Lesson 11.4*	*Chapter 11* *Lesson 11.5* *Lesson 11.6* *Lesson 11.7*	*Chapter 11* *Writer's Workshop: Research Report*
Week 33	**Week 34**	**Week 35**	**Week 36**
Chapter 11 Review and reteaching as needed	*Chapter 12* *Lesson 12.1* *Lesson 12.2* *Lesson 12.3* *Lesson 12.4*	*Chapter 12* *Lesson 12.5* *Writing Application: Essay Question Response*	*Chapter 12 Review and reteaching as needed*

Integrating Grammar and Writing

Teachers know that knowledge of grammar is essential to improve their students' writing and communication skills.

Why is grammar integral to instruction in writing?

- Grammar helps students construct and vary sentences.
- Grammar helps students write correctly and effectively.
- Grammar provides clues to standard English usage.

Why is writing integral to instruction in grammar?

- Writing personalizes grammar and makes it meaningful through opportunities for students' own expression.
- Writing provides immediate application of grammar topics.
- Writing provides the practice that helps students acquire grammar skills.

How does *Grammar for Writing* integrate grammar and writing?

- Every chapter culminates in a Writing Workshop or Writing Application, each with grammar features.
- Connecting Grammar and Writing features integrate grammar tips into writing lessons.
- In the grammar chapters, writing exercises allow students to apply grammar rules to their writing.

Part 1: Composition Overview

The lessons in Part 1 focus on:

- the writing process
- writing effective sentences and word choice
- sentence variety and structure
- writing effective paragraphs
- writing effective essays

Writing Workshops and Applications cover descriptive, narrative, expository, persuasive, and real-world writing.

LESSON 2.5

Using Sensory Details

Sensory details are what we experience through our five senses—sight, sound, smell, taste, and touch.

Five Senses	
Sight	sparkling blue water, tiny oval stones
Sound	roar of the ocean, bird's high-pitched cry
Smell	burned toast, scent of flowery perfume
Taste	salty water, sour pickles
Touch	powdery sand, smooth cotton

➡ Use sensory words and details to grab your readers' interest and create a clear, vivid picture of your subject.

Notice how the author of the following passage includes sensory details in her description.

Literary Model

[1]Lucille led Jake to the kitchen. [2]Randolph was standing at the stove, frowning ferociously and poking at a pan of frying bacon with a long fork, a steaming coffee mug in his other hand. [3]He glowered at them as they came in. [4]A towheaded boy who looked about four years old was sitting on a tall stool at the counter, singing about an itsy-bitsy spider at the top of his lungs. [5]The moment he saw Jake, he stopped singing and stared, his mouth open, his blue eyes wide and round.

—Excerpt from *Surviving the Applewhites* by Stephanie S. Tolan

Smell and taste

Sound

Sight

Reading as a Writer

1. How well can you picture this scene? Which details are the most effective?
2. What other sensory details could the author have added?
3. The author does not tell us how Randolph is feeling. What details show us his mood?

Lessons focus on core **writing standards**.

Lesson vocabulary in boldface helps students learn key academic terms.

Organized **teaching points** are supported by clear examples.

Literary Models provide strong, effective examples of lesson topics—and encourage reading!

Reading as a Writer encourages students to analyze and evaluate professional models.

Additional features:

✔ **Sidebar features** offer writing hints, connect writing and grammar, cross-reference related lessons, and provide tips by published writers.

✔ **Scaffolded exercises** provide several opportunities for practice.

✔ **Diverse exercise topics** cover grade-level content area topics and include a variety of genres, such as real-world writing and nonfiction.

Part 2: Grammar Overview

The lessons in Part 2 focus on:

- parts of a sentence
- parts of speech
- subject-verb agreement
- punctuation
- capitalization and spelling

Lessons focus on core **grammar standards**.

Boldface **lesson vocabulary** defines key academic terms.

Sidebar features offer tips and cross-reference related lessons.

Step by Step guidance helps students master difficult grammar topics.

LESSON 10.1

Agreement of Subject and Verb

The **subject** of a sentence is the person or thing that performs the action of the sentence. The **verb** is the word that expresses the action.

➡ The subject and verb of a sentence must **agree** in number. Use a singular verb with a singular subject. Use a plural verb with a plural subject.

Remember

A **singular** subject names one person, place, thing, or idea. A **plural** subject names more than one.

Singular	Plural
Marty speaks quickly.	**My friends speak** quickly.
I am late for school.	**We are** late for school.
She wants three cats.	**They want** three cats.

➡ In a **verb phrase,** the first helping verb (HV) must agree with the subject (S).

Our car (S) has (HV) been making strange noises.
We (S) are (HV) leaving soon.
My parents (S) do (HV) not know any mechanics.

See **Lesson 8.1** for more about verb phrases.

STEP BY STEP

To decide whether a verb agrees with its subject:

1. Find the verb or verb phrase.
   My grandparents' neighbor collects coins.
   VERB *collects*
2. Ask *Who?* or *What?* before the verb to find the subject.
   WHO COLLECTS? *neighbor*
3. Use a singular verb with a singular subject and a plural verb with a plural subject.

Remember: The verb needs to agree with only the subject, not with any other word in the sentence.

Chapter 10 • Subject-Verb Agreement **201**

ONLINE PRACTICE
www.grammarforwriting.com

Exercise 1 Choosing Correct Verbs

Present Tense Forms of *Be*

Singular
I **am** hungry.
You **are** hungry.
He **is** hungry.

Plural
We **are** hungry.
You **are** hungry.
They **are** hungry.

Underline the subject of each sentence. Then circle the verb in the parentheses that agrees with the subject.

1. Video-sharing Web sites (have, has) become popular recently.
2. People (are, is) using them to post their own videos.
3. Many users (watch, watches) other people's videos.
4. One popular site now (air, airs) 100 million videos a day.
5. Many new videos (are, is) added each day.
6. No fancy equipment (are, is) needed.
7. My friends (like, likes) to find funny clips.
8. Even my dad (enjoy, enjoys) online videos.
9. The content (range, ranges) from the silly to the serious.
10. My neighbors (have, has) made several videos.

Exercises in every lesson give plenty of **scaffolded practice**.

Exercise 2 Editing an Article

As you read the article below, find five errors in subject-verb agreement. Rewrite the paragraph to correct the errors.

[1]DVD players were introduced in 1997. [2]They offers high-quality images. [3]This technological breakthrough have slowly beaten VCRs. [4]Today most American consumers own DVD players. [5]In fact, more people has DVD players in their homes than they do computers, VCRs, or cable television. [6]New models is becoming cheaper. [7]High-definition (HD) DVD players produces extremely sharp pictures.

Exercises provide opportunities for applying the grammar skill to a **variety of formats**.

Real-world formats allow students to see the connection between grammar topics and their lives.

Write What You Think

On a separate piece of paper, write at least five sentences that explain your answer to the question below. Check that each verb agrees with its subject.

Is lying ever the right thing to do?

Write What You Think exercises integrate grammar and writing and provide opportunities for writing persuasive and expository paragraphs.

Writing Workshops and Writing Applications

Writing Workshops and Writing Applications at the end of each chapter cover:

- writing modes and forms, such as descriptive paragraphs, autobiographical incidents, compare-contrast essays, and persuasive essays
- writing purposes, such as to describe, to entertain, to explain, and to persuade

Writing Workshops guide students through each step of the writing process, offering step-by-step instruction, Writing Models, tips, Revising checklists, and Editing and Proofreading checklists.

Each page in a Writing Workshop is dedicated to a different **step of the writing process**.

Step-by-step, easy-to-read instruction walks through each step of the writing process.

Visuals, such as graphic organizers and charts, provide effective models for students.

WRITER'S WORKSHOP continued

Drafting

Include All the Parts As you draft, include all three parts of an essay.

1. The **introduction** should identify the title and author of the work. Include your thesis statement and summary.
2. The **body** of your essay should explain your response. Include at least two key points, each one supported by specific evidence, such as examples or quotations. Explain each point in a separate paragraph.
3. Your **conclusion** should summarize your response and restate your thesis, using different words.

WRITING HINT

Skim the work to find specific details that will help you explain your points. Your teacher may ask you to include a page number in parentheses for quotations or details you use.

Introduction Thesis	Although the plot is full of weird events, I can connect to many characters in <u>James and the Giant Peach.</u>
Body Point 1 Evidence	James seems like a normal kid in a strange world. • parents eaten by rhino (p. 1) • gets magic crystals (p. 9) • scared and hopeless at beginning (p. 13) • fights with Cloud-Men (p. 85) • excited at end just the way I would be (p. 117)
Point 2 Evidence	James's peculiar friends look bizarre and scary, but they are a lot like my friends and me. • different personalities and skills • Glow-worm = gives light, is shy (p. 34) • Earthworm = gloomy (p. 49) • Centipede's jokes and funny song about "smelly jelly" and "mudburgers" (p. 52)
Conclusion	Although what happens to James and his insect friends is extraordinary, they seem like ordinary people to me.

192 *Chapter 9 • Writer's Workshop: Personal Response to Literature*

Revising

Use the Revising Questions below to improve your draft. The model shows how one writer began revising the introduction.

As you revise, keep in mind the traits of good writing. See **Lesson 1.3.**

Revising Questions

- ❑ How clear is my overall response to the work?
- ❑ How effective is my summary?
- ❑ Where should I add supporting text evidence?
- ❑ How clearly have I organized my ideas?
- ❑ How effective are the introduction, body, and conclusion?

Specific Revising Questions help students evaluate their drafts.

CONNECTING Writing & Grammar

Use the present tense when you write about a work of literature.

James **is** a hero.

The author **describes** the scene in detail.

Connecting Writing & Grammar integrates key grammar topics.

Writing Model

[1]James and the Giant Peach, by Roald Dahl, is one of my favorite novels. [2]The main character is James Trotter, an orphan who lives in England with his two horrible aunts. [3]~~They are mean and lazy.~~ [4]James's life changes when he climbs inside an enormous peach and discovers some huge talking creatures. [5]The book describes their amazing adventures. [6]~~For example, the peach rolls into the ocean, and sharks attack it.~~ [7]Although the plot is full of weird events, I can connect to ~~many~~ characters ^like James and his new friends.

Cut details from the summary.

Make the thesis more specific.

Annotated Writing Models demonstrate effective ways to improve writing.

Writing Applications are short, step-by-step lessons for crafting writing pieces, such as friendly letters, opinion paragraphs, and summaries.

Steps to Finalize Writing

Grammar for Writing provides several teaching and practice opportunities for students to finalize their drafts.

1. Revising Questions

Revising Questions in the Writing Process Chapter and in each Writing Workshop help students focus on improving their drafts by using five of the six traits of good writing. (The sixth trait, conventions, is taught in the Editing and Proofreading lesson and in each workshop.)

Ideas and Content	• How clear are my ideas? • Where should I add or delete details?
Organization	• How easy is it to follow the order of my ideas? • How well does one sentence connect to the next?
Sentence Fluency	• How do my sentences sound when I rea aloud? Where should I rearrange words? • Which short sentences should be combi
Word Choice	• Where can I add more precise words? • Which words should I replace?
Voice	• How natural does my writing sound? • How interested do I seem in my topic?

Revising Questions

- ❑ How clear is my use of spatial order?
- ❑ Where can I add figurative language and imagery?
- ❑ How effective is my use of sensory details?
- ❑ How clearly have I expressed my feelings about the place?
- ❑ How clear is the overall impression I have created?

2. Peer Review Form

Peer Review guidelines and tips are taught in the Writing Process chapter and in several Writing Workshops. An online Peer Review Form provides specific questions peers may ask each other in an easy-to-use format.

Peer Review Questions

Peer Reviewer's Name: ____________________

Writer's Name: ____________________

1. Are the ideas in the paper easy to understand?

____

____

2. Does the writer include enough details?

____

____

3. Are there any details that are not relevant?

____

____

3. Publishing

Publishing tips are provided in the Writing Process chapter and in every Writing Workshop.

- Submit your work to a school or local newspaper.
- Send it to friends or family in an e-mail.
- Read your work aloud to several classmates. Discuss their reactions and questions.
- Add photos or illustrations, and display your writing in your class or at the school library.
- Share it as part of a formal or informal oral presentation or speech to another class.
- Post it on a blog, or send it to a Web site that publishes student writing.

4. Presenting

A variety of tips and guidelines for presenting are provided in the Writing Process chapter and in every Writing Workshop. Suggestions are based on listening and speaking standards.

Publishing and Presenting

Choose one of these ways to share your personal response.

- **Collect it.** With your classmates, create a booklet of responses for the school library.
- **Talk about it.** Turn your paper into an oral presentation for the class or for your family. Include visual aids when appropriate.
- **Add it to your portfolio.** Keep a writing portfolio to track how you've grown as a writer throughout the year. To decide whether to add a piece to your portfolio, ask yourself, "Why is this one of my best pieces of writing?"

Remember

When you make a presentation, follow these tips:

- Speak loudly so that everyone can hear you.
- Look at your audience as you speak to them.
- Practice several times beforehand.

Assessment

Grammar for Writing offers two effective ways to assess students' understanding of key writing and grammar skills: Chapter Reviews and the Test Booklet (optional purchase).

Chapter Reviews

Chapter Reviews in the Student Edition provide a **variety of standardized test formats** for students to master.

CHAPTER 1

Chapter Review

A. Practice Test

In the passage below, there is a question *for each numbered item*. Read the passage carefully, and circle the best answer to each question.

Raising a Guide Dog

Guide dogs provide an invaluable service to people who are blind. They are trusted companions. They [1] protect their owners. You can help improve the quality of life for the blind by volunteering to raise a guide dog puppy. Becoming a puppy-raiser is a big responsibility. It [2] is extremely rewarding. Volunteers take potential guide dogs home with them when the puppies are several weeks old. The puppy-raiser's job is to teach the dog how to behave around people, among other skills [3]. When the puppy grows to be about fifteen months old, it leaves the puppy-raiser's home to go

1. What is the best replacement for the underlined section?
A. NO CHANGE
B. trusted companions who
C. trusted loyal reliable companions who
D. trusted. They are loyal. They

2. What is the best replacement for the underlined section?
A. NO CHANGE
B. Becoming a puppy-raiser is a responsibility, it
C. Becoming a puppy-raiser,
D. Although becoming a puppy-raiser is a big responsibility, it

3. How could this part of the sentence be improved?
A. Delete it.
B. Insert a transition.
C. Add specific details.
D. Combine it with the previous sentence.

Test-Taking Tips guide students as they complete the Chapter Review.

TEST-TAKING TIP

- Always read *every* answer choice, even if you think you spot the correct answer right away.
- Watch out for answer choices that fix one error but introduce another.

Chapter Review

Chapter 1 • The Writing Process 27

Various **short-answer response exercises** allow students to demonstrate mastery in a short, easy-to-grade way.

C. Identifying Topics

For each topic idea below, write *B* if the topic is too broad, *N* if it is too narrow, or *S* if it is suitable for a three-page paper. Revise topics you marked *B* or *N*.

___ **1.** The History of Dance

___ **2.** How to Tie-Dye

___ **3.** The Height of the Washington Monument

___ **4.** What to Feed a Pet Parakeet

___ **5.** Africa and Its People

Test Booklet*

Diagnostic Test

Diagnostic Test

A. Identifying Errors

Read each sentence below carefully. If you find an error, choose the underlined part that must be changed to make the sentence correct. Fill in the circle for the corresponding letter. If there is no error, fill in circle *E*.

1. ⒶⒷⒸⒹⒺ

Mara and me (A) want (B) to learn how to surf when we go (C) on vacation in July. (D) No error (E)

2. ⒶⒷⒸⒹⒺ

Verzell prefers (A) hiking, he's (B) ready to spend (C) the day in a national park. (D) No error (E)

3. ⒶⒷⒸⒹⒺ

Rose and Max (A) wants to go to the (B) National Civil Rights Museum (C) on Tuesday. (D) No error (E)

4. ⒶⒷⒸⒹⒺ

We looked at (A) posters of Florida and (B) Jamaica when we stopped by (C) the Travel Agency. (D) No error (E)

5. ⒶⒷⒸⒹⒺ

Everyone in my class (A) wants to talk (B) about their favorite (C) place to relax. (D) No error (E)

6. ⒶⒷⒸⒹⒺ

Fred begun talking (A) about his weekend plans before (B) Tasha had finished (C) speaking. (D) No error (E)

7. ⒶⒷⒸⒹⒺ

Fred is takeing (A) a long trip to see his (B) cousins in South Carolina (C) over the (D) summer. No error (E)

8. ⒶⒷⒸⒹⒺ

Just between you and me, (A) he is incredible excited (B) about traveling (C) such a long distance. (D) No error (E)

9. ⒶⒷⒸⒹⒺ

If you could travel (A) anywhere in the (B) world, where do you think (C) you would (D) like to go? No error (E)

10. ⒶⒷⒸⒹⒺ

Is a long (A) vacation always (B) more better (C) than a short one? (D) No error (E)

Diagnostic Test 1

Diagnostic Tests and Mastery Tests allow teachers to assess students' skills at the beginning of the year and assess their growth at the end of the year.

Chapter Tests help teachers **measure student progress** throughout the year.

Chapter Tests rotate four **standardized test formats** and include **short-answer response exercises**.

* Available for additional purchase

Standards Content

The standards-based curriculum in the ***Grammar for Writing*** program focuses on core language arts standards.

Part I: Composition, the first half of the book, teaches essential writing standards.

Part II: Grammar, Usage, and Mechanics focuses on key standards in these areas.

In addition to teaching writing and grammar standards, ***Grammar for Writing*** also covers the following standards:

✔ **Listening and Speaking** standards through:

- Peer Review activities
- Publishing and Presenting guidelines and tips
- Writing Applications on writing effective speeches

✔ **Literature and Reading** standards through:

- Literary Models throughout the book
- Reading as a Writer questions that ask students to analyze passages

✔ **Test-taking** standards through:

- Writing Applications on taking writing tests
- Test-Taking Tips in the Chapter Reviews
- Chapter Reviews that include a variety of standardized test formats and short-answer responses

✔ **Academic and Study Skills** standards through:

- Guidelines for using a variety of graphic organizers
- Tips for using note cards and source cards when researching
- Note-taking guidelines for paraphrasing, summarizing, and quoting sources and tips for avoiding plagiarism
- Finding and evaluating primary and secondary sources

Standards-Based Curriculum

Aligns With Standards

Grammar for Writing teaches a core of the most widely taught standards. Lessons in the student edition derive from a detailed analysis of the language arts standards across the country, focusing on the core standards.

Chapter 1 The Writing Process

Lesson	Core Standards
1.1 Prewriting	✓ **Writing:** Uses a variety of prewriting strategies (e.g., makes outlines, uses published pieces as writing models, constructs critical standards, brainstorms, builds background)
1.2 Drafting	✓ **Writing:** Uses a variety of strategies to draft (e.g., uses an organizational scheme, uses sensory words and figurative language, thinks and writes for different audiences and purposes) ✓ **Writing:** Uses content, style, and structure (e.g., formal or informal language, genre, organization) appropriate for specific audiences (e.g., public, private) and purposes (e.g., to entertain, to persuade, to inform)
1.3 Revising	✓ **Writing:** Uses a variety of strategies to revise written work (e.g., analyzes and clarifies meaning, makes structural and syntactical changes, uses an organizational scheme, uses sensory words and figurative language, rethinks and rewrites for different audiences and purposes, checks for a consistent point of view and for transitions between paragraphs) ✓ **Writing:** Evaluates own and others' writing ✓ **Listening & Speaking:** Asks questions to seek elaboration and clarification of ideas
1.4 Editing and Proofreading	✓ **Writing:** Uses a variety of strategies to edit written work (e.g., eliminates slang; edits for grammar, punctuation, capitalization, and spelling at a developmentally appropriate level, proofreads using reference materials, word processor, and other resources; edits for clarity, word choice, and language usage) ✓ **GUMS:** Uses grammatical and mechanical conventions in written compositions

Source of Standards: Marzano, Robert, Kendall, John (...
Standards and Benchmarks for K-12 Education, 4th ed...
Online: www.mcrel.org/standards-benchmarks/

Chapter 1 The Writing Process

Lesson	Core Standards
1.5 Publishing and Presenting	✓ **Writing:** Uses a variety of strategies to publish written work (uses a word processor or other technology to publish written work) ✓ **Listening & Speaking:** Makes oral presentations to the class
Writer's Workshop: Description	✓ **Writing:** Uses the general skills and strategies of the writing process ✓ **Writing:** Uses descriptive language that clarifies and enhances ideas (e.g., establishes tone and mood, uses figurative language, uses sensory images and comparisons) ✓ **Reading:** Understands specific devices an author uses to accomplish his or her purpose (e.g., persuasive techniques, style, word choice, language structure) ✓ **GUMS:** Uses conventions of punctuation in written compositions (e.g., uses commas in a series)
Chapter Review	✓ **Test-taking:** Use a variety of test-taking strategies.

Chapter 7 Nouns and Pronouns

7.1 Nouns	✓ **GUMS:** Uses nouns in written compositions (e.g., forms possessives of nouns; forms irregular plural nouns)
7.2 Pronouns	✓ **GUMS:** Uses pronouns in written compositions (e.g., uses personal [i.e., possessive] pronouns)
7.3 Subject and Object Pronouns	✓ **GUMS:** Uses pronouns in written compositions (e.g., uses personal [i.e., subject, object] pronouns)
7.4 Pronoun Agreement	✓ **GUMS:** Uses pronouns in written compositions (e.g., uses pronouns that agree with their antecedent)
Writer's Workshop: How-to Essay	✓ **Writing:** Writes expository compositions (e.g., states a thesis or purpose; presents information that reflects knowledge about the topic of the report; organizes and presents information in a logical manner, including an introduction and conclusion; uses own words to develop ideas; uses common expository structures and features, such as compare-contrast or problem-solution) ✓ **Writing:** Uses the general skills and strategies of the writing process ✓ **Writing:** Uses explicit transitional devices ✓ **GUMS:** Uses pronouns in written compositions (e.g., uses pronouns that agree with their antecedent)
Chapter Review	✓ **Test-Taking:** Uses a variety of test-taking strategies

Examples from grade 6 standards correlation charts

Differentiating Instruction

Students whose first language is not English need special support, and teachers will want to differentiate their instruction to accommodate this need. Some native English speakers also need extra help as they strive for excellence in their academic studies.

English Learners

Research has established specific methods for helping English learners succeed.

Develop Vocabulary

- Model correct pronunciation and have students repeat after you.
- Invite students to point to examples.
- Give students varied activities that provide numerous exposures to each new word, such as vocabulary games with flash cards.
- Have students use vocabulary terms in sentences.

Flash Card Games

- Bingo
- Part of Speech Match
- Definition Challenge
- Find Your Partner

Model Concepts

- Use lesson **EXAMPLES** to demonstrate key points.
- Use think-alouds; say what you go through mentally in completing an exercise.
- Use gestures, pictures, diagrams, and graphic organizers in explanations.

Say "Yes" not "No"

To correct a student's pronunciation, restate and model the right way to say things. For example, "Yes, Juana, a conjunction joins sentences."

Form Pairs and Small Groups

Increase students' comfort level when they respond aloud by giving them the security of working with a partner or a small group.

Provide opportunities for all students to use their developing English by having them talk over and complete activities with a partner or small group, discussing how they came up with their answers.

Invite Students to Show What They Know

English Learners have broad experience and much knowledge, just as their English-speaking peers do. Rather than doing all the teaching and demonstrating yourself, invite students to write on the board, demonstrate or provide examples, and explain how they went about completing an exercise or solving a problem.

Striving Learners

These learners respond well to many of the same techniques as English Learners. In addition, they benefit from a strong focus, consistent modeling, extended repetition, and a slower pace.

Both groups should be expected to develop all the skills of the course. Neither group should be kept from learning what all students need to know to succeed in school and in life.

Chapter Vocabulary

- prewriting
- writing process
- brainstorming
- *5-W and How?* questions
- clustering
- drafting
- revising
- traits of good writing
- conventions
- peer reviews
- editing and proofreading
- proofreading symbols
- publishing and presenting

Chapter 1

Lesson	English Learners	Striving Learners
Lesson 1.1	Discuss *pre-* meaning "before," and explain that it's a clue to the meaning of many English words.	Explain prewriting as making a plan and tell students they will learn 4 skills to help them.
Lesson 1.2	Point out the 2 meanings of *draft*: "an air current" and "the first version of a piece of writing."	Have students make a 3-column chart headed Beginning, Middle, and End to organize their notes.
Lesson 1.3	Read the Writing Model aloud. Have students work in small groups to discuss the Writing Model and their revisions to the paragraph in Exercise 1.	Explain the 6 traits and introduce the chart on page 14. Have students use the sidebar notes on page 15 to explain the revisions to the Writing Model.
Lesson 1.4	Explain *proofread*: "to read and mark corrections in a piece of writing." Read the Checklist aloud.	In Exercise 2, have students find an example of each mark shown in the chart on page 18 and tell why the correction was needed.
Lesson 1.5	In small groups, have students discuss the ways they would like to present their writing.	Review your requirements for student writing. Then have students practice and present a piece of writing.
Writer's Workshop: Description	Simplify the 5 Key Features from page 21 to: main impression, organization, language, feelings, and details.	Assign small groups each a step in the writing process. Have them plan and present the important ideas to remember about their step.

Chapter 2

Lesson	English Learners	Striving Learners
Lesson 2.1	Tear a sheet of paper to demonstrate *complete* and *fragment*. Have students write subjects on a strip of paper and verbs on another and use their strips to form sentences.	Review subjects and verbs. Have partners complete Exercises 1 and 2. Invite volunteers to share their responses and discuss them as a group before doing other Exercises independently.
Lesson 2.2	Pronounce *coordinating conjunction* in syllables and then again as a phrase. Have students repeat after you.	Work through Exercises 1 and 2 as a whole group. Invite students who give correct answers to explain their thinking.
Lesson 2.3	Review the verb *to be* and help students recognize it in passive constructions.	Invite students to give examples of wordiness and come up with concise replacements.
Lesson 2.4	Have small groups each take a general word from the example on page 40 and brainstorm a list of specific words.	Read the Literary Model aloud. Ask: *How do such words as* struggled, clawed, *and* shrieked *help you picture Sam's trouble?*
Lesson 2.5	Read the Literary Model aloud, pantomiming *frowning, poking*, etc.	Help students brainstorm words to complete a details chart for the 5 senses.
Writing Application: Friendly Letter	Use the model letter on page 49 to point out the 5 parts of a friendly letter. Then have small groups work through the application together.	Preview the Writing Application with students to clarify its parts, what students should get from each part, and how to respond to it.

Chapter Vocabulary

- sentence fragment
- run-on sentence
- coordinating conjunction
- wordy sentences
- active voice
- precise words
- sensory details

Chapter Vocabulary

- declarative sentence
- imperative sentence
- understood subject
- interrogative sentence
- exclamatory sentence
- sentence variety
- clause
- independent (main) clause
- subordinate (dependent) clause
- sentence fragment
- simple sentence
- compound sentence
- complex sentence
- combining sentences
- compound subject
- compound verb
- key word

Chapter 3

Lesson	English Learners	Striving Learners
Lesson 3.1	Say aloud, slowly, the names of the 4 kinds of sentences. Have students repeat after you.	Have students brainstorm examples and complete a 4-column chart for the 4 kinds of sentences.
Lesson 3.2	Read aloud the examples on page 57 and the Literary Model on page 58. Clarify words and expressions as needed.	Ask volunteers to identify the kinds of sentences in the DIFFERENT examples on page 57. Do the same for the Literary Model.
Lesson 3.3	Help students generate example sentences using the sidebar words on page 60.	Have students give examples of subordinate clauses and tell why they aren't complete sentences.
Lesson 3.4	Assign each group a kind of sentence. Have them discuss ways to explain their kind and brainstorm examples. Then have groups present to the class.	Review clauses and give examples of each kind. Work on Exercise 2 with the group. Invite volunteers to share Exercise 3 revisions, and discuss as a group.
Lesson 3.5	Read the ORIGINAL and COMBINED passages aloud, and ask students to listen to the differences and explain what they hear.	Explain that subjects and verbs can be compound, just like sentences. Have students locate the compound subject and verb in the examples on page 65.
Writer's Workshop: Autobiographical Incident	Tell students they will use the steps of the writing process to write about a time that changed how they felt about something.	Have students help each other choose a topic and then tell their stories to each other prior to writing them.

Chapter 4

Lesson	English Learners	Striving Learners
Lesson 4.1	Pronounce the names of the 4 types of paragraphs, and have students repeat after you. Read aloud the Literary Model and Exercise paragraphs, and clarify unfamiliar terms.	Use a think-aloud for Exercise 1: *I think sentence 3 is the topic sentence because not all the sentences are about mother and baby dolphins, but they all are about dolphin communication.*
Lesson 4.2	Ask students to provide examples for *topic, detail, fact, example, sensory detail,* and *quotation.*	Review the difference between main idea and supporting details.
Lesson 4.3	Have students work with partners, discussing their thinking about the unnecessary details in Exercise 1.	Have partners discuss their Exercise 1 deletions. Then discuss revision choices as a group.
Lesson 4.4	Read aloud the lesson models while students follow along. Clarify unfamiliar words.	Have partners write the sentences in the first model on page 87 on strips of paper, arrange them, and explain their thinking.
Lesson 4.5	Have partners provide example sentences for each word or phrase in the Transitions chart on page 90.	Explain that transitions help relate sentences to one another. Focus on only one or two kinds of transitions in a session.
Writing Application: Opinion Paragraph	Provide a dictionary or thesaurus for students to use in writing.	Have groups choose their best paragraph and tell what makes it strong.

Chapter Vocabulary

- paragraph
- main idea
- topic sentence
- supporting sentences
- body
- concluding sentence
- clincher
- topic
- supporting details
- unity
- organization
- patterns of organization
- coherence
- transitions

Chapter Vocabulary

- essays
- introduction
- body
- conclusion
- thesis statement
- body paragraphs
- unity
- topic sentence
- coherence
- transitions

Chapter 5

Lesson	English Learners	Striving Learners
Lesson 5.1	Read aloud the essay on page 102. Have small groups discuss ancient influences and then write independently.	In the essay on page 102, discuss how to recognize the introduction, body, or conclusion. Lead a group-write about ancient contributions.
Lesson 5.2	Have partners read the Exercise 1 paragraphs together and talk about which sentence is the thesis statement. Clarify unfamiliar terms as needed.	Review main ideas and topic sentences. Explain that a thesis statement is a group of sentences that states the main idea of an essay.
Lesson 5.3	Ask volunteers to explain each of the dark-print vocabulary terms on page 105. Then read the Models aloud.	Refer students to the common transitions back on page 90. Help students create sentences that use these terms.
Lesson 5.4	The prefixes *in-* and *con-* can help students learn many English words. Have students complete a 2-column chart with examples for each prefix.	Work on Exercises 1 and 2 with the whole group. Ask students to identify the parts of each paragraph that are weak. Use think-alouds to help them if they get stuck.
Writer's Workshop: Persuasive Essay	For each step in the Workshop, read aloud or restate the directions. Have students work in small groups to give each other feedback.	Guide students through the Workshop: text, examples, checklist, hints, graphic organizers, and directions. Ask: *How will this help you write your essay?*

Chapter 6

Lesson	English Learners	Striving Learners
Lesson 6.1	Have students identify the verbs in the chart on page 121.	Make a 2-column Subjects and Verbs chart, and have students complete it.
Lesson 6.2	Explain that *simple* means "having only one part." Other meanings include "easy," "bare," "plain," and "ordinary."	Have students brainstorm sentences with the Helping Verbs on page 123 and identify the simple predicates and verb phrases.
Lesson 6.3	Have students work on the Exercises with a partner, explaining their work to each other.	Spend time with each of the 4 explanations on page 125. Provide additional examples for each.
Lesson 6.4	Stress the prefix *com-* (meaning "together") in *combined* and *compound.* Ask: *What has been put together?*	Work on the first 2 Exercise 1 items as a group, and then have students work independently. Talk through Exercise 2 before students write.
Lesson 6.5	Explain that the term *object* is used often to describe how English works.	For the first 3 items in Exercise 1, ask *what* and *whom* questions. Then have students work on their own.
Lesson 6.6	Pronounce the dark print vocabulary words and have students repeat after you.	Review subjects and predicates. Have students locate subject complements in the sample sentences.
Writing Application: Story	Have groups discuss each lesson part, and then have students share their stories with the group.	Monitor students' lists of ideas, characters and their types, the conflict, and Story Maps.

Chapter Vocabulary

- sentence
- subject
- predicate
- verb
- complete subject
- complete predicate
- simple subject
- simple predicate
- verb phrase
- understood subject
- inverted sentences
- compound subject
- compound verb
- action verbs
- direct object
- subject complement
- linking verbs
- predicate nominative
- predicate adjective

Chapter Vocabulary

- parts of speech
- noun
- common noun
- proper noun
- pronouns
- antecedent
- personal pronouns
- possessive pronouns
- indefinite pronouns
- subject pronoun
- predicate nominative
- object pronoun
- direct object

Chapter 7

Lesson	English Learners	Striving Learners
Lesson 7.1	Explain that to identify the part of speech, students need to look at what the word is doing—naming, describing, and so on.	Have students name some people, places, and things they see. Then have the group decide which are common nouns and which are proper nouns.
Lesson 7.2	For each pronoun in the lists on page 143, have partners generate a sentence and then replace the pronoun with a noun.	Have students check their Exercise 1 answers against the lists of pronouns on page 143. Have them use the lists also for Exercise 2.
Lesson 7.3	Tell students that being able to tell subjects from objects can solve such problems as when to use *I* or *me* and *who* or *whom.*	Talk through the Writing Hints and give students more examples, as these provide important practice for high-stakes tests.
Lesson 7.4	Discuss the prefixes *ante-* meaning "before" and *in-* meaning "not." Introduce *antecedent* and *indefinite.* Review singular and plural, and explain agreement.	Review the lists of subject and object pronouns on page 145. Have students identify which are singular and which are plural. Then have them make reference charts to use as they write.
Writer's Workshop: How-to Essay	In small groups, have students pick topics and plan their essays. Have them use the questions on page 153 and the Checklist on page 154 to review each other's work.	The Process Notes organizer on page 151 is a strong tool for organizing the information students will use in their essays. Guide students in making their own.

Chapter 8

Lesson	English Learners	Striving Learners
Lesson 8.1	Pantomime action and linking. Have students create sentences using the Linking Verbs list on page 161.	With students, generate examples of action verbs. Then analyze the list of Linking Verbs to explain "state of being."
Lesson 8.2	Explain that the present describes a habit or fact; both present and past are for ongoing events, those now and those that have ended.	Help students identify participles by pointing out that they take a helping verb. Suggest students memorize the Remember sidebar on page 163.
Lesson 8.3	Point out that the prefix *ir-* can mean "not" just as *in-* can. An irregular verb does not follow the usual pattern of past and past participle endings.	Explain that the helping verb in participle forms changes with the number (singular or plural) of the subject and the time (past or present).
Lesson 8.4	Read aloud Exercise 2. Then have partners identify the verbs and discuss how to change them to the past tense.	Have students use the 6 tenses in sentences about classroom events. Have them explain how they chose the verb form they used.
Lesson 8.5	Read aloud the Literary Model. Then guide students in identifying the types of verbals in it.	Teach gerunds, then Exercise 1; teach participles, then infinitives and Exercise 2. End with the Literary Model.
Writing Application: Summary	Have students share their summaries and check for correct use of verb tenses.	Focus students on finding the main idea and identifying 3 details in the article they will summarize.

Chapter Vocabulary

- verb
- action verbs
- linking verbs
- verb phrase
- helping verb
- main verb
- principal parts
- regular verb
- present
- present participle
- past
- past participle
- irregular verbs
- tense
- simple tenses
- present
- future
- perfect tenses
- verbals
- noun
- adverb
- adjective

Chapter Vocabulary

- modifiers
- adjectives
- modify
- proper adjectives
- adverbs
- degrees of comparison
- positive
- comparative
- superlative
- irregular degrees of comparison
- double comparisons
- preposition
- prepositional phrase
- object of a preposition
- compound object
- adjective phrase
- adverb phrase
- conjunction
- coordinating conjunctions
- interjection
- exclamation point
- comma

Chapter 9

Lesson	English Learners	Striving Learners
Lesson 9.1	Have partners generate more example sentences for the second chart on page 179.	Teach adjectives and adverbs in separate sessions.
Lesson 9.2	Focus on the 3 degrees of comparison, and have students discuss when to use each.	Focus on the rules in the chart on page 181 and on the spelling tip in the Remember sidebar.
Lesson 9.3	Point out the prefix in *irregular* and tell what it means (*ir-* means "not"). Use the chart on page 183 to develop vocabulary. Have students make sentences using each word.	Have students tell which irregular adjectives and adverbs give them the most trouble. Focus on these. Explain that *most, least, best,* and *worst* never have *-est* added as an ending.
Lesson 9.4	Have small groups draw or demonstrate the meaning of each word in the list of Commonly Used Prepositions.	Suggest students use the list on page 185 to help them with the Exercises on page 186.
Lesson 9.5	Pronounce *conjunction* and *interjection,* and have students repeat after you. Discuss the prefixes.	Teach conjunctions and interjections in separate sessions. Review punctuation marks.
Writer's Workshop: Personal Response to Literature	Have partners quiz each other using the checklist on page 190. After writing independently, partners should give feedback, and then revise.	Have students pick a work they feel strongly about. With a partner, they should discuss what details make them feel strongly.

Chapter 10

Lesson	English Learners	Striving Learners
Lesson 10.1	Explain that number means "one (singular) or more than one (plural)." Refer students to the sidebar on page 202 to see the verb forms that agree in number with various pronouns. Suggest students substitute a pronoun for the subject to decide which verb to use.	Use a think-aloud technique for item 1 in Exercise 1: Video-sharing describes *Web sites*, so it must be an adjective, not the subject. That means *Web sites* is the subject. It's plural. If I substituted a pronoun for *Web sites*, I'd use *they*. I would say, "they have," so *have* is the answer.
Lesson 10.2	Have students use the list of common prepositions on page 185 as a reference for this lesson.	Talk through the first 5 items in Exercise 1 before students work on their own.
Lesson 10.3	Pronounce the unfamiliar words *parasailing, helmets, solar,* and *silicon* as students repeat after you. Give meanings as needed.	Review *and, or,* and *nor,* and lead a discussion about why *and* makes subjects plural, but *or* and *nor* do not. Give additional examples of the 4 situations on page 205.
Lesson 10.4	Have teams generate sentences using the indefinite pronouns listed in the sidebar.	Focus separately on each of the 3 agreement problems. Discuss the answers to Exercise 2 with the group.
Writing Application: Business E-mail	Have the group decide on a business and what they want to ask. Discuss how to word the e-mail, and then assign the Workshop.	After reading and before writing, have students discuss the differences between a business e-mail and an e-mail between friends.

Chapter Vocabulary

- subject
- verb
- agree
- verb phrase
- singular
- plural
- prepositional phrases
- compound subject
- indefinite pronouns

Chapter Vocabulary

- end marks
- period
- declarative sentence
- imperative sentence
- question mark
- interrogative sentence
- exclamation point
- exclamatory sentence
- abbreviations
- comma
- semicolons
- colons
- compound sentence
- quotation marks
- direct quotation
- speech tag
- apostrophes
- possession
- ownership
- possessive nouns
- contraction
- hyphen
- dash

Chapter 11

Lesson	English Learners	Striving Learners
Lesson 11.1	Pronounce the lesson vocabulary words slowly, and have students repeat after you.	Invite students to provide other sentences for each of the 4 types and write them on the board.
Lesson 11.2	Read aloud the example sentences, pausing slightly for the commas to let students hear them.	Teach the 2 comma uses in this lesson in 2 different sessions. Review compound sentences.
Lesson 11.3	Have students discuss Exercise 1 answers within a small group.	With students, brainstorm sentences for each of the 5 comma uses.
Lesson 11.4	Have students use the checklist on page 211 to review each other's answers to Exercise 3.	Show a compound sentence with a conjunction and a comma and one without a conjunction but with a semicolon.
Lesson 11.5	Clarify *direct quotation* and *speech tags.* Vary your tone as you read.	Teach the punctuation of titles separate from that of dialogue.
Lesson 11.6	Play a contraction flash card game. Students draw a card and use its word in a sentence.	Teach the 2 uses of apostrophes in different sessions.
Lesson 11.7	Clarify unfamiliar terms in the Exercises.	Show syllables and hyphens in a dictionary.
Writer's Workshop: Research Report	Have students work in small groups but require each person to write his or her report independently.	Monitor the different steps of students' work: topic selection, note cards, outline, etc.

Chapter 12

Lesson	English Learners	Striving Learners
Lesson 12.1	Demonstrate and explain *capital letter, capitalize,* and *capitalization.* Use volunteers to demonstrate *specific* and *general*; for example, *Anna/girls*.	Explain that this lesson is about rules for when to use capital letters. Work through the first 2 items of Exercise 1 as a group. Then have students complete it independently.
Lesson 12.2	Read aloud the sentences in Exercise 1, and clarify words and concepts as needed.	Spend extra time on the second point (in quotations, when a capital letter is required and when it is not).
Lesson 12.3	Remind students that a dictionary can often help with capitalization.	After students have completed Exercise 2, ask: *When did you capitalize* port? *Why?*
Lesson 12.4	Encourage students to keep a book of words they have trouble spelling. Have them organize it alphabetically, like a dictionary.	Urge students to use the chart on page 249 to help them do Exercises 1 and 2. Have them work with a partner to check their answers against the chart.
Lesson 12.5	Have students complete the Exercises with a partner. Review Exercise answers and students' reasoning as a group.	On the chart on page 251, have students put a check-mark by plurals they know and circle those they don't to provide a focus for study.
Writing Application: Essay Question Response	If needed, provide the historical background for the Writing Model on page 255. Then discuss its key features.	To help students clarify their thinking, have them discuss their responses in small groups before planning their writing.

Chapter Vocabulary

- proper nouns
- proper adjectives
- plural nouns

Online Program Support

Grammar for Writing provides several online resources for teachers and students.

For Teachers	For Students
✔ password-protected supplemental Answer Key ✔ full-length research-based article by Beverly Chin ✔ Writing Rubrics	✔ additional practice for grammar lessons ✔ work-in-progress writing models for each step of the Writing Process ✔ full-length writing models for each writing workshop

1. Writing Rubrics

Writing Rubrics are provided for each grade for the main writing purposes: to describe, to entertain, to explain, and to persuade.

Criteria	Not Effective				Effective
How clearly are the steps organized?	1	2	3	4	5
How complete is the list of materials?	1	2	3	4	5
How effectively have transitions been used?	1	2	3	4	5
How interesting is the introduction?	1	2	3	4	5
How precise are the word choices?	1	2	3	4	5

2. Additional Grammar Exercises

Additional practice blackline masters are provided for each grammar lesson. Exercises allow teachers to reinforce the grammar topic or provide additional support for striving learners.

Name: ______________________________

Exercise 1 Recognizing Irregular Verbs

Underline five irregular verbs in the following paragraph.

[1]Conservation efforts began as early as the seventeeth century. [2]In the English colony of Pennsylvania, William Penn set limits on the amount of land available for settlement. [3]He made sure that one acre of forest was preserved for every five acres. [4]During the nineteenth century, Britain sent a strong message to industries. [5]New laws protected the environment against types of air pollution. [6]In the early twentieth century, countries felt that animals, such as migratory birds, needed protection under the law.

3. Writing Models

For each Writing Workshop in the Student Edition, full-length Writing Models are provided online. Work-in-progress Models for each step of the writing process accompany the Writing Process chapter.

Writing Model

[1]The octopuses swimming next to the weird, dark caves tower over me like bright planets. [2]In front of these purple giants, a blue whale glides along the ocean current, feeding on tiny krill. [3]The current trembles under the blue beast's deep call. [4]Behind the whale, strange glow-in-the-dark fish scurry away, leaving only a trail of bubbles. [5]My eyes widen as big as my smile as I try to capture this mysterious scene like a photograph.

4. Online Answer Key

While the Teacher's Edition provides a comprehensive answer key, the Online Answer Key provides sample answers for writing exercises and Write What You Think exercises.

Online Answer Key

Chapter 2, Lesson 1, Exercise 3

Answers will vary. Sample answers are shown.

You don't have to travel far to enjoy a good hike. Last summer, my best friend and I went on a different hike each week. We found interesting places right in our own neighborhood! We explored a different area on each hike. We saw something new on the back roads. Just by paying more attention than usual, we saw many birds, trees, and flowers we had never seen before. Of course, we found plenty of bugs. I will never forget insect repellent again!

Test Booklet Answer Key

Diagnostic Test, Exercise A

1. A **2.** B **3.** A **4.** D **5.** C

6. A **7.** A **8.** B **9.** E **10.** C

Diagnostic Test, Exercise B

1. A **2.** C **3.** D **4.** B **5.** A **6.** D

7. A **8.** C **9.** A **10.** C **11.** B **12.** B

Diagnostic Test, Exercise C

1. B **2.** C **3.** A

Chapter 1, The Writing Process, Exercise A

1. C **2.** D **3.** A **4.** C **5.** E

Chapter 1, Exercise B

1. B **2.** E **3.** B **4.** N **5.** E

6. E **7.** B **8.** E **9.** E **10.** B

11. B **12.** N **13.** B **14.** N **15.** N

Chapter 1, Exercise C

Answers may vary slightly. Students should be able to support their choices with reasons.

2 Write a script.

5 When you have decided where you will film, borrow a video camera.

1 You and your friends can make your own movie.

3 Ask friends to read your script, and practice acting it out.

4 Find a place to film your movie.

~~Some Hollywood movies cost tens of millions of dollars.~~

6 Test the camera to make sure the lighting and sound are okay.

7 Film the scenes in order.

Chapter 1, Exercise D

1. e **2.** c **3.** b **4.** d **5.** a **6.** f

Chapter 1, Exercise E

1. entertain **4.** persuade

2. persuade **5.** inform

3. entertain

Chapter 1, Exercise F

[1]They are dusty, torn, and almost worn out. [2]They are my old green sneakers. [3]I love them! [4]The bo^t^toms of the sneakers are scuffed, and there is^#^a small hole in ^the^ left sneaker. [5]The insides (the)(of) sneakers are squishy, and my mom says they don't smell to^o^ good. [6]The tops of the sneakers are faded in some places, and the laces are ragged at the ~~the~~ ends. [7]my mom wants me to ~~to~~ get a new pair. [8]How could I love any other pair of Sneakers as much? [9]with these sneakers, I won the all-city basketball tournament last friday! [10]I'll never (them)(give) up.

Chapter 1, Exercise G

Students' paragraphs should focus on one item of clothing and should use spatial order and exact, specific words to describe that item.

Chapter 2, Effective Sentences and Word Choice, Exercise A

1. C **2.** B **3.** E **4.** D **5.** C

6. D **7.** E **8.** A **9.** C **10.** C

Chapter 2, Exercise B

Answers will vary. Sample replacement words or phrases are shown.

1. football player, baseball cap
2. hurried, library
3. social studies, article
4. San Francisco, gorgeous
5. suspension bridges, cornfields
6. pears, carrots, delicious
7. At night, howls
8. burning, icy
9. basketball and soccer, community service and participate on the debate team
10. comic-book shop, crowded with
11. soccer player, flew
12. crow, cawed, flew
13. ordered, absolutely silent
14. gigantic, dazzling
15. tells, dramatic

Chapter 2, Exercise C

Answers will vary. If you wish, have students underline the sensory details they used.

Chapter 2, Exercise D

Students' corrected sentences may vary slightly. A sample answer is shown.

One of my favorite bands is the Beatles. They used a variety of instruments and produced original sounds. Even though they were most famous in the 1960s, I think they are still one of the best bands. They have so many different sounds! For example, on the album *Sgt. Pepper's Lonely Hearts Club Band*, they use a sitar, which is a type of guitar played in India.

The Beatles were from England, but their popularity was worldwide. The band played sold-out shows from the United States to Japan! When band member John Lennon died, it was an international tragedy.

I don't think that any band influenced rock and roll as much as the Beatles did. They were just four boys from Liverpool, but they wrote their own lyrics, and they set the bar high for musical success.

Chapter 2, Exercise E

Answers will vary. If you wish, have students number the sensory details they used.

Chapter 3, Sentence Variety and Structure, Exercise A

1. C **2.** D **3.** B **4.** A **5.** B

6. B **7.** D **8.** B **9.** A **10.** A

Chapter 3, Exercise B

Answers will vary.

Chapter 3, Exercise C

1. S **2.** I **3.** I **4.** I **5.** I

6. S **7.** S **8.** S **9.** S **10.** I

Chapter 3, Exercise D

1. complex; underline "who was a sculptor,"
2. compound
3. complex; underline "Although her full name was Mary Edmonia Lewis,"
4. complex; underline "which is what her Chippewa relatives called her."
5. simple
6. compound
7. simple
8. simple
9. compound
10. complex; underline "Although it was not until after her death,"

Chapter 3, Exercise E

Answers may vary slightly. A sample answer is shown.

This morning we left Grandma's apartment and drove to the shore. We saw dolphins, crabs, and tiny minnows in the bay. I forgot my sunscreen, so I ended up with quite a sunburn. Will you be home when we get back on Tuesday afternoon? I'm having a fun vacation, but I miss my dogs and my hamsters.

Chapter 3, Exercise F

Answers will vary. A sample answer is shown.

When I was five-and-a-half years old, I got lost at the Kingston Shopping Plaza. My mother and brother looked for me, but they couldn't find me. I remember hearing the echo of shoppers' footsteps and smelling hot pretzels from the pretzel stand. Eventually, my family found me. I was sitting on the floor behind the counter at the pretzel stand. The teenagers working at the stand felt sorry for me, so they gave me three huge, salty pretzels to eat.

Chapter 4, Effective Paragraphs, Exercise A

1. A **2.** D **3.** B **4.** B **5.** C

Chapter 4, Exercise B

1. N **2.** D **3.** P **4.** N **5.** E

Chapter 4, Exercise C

1. c **2.** b **3.** a **4.** d **5.** e

Chapter 4, Exercise D

Students' opinion paragraphs should be focused, specific, and logical. If you wish, have students circle the topic sentence and underline the transitions.

Chapter 5, Writing an Essay, Exercise A

1. A **2.** C **3.** D **4.** A

Chapter 5, Exercise B

1. B **2.** A **3.** A **4.** C **5.** A

Chapter 5, Exercise C

1. B **2.** N **3.** E **4.** B **5.** E

Chapter 5, Exercise D

1. SI **2.** TS **3.** SI **4.** C **5.** SI

Chapter 5, Exercise E

1. Underline "The second stage in a butterfly's life cycle is the larva stage." Circle "During this stage" and "In fact." Cross out "Butterflies don't develop wings until this next stage, which is called the pupa stage."
2. Underline "The first step to starting your own babysitting business is to make a plan." Circle "First," "For example," and "Then." Cross out "Just like starting a babysitting business, starting a lawn-mowing business is easy, too."

Chapter 5, Exercise F

Students' responses should include at least two supporting details. If you wish, have students number the supporting details they used.

Chapter 5, Exercise G

Concluding sentences will vary. A sample answer is shown.

[1]Students who are taking part in after-school sports programs should be ecxused from gym classes. [2]Physical education is an important part of the school day. [3]~~Not everybody likes gym class, of~~

~~course.~~ [4]Students who get some exercise often feel less stressed and are able to concentrate better. [5]However, those of us who participate in after-school sports get plenty of exercise. [6]An extra Study Hall Period makes more sense for us. [7]We could get more homework done during the school day, which would give us more time to learn a sport. [8]opponents of this plan say that it would be tooo difficult to keep track of who needed to be in gym class and who didn't. [9]There is a simple solution to this problem, though. [10]Coaches could give their players study hall passes. [11]Any student who drops out of ~~of~~ after-school sports would stop getting the passes. [12]Excusing student athletes from gym class would give us plenty of time to study and to exercise.

Chapter 6, Parts of a Sentence, Exercise A

1. A **2.** D **3.** B **4.** A **5.** C

Chapter 6, Exercise B

Avalanche means "snow sliding down a mountain." Avalanches can be deadly. Experts have trouble predicting them. The weather, the snow depth, and the angle of the mountain are all important. Pay attention to the weather and to your environment in the mountains. (you)

Chapter 6, Exercise C

Answers will vary. Sample answers are shown.

1. My new shoes are comfortable.
2. Delicious bacon and eggs sizzle in the frying pan.
3. My dog will whine and howl if I leave her.
4. Will you and your cousin visit Tulsa, Oklahoma?
5. Watch out! (you)

Chapter 6, Exercise D

The 23rd Street Bridge is a wreck (PN). People in the neighborhood are nervous (PA). The bridge seemed unstable (PA) yesterday before the collapse. Cracks in the bridge appeared larger (PA) and deeper (PA) than normal. The new mayor is Caroline Olson (PN). Mayor Olson looks tired (PA) but calm (PA). The rescue workers will arrive very soon. The city's public safety officers are Dan Hansen (PN) and Verzell Little (PN). The builder of the bridge is McAllister Construction (PN).

Chapter 7, Nouns and Pronouns, Exercise A

1. A **2.** D **3.** C **4.** C **5.** B

Chapter 7, Exercise B

Students' examples of proper nouns will vary.

1. My hero is an athlete.
2. I'm going to bring a friend to the city.
3. Our school is great.
4. The building is amazingly beautiful.
5. Will my team win?

6. Felipe wants to climb that (mountain).
7. My (brother) will bathe the (dog) for us.
8. Let's have (dinner) at the (restaurant).
9. The (street) was crowded.
10. Did Tameka or the (boy) run faster?

Chapter 7, Exercise C

Hi Jelena,

[1]You will not believe what happened to Meredith and ~~I~~ me. [2]We took a cooking class together, and both of ~~we~~ us had a great time! [3]The chef taught us how to make breakfasts, lunches, and dinners. [4]At the start of class, everyone gathered ~~their~~ his or her ingredients. [5]~~Her~~ She and ~~me~~ I were in charge of chopping the vegetables. [6]The chef told us to leave the sharp knife in ~~it's~~ its case. [7]Some of the students didn't want to eat their salads, so I ate ~~mines~~ mine and ~~theirs's~~ theirs. [8]Neither Meredith nor ~~me~~ I knew how to cook before we took the class, but now we are experts. [9]The best cooks in the class were she and ~~me~~ I (and the chef, of course)!

Chapter 7, Exercise D

Students' responses should describe the steps in order. If you wish, have students underline the transitions they used.

Chapter 8, Verbs, Exercise A

1. E **2.** C **3.** A **4.** B

5. A **6.** A **7.** C **8.** A

Chapter 8, Exercise B

Answers will vary. Sample answers are shown.

1. Dancing is my favorite weekend activity.
2. I want to eat one more slice of pizza, please.
3. The frowning hall monitor wanted to know where we were going.
4. Spelling irregular verbs can be a challenge.
5. Don't ask me to hold a place in line for you!
6. Surprised, I wondered where all the pizza had gone.
7. Relaxing is my favorite thing to do on Saturday nights.

Chapter 8, Exercise C

1. will enjoy **4.** was

2. discussed **5.** have read

3. will have been

Chapter 8, Exercise D

[1]The story of the boy who cried wolf ~~have~~ has been told since ancient times. [2]The boy in the story was watching over a flock of sheep. [3]Bored, he yelled, "Wolf! Wolf!" even though no wolf had ~~came~~ come. [4]~~Watching a bunch of sheep sounds pretty boring!~~ [5]The villagers ~~come~~ came running. [6]They discovered that the sheep and the boy ~~was~~ were safe. [7]On the next day, he ~~done~~ did exactly the same thing. [8]On the third day, a wolf really did ~~to~~ appear. [9]Nobody in the village ~~helps~~ helped the boy.

[10]When the boy complained, a wise old woman ~~telled~~ told him, "Nobody believes a liar, even when the liar is telling the truth!"

Chapter 9, Adjectives, Adverbs, and Other Parts of Speech, Exercise A

1. C **2.** A **3.** D **4.** E **5.** B

6. D **7.** D **8.** B **9.** A **10.** C

Chapter 9, Exercise B

Answers will vary. If you wish, have students number the modifiers or prepositions they used.

Chapter 9, Exercise C

1. successfully	**9.** usually
2. real	**10.** famous
3. clever	**11.** extremely
4. wisely	**12.** eventually, secret
5. quickly	**13.** simple
6. bravely	**14.** Recently
7. carefully	**15.** well
8. various	

Chapter 9, Exercise D

1. <u>on</u>
2. <u>on the kitchen table</u>
3. <u>chair</u>
4. <u>Hey</u>
5. <u>best</u>
6. <u>or</u>
7. <u>most</u>
8. <u>talk and eat</u>
9. <u>complex</u>
10. <u>seven or eight</u>

Chapter 9, Exercise E

[1]The ~~most~~ best book I have read this year is *The Kite Fighters* by Linda Sue Park. [2]Because of the time and place where the book happens, I thought I would not have anything in common with the characters. [3]I was wrong. [4]This novel takes place in Korea in 1473. [5]The main character has ~~a more old~~ an older brother. [6]The ~~more young~~ younger brother and the ~~more old~~ older brother sometimes fight. [7]My two brothers and I sometimes fight over which of us is ~~stronger~~ strongest, just like the characters in this book. [8]Chapter 13 is the ~~most long~~ longest chapter and the ~~excitingest~~ most exciting one. [9]The younger brother, Young-sup, competes in a kite-flying contest. [10]In Korea, kites had sharp pieces of glass glued to the kite string. [11]The ~~talentedest~~ most talented kite flyer could use the glass to cut the strings of the other kites. [12]Young-sup wants to fly his kite ~~good~~ well.

Chapter 9, Exercise F

Responses will vary. A sample response is shown.

I liked this blog entry. The writing is clear. The details about the kite fighting are <u>surprising</u> and <u>interesting</u>. I would like to know more about what the main character is like. Also, I would like to know what Korean kites look like.

Chapter 10, Subject-Verb Agreement, Exercise A

1. D **2.** D **3.** A **4.** A **5.** E

6. C **7.** C **8.** A **9.** D **10.** B

Chapter 10, Exercise B

1. The Web site ~~on the school's activities~~ is important to students.
2. Students ~~in each different organization~~ are excited to see their clubs online.
3. The content ~~on the Web site~~ includes group pictures and announcements.
4. A map ~~of the site's contents~~ guides the user through various sections.
5. Students ~~in our club~~ click on the club's logo.
6. The president ~~of the Internet club~~ thinks the Web site is a good idea.
7. Facts and details ~~on the site~~ are always available.
8. Teachers ~~at the school~~ believe parents can also benefit from the Web site.
9. Now, parents ~~of each club member~~ know about events sooner.
10. Announcements ~~on the "School News" page~~ keep all students up to date.
11. Members ~~of our club~~ access club calendars from any computer.
12. The home page ~~of our school's site~~ has a picture of the school mascot.
13. Links and icons ~~on the Web site~~ connect students to different parts of the site.
14. My friends ~~at another school~~ want to create their own Web sites.
15. One ~~of them~~ borrows some of our ideas for her school's new club.

Chapter 10, Exercise C

1. ✓	**11.** ✓
2. like	**12.** find
3. sharpens	**13.** makes
4. checks	**14.** ✓
5. comes	**15.** writes
6. require	**16.** helps
7. is	**17.** starts
8. carry	**18.** make
9. is	**19.** give
10. are	**20.** ✓

Chapter 10, Exercise D

Students should add a subject.

To: d.klonoski@xy2school.com

From: c.dewitt@xy2school.com

Subject: Information about Space Camp

[1]Dear Dr. Klonoski:

[2]Please e-mail me information on the space camp that you will be running at the university this summer. [3]My best friend and I ~~am~~ are interested in a one-week stay. [4]Both of us think~~s~~ it would be ~~sooooo coooool~~ fascinating to go to space camp. [5]~~Is~~ Are there any sessions in May or June? [6]~~June is my favorite month of the year.~~ [7]Everyone I know who attended the camp says it is well worth the cost.

[8]Sincerely,
[9]Chris DeWitt

Chapter 10, Exercise E

Answers will vary.

Chapter 11, Punctuation, Exercise A

1. A **2.** D **3.** A **4.** B **5.** C

Chapter 11, Exercise B

1. IN **2.** D **3.** D **4.** IMP **5.** E

6. D **7.** E **8.** IN **9.** IMP **10.** D

Chapter 11, Exercise C

[1]I watched a movie called *The Goonies* this weekend. [2]I've seen it six ~~time's.~~ times. [3]The movie is about a group of kids~~,~~ who go on an adventure after they find a treasure map. [4]One scene, which is my favorite, was filmed on a real ship. [5]I laughed when one of the characters in the movie said, "Hey, you guys!" ~~!~~ [6]The movie is older than I am, but I still enjoyed it. [7]Have you seen it? ~~.~~

Chapter 11, Exercise D

1. Student council elections are on Thursday; I am nervous just thinking about them.

2. I wasn't sure if I wanted to run for vice president; Marta talked me into it.

3. Marta isn't nervous; she is running unopposed for treasurer.

4. Marta, Phil, and I are tired; we spent all weekend making campaign posters.

5. I hope you will vote for us; but even if you don't, we can still be friends.

Chapter 11, Exercise E

1. We all shouted, "Run!"

2. In the book I am reading about ancient Egypt, the author states, "The Nile is the longest river in the world."

3. My mother's favorite song is "The Star-Spangled Banner."

4. The Italian word *ciao* means "hello."

5. The sign read, "Store open from nine to noon."

Chapter 11, Exercise F

1. H; I need to write a four-page research report by Tuesday.

2. D; I'm not sure which topic I want to write about—the history of baseball or careers in computer animation.

3. H; Our school's media center has twenty-six books about baseball.

4. D; One book—*Baseball's Glorious Past* by Carla McKissack—is my favorite.

5. H; The book has forty-four photographs.

Chapter 11, Exercise G

1. A **2.** NA **3.** A **4.** NA **5.** NA

Chapter 11, Exercise H

Answers will vary. Sample answers are shown.

1. The artwork of the Shoshone people is complex and beautiful for several key reasons.

2. During the presidential election of 2008, many young people became interested in politics for the first time.

3. Scientists are investigating the fascinating subject of how dolphins communicate with each other.

Chapter 11, Exercise I

[1]The Rolling Stones a British rock band, started playing music in the mid-1960s. [2]They have been popular ever since. [3]Most of their songs have been written by Mick Jagger who is the lead singer and Keith Richards the lead guitarist [4]Here are the names of two great songs by the Stones Paint It Black and Satisfaction. [5]Despite their age they still continue to perform at sold-out concerts throughout the world.

Chapter 12, Capitalization and Spelling, Exercise A

1. A **2.** C **3.** D **4.** C **5.** A
6. B **7.** D **8.** B **9.** D **10.** C

Chapter 12, Exercise B

1. ceiling
2. running
3. shyness
4. penniless
5. slipping
6. silliest
7. trying
8. timeless
9. truly
10. wives
11. deer
12. friend
13. field
14. carefully
15. caring

Chapter 12, Exercise C

1. England
2. However
3. game
4. piece
5. Japanese
6. ✓
7. Roman
8. likely
9. ✓
10. men

Chapter 12, Exercise D

Check students' reviews for correct capitalization and spelling. Make sure that students support their opinions with reasons and examples.

Chapter 12, Exercise E

[1]Parents should not restrict their children's ~~childrens'~~ Television watching time if the children are getting passing grades in their classes. [2]~~We learned in social studies class that television was invented in 1927.~~ [3]Part of becomming mature is learning how to budget time. [4]If parents control television time, children will not learn how to budget time for Homework, Chores, and Fun. [5]For that reason, I beleive it would be unfair to limit children's time. [6]If a child is failing one or more Classes, then parents should take away television until the grades improve.

Mastery Test, Exercise A

1. A **2.** B **3.** E **4.** C **5.** D
6. C **7.** B **8.** D **9.** B **10.** E

Mastery Test, Exercise B

1. C **2.** A **3.** B **4.** D **5.** B **6.** D
7. C **8.** A **9.** D **10.** B **11.** B **12.** C

Mastery Test, Exercise C

1. A **2.** C **3.** C

Level Red

GRAMMAR for Writing

Senior Series Consultant
Beverly Ann Chin
Professor of English
University of Montana
Missoula, MT

Series Consultant
Frederick J. Panzer, Sr.
English Dept. Chair, Emeritus
Christopher Columbus High School
Miami, FL

Series Consultant
Anthony Bucco
Language Arts Literacy Teacher
Pierrepont Middle School
Rutherford, NJ

Series Editor
Phyllis Goldenberg

Sadlier

Reviewers

Maria Davis Baisier
English Teacher
Holy Cross School
New Orleans, LA

Joan Borrasso
English Teacher
Aquinas Academy
Gibsonia, PA

Melissa Churchwell
Language Arts Teacher
Brooklawn Middle School
Parsippany, NJ

Jay Falls
Language Arts Teacher
Solon Middle School
Solon, OH

Stephanie Jones
Sixth Grade Teacher
Saint Francis of Assisi
Cordova, TN

Sister Rita Ann Keller, IHM
Language Arts Teacher
St. Gregory the Great
Virginia Beach, VA

Cheryl Kordes
Language Arts Teacher
St. Peter in Chains
Hamilton, OH

John T. Ludwig
Language Arts Teacher
Our Lady of Lourdes
Melbourne, FL

Darbie Dallman Safford
Language Arts Teacher
St. Monica School
Dallas, TX

Joan Sieja
Language Arts/Reading Teacher
Mary Queen of Heaven
Brooklyn, NY

Sister June Clare Tracy, O.P., Ed.D.
District Superintendent
Manhattan Catholic Schools
New York, NY

Mollie Mumau Williams
Language Arts Teacher
James W. Parker Middle School
Edinboro, PA

Acknowledgments

Every good faith effort has been made to locate the owners of copyrighted material to arrange permission to reprint selections. In several cases this has proved impossible. Thanks to the following for permission to reprint copyrighted material.

Excerpt from *Becoming Naomi León* by Pamela Muñoz Ryan. Copyright © 2004 by Pam Muñoz Ryan. Published by Scholastic Press, an imprint of Scholastic Inc.

Excerpt from *Blizzard*. Copyright © 2000 by Jim Murphy. Published by Scholastic Press, an imprint of Scholastic Inc.

Excerpt from *BREAKING THROUGH* by Francisco Jiménez. Copyright © 2001 by Francisco Jiménez. Reprinted by permission of Houghton Mifflin Harcourt Publishing Company. All rights reserved.

Reprinted with the permission of Simon & Schuster Books for Young Readers, an imprint of Simon & Schuster Children's Publishing Division from *THE HOUSE OF DIES DREAR* by Virginia Hamilton. Copyright © 1968 Virginia Hamilton.

Excerpt from *A Friendship for Today*. Copyright © 2007 by Patricia McKissack. Published by Scholastic Press, an imprint of Scholastic Inc.

Excerpt from "The Jacket" from *The Effects of Knut Hamsun on a Fresno Boy: Recollections and Short Essays* by Gary Soto. Copyright © 1983, 2001. Reprinted by permission of Persea Books, Inc. (New York)

Excerpt from *LINCOLN: A Photobiography* by Russell Freedman. Copyright © 1987 by Russell Freedman. Reprinted by permission of Clarion Books, an imprint of Houghton Mifflin Harcourt Publishing Company. All rights reserved.

From *MANIAC MAGEE* by Jerry Spinelli. Copyright © 1990 by Jerry Spinelli. By permission of LITTLE, BROWN & COMPANY.

Our Poisoned Waters by Edward Dolan. Copyright © 1997 by Edward Dolan. Published by Cobblehill Books.

Excerpt from *SILENT SPRING* by Rachel Carson. Copyright © 1952 by Rachel L. Carson, renewed by Roger Christie. Reprinted by permission of Houghton Mifflin Harcourt Publishing Company. All rights reserved.

Excerpt from *Surviving the Applewhites*. Copyright © 2002 by Stephanie S. Tolan. Published by Harper Collins Children's Books, a division of Harper Collins *Publishers*. All rights reserved.

Excerpt from "Taste of Snow" from *Beyond Manzanar* (Capra Press), by Jeanne Wakatsuki Houston. Copyright © 1985 by Jeanne Wakatsuki Houston.

Excerpt from *Ties That Bind, Ties That Break*. Copyright © 1999 by Leslie Namioka. Published by Delacorte Press, a division of Random House, Inc.

Excerpt from *The Treasure of Lemon Brown*. Reprinted by permission of Miriam Altshuler Literary Agency, on behalf of Walter Dean Myers. Copyright © 1983, by Walter Dean Myers.

Excerpt from *World War II's Tuskegee Airman*, © 2001 Perfection Learning Corporation.

Excerpt from *Yao Ming: Gentle Giant*. Used by permission of Avisson Press, Inc.

Credits

Cover Art and Design
William H. Sadlier, Inc. and Studio Montage

Cover Photos
Getty Images/Minden Pictures/Tui de Roy: penguins in Antarctica; Punchstock/Corbis: Colosseum; Punchstock/PhotoAlto: bottom three teenagers in winter clothing; Punchstock/Rubberball: girl jumping; Punchstock/Purestock: top teenager in winter clothing

Chapter Opener Photos
Alamy/Glow Images: 120 background; ImageGap: 30 background; Gunter Marx: 200 background; Robert Harding Picture Library Ltd/Adina Tovy: 54 background; Robert Harding Picture Library Ltd/RH Productions: 140 background; Rubberball: 200. Getty Images/Digital Vision/Roger Weber: 140; Minden Pictures/Tui de Roy: 78 background; Photodisc/SW Productions: 100; Photographic Choice RR/Geri Lavrov: 242; Photonica/Vincent Ricardel: 216. Jupiter Images/PhotoAlto Agency/Laurence Mouton: 160. Punchstock/BananaStock: 178; Corbis: 8 background; MIXA: 178 background; PhotoAlto: 78; Photodisc: 54, 216 background; Photosindia.com: 30; Rubberball: 8; Punchstock/Purestock: 78 inset top. Used under license from Shutterstock.com/Thomas Barrat: 100 background; David Hughes: 160 background; Graca Victoria: 242 background

Interior Photos
Getty Images/Tim Boyle: 16; Marc Carter: 226; ColorBlind Images: 10; Getty Images: 126, 142, 224; Dario Mitidieri: 243; Arnold Newman: 122; Erin Patrice O'Brien: 89; Purestock: 188; Tui De Roy: 234; Stringer/Joe Patronite: 170; Stockbyte: 59; Time & Life Pictures: 222; David Young-Wolff: 128; Norbert Wu: 22; istock International Inc/Anna Chelnokova: 104; Robert Churchill: 186; Matt Craven: 162; Christa Brunt: 92; Karen Hogan: 82; istock International Inc.: 42; Bonnie Jacobs: 149, 182; Paul Kline: 189; Evgeniya Lazareva: 219; Rich Legg: 231; Jakob Leitner: 62; MyShotz.com: 252; Jane Norton: 67; Shelly Perry: 148; Ray Roper: 230; Beth Skwarecki: 109; Nancy Catherine Walker: 21; Jan Will: 248; Monika Wisniewska: 103; Jupiterimages Corporation/AbleStock.com: 39, 45; Brand X Pictures: 133; Comstock Images: 20, 38, 79, 171; Creatas Images: 146; Liquidlibrary: 36, 164; Photos.com: 57, 168, 174, 228; Thinkstock Images: 64, 69; Library of Congress: 41; 86; NASA: 34; Shutterstock Images/John Bell: 204; Carlos Caetano: 68; Markus Gann: 87; Salvador Garcia Gil: 179; Vladislav Gurfinkel: 246; Andrew Kua Seng How: 130; Kostyantyn Ivanyshen: 203; Brandon Jennings: 31; Karl Keller: 81; Le Loft: 250; William J. Mahnken: 90; Mikhail Nekrasov: 65; Plastique: 106; Sasha Radosavljevich: 110; Franziska Richter: 202; Gina Sanders: 55; Vnlit: 85; Lisa F. Young: 61; SuperStock/ZSSD: 35

Printed in the United States of America
Student Edition: ISBN: 978-0-8215-0216-7
1 2 3 4 5 6 7 8 9 / 13 12 11 10 09 08

Dear Student:

As a student, you are constantly being challenged to write correctly and effectively in a variety of subjects. From homework to standardized tests, more and more assignments require that you write in a clear, correct, and interesting way.

Grammar for Writing teaches composition and grammar in an effective and appealing way. The first half of the book focuses on **Composition** and tells you about the important traits of good writing. In this section, you'll learn how to write correct and effective sentences, choose the best words to get your message across, and write strong paragraphs and essays. The second half of the book presents **Grammar** lessons in a way that is entertaining and easy to understand. You'll learn how grammar is used in everyday writing and how grammar mistakes can lead to funny misinterpretations that you'll want to avoid. Also, **Writing Workshops** show you how to craft different types of writing, such as stories and how-to essays.

Writing and grammar are subjects that you use every day. Whether you are writing a paper for class or emailing your friend about your weekend, you can express yourself best if you know how to write effectively. *Grammar for Writing* will help you do that. This program was created with you in mind, and it includes topics that will inspire you and spark your curiosity.

While no textbook can make writing easy, *Grammar for Writing* breaks down the essential steps of writing in a way that makes sense. Throughout the book, there is a **Write What You Think** feature that helps you develop clear arguments and sharpen your thinking skills. There are also **Literary Models** that draw examples from popular literature. Exercises are interesting and easy to understand. If you need help, **Hint** features point you in the right direction and ensure that you get the most out of the practice.

The point of *Grammar for Writing* is to sharpen the way you speak and write. By explaining grammar rules and writing techniques in a simple way, this book will help you become a better writer.

Good luck!
The Authors

CONTENTS

Part I: Composition

Part II: Grammar, Usage, and Mechanics

CHAPTER 1

The Writing Process

LESSON 1.1

Prewriting

During **prewriting,** you plan your writing. Prewriting means you explore possible topics, decide on your purpose and audience, and gather and organize your ideas.

Choose a topic you care about. You can find an idea almost anywhere—in magazines, movies, or personal experiences and imagination. Use a journal to record your ideas.

Try **brainstorming** to come up with a lot of topics quickly. Focus on one word or phrase, and list everything that comes to mind. Continue for three to five minutes.

Writing Model

interesting person

Mr. Kreisher, coach	J.K. Rowling	Pocahontas
Carlos, friend	Blackbeard	Anne Frank
Mrs. Belmonti, neighbor	Helen Keller	Tiger Woods

Narrow your topic. Sometimes a topic is too broad to cover in a short piece of writing. Asking ***5-W and How? questions*** is one way to divide a big topic into smaller parts.

Writing Model

Whom does Mrs. Belmonti remind me of?

What are her hobbies? What is she like?

Where does she work?

When did she move to the United States?

Why do I think she is funny?

How did I first meet her?

Remember

The **writing process** consists of five stages.

Prewriting → Drafting → Revising → Editing and Proofreading → Publishing and Presenting

Choose a topic on which you can elaborate.

Consider purpose and audience. As you plan your writing, ask yourself questions to help identify *why* you are writing and *who* your readers are.

- What is my goal? Is it to describe, inform, persuade, or entertain?
- Am I writing for my teacher, my class, or someone else?
- How much do my readers already know about the topic?
- How can I capture their interest?

Complete an "I want to" sentence like the one below. The more specific it is, the more it will help you stay on track as you start writing.

I want to describe my neighbor's crazy sense of humor to readers of my school newspaper.

Gather and organize details. Finish your prewriting by exploring which specific ideas and details to include. Try the strategy of **clustering** to explore your topic and connect different details.

Write your topic in a big circle. As you think of specific details, write them in separate circles.

Once you have developed your ideas, decide how best to organize them. For instance, you can order ideas in a simple list or create an outline. (See example on page 12.)

Exercise 1 Brainstorming Topics

What words or images does the photo make you think of? On a separate sheet of paper, make a list of words. Then turn your word list into a list of possible topics for a one- to two-page paper.

Answers will vary but should include a variety of topics. See www.grammarforwriting.com for writing models for each stage of the writing process.

WORDS lunch, friendship, fast food

POSSIBLE TOPIC vending machines at school

Exercise 2 Narrowing Topics

When choosing a topic, consider the length of your final product. Students' topics will vary but should be appropriate for a one- to two-page paper.

1. Look back at the list of topics you created for Exercise 1. If any of the topics are too broad to cover in a one- to two-page paper, narrow them by choosing one aspect of the topic to write about. If any of the topics are too specific, expand on them.
2. Create a new list of your revised topics.

BROAD TOPIC friendship

NARROWED TOPIC how I met my best friend

Exercise 3 Thinking of Audience and Purpose

Look at the list you created in Exercise 2. Choose two topics, and write an "I want to" statement for each. The audience and purpose should be different for both topics.
Students' statements should include a single purpose and audience.

TOPIC 1 I want to make a speech to my classmates to persuade them that we should not have vending machines at school.

TOPIC 2 I want to entertain my teacher with the story of how my friends and I saw a frog hopping in the mall.

Exercise 4 Gathering and Arranging Details

Now select one statement you created in Exercise 3. You will develop this topic as you move through the following lessons. Use the clustering strategy to gather details. Number each circle to show the order in which you will present your details.
Answers will vary but should be similar to the example.

For more on organizing ideas, see **Lesson 4.4.**

LESSON 1.2

Drafting

The most important goal of **drafting** is to get your ideas down on paper. When you write a draft, you organize your thoughts about a topic into sentences and paragraphs.

➡ Facing a blank page can be scary. Remember, you don't have to get everything perfect the first time.

➡ Organize your ideas into a beginning, a middle, and an end. Group related details together. Grab your readers' attention right away, and wrap things up at the end.

➡ Refer to the notes you made during prewriting, but feel free to add details or make changes to your writing plan as you go.

Writing Model

Outline:
Mrs. Belmonti's sense of humor

1. clothes
2. jokes
3. stories
4. surprises

Below is part of a first draft about an interesting person. It is based on the list of details to the left.

Writing Model

Introduction that focuses on one characteristic

Note to check spelling later

Arrow to add a detail

Mrs. Belmonti is a woman who has been my neighbor for the past four years. She is eighty years old. She seems much younger. She has a crazy sense of humor. Her choice of clothes is crazy and definitely out of the ordanary.sp? For instance, she loves to wear all kinds of hats everywhere she goes. She likes us to tell her crazy jokes. My parents hardly ever laugh out loud at jokes. Mrs. Belmonti laughs so hard that she cries. A huge one with orange ribbons is my favorite.

➡ Don't interrupt the flow of ideas to correct mistakes or stop and start over. It's okay for drafts to be messy.

Exercise 1 Describing How You Draft

Think about a paper you drafted recently.

Students' lists will vary but should include specific details.

1. Make a list that describes how you drafted the paper. For instance, did you write it first on paper or on a computer?
2. Think about what worked well and what did not. Make a second list describing how you will draft this paper. What might you do differently? What will you do in the same way?

WRITING HINT

When you draft, leave room for changes. Skip every other line if you are using a pen and paper. Double-space between lines if you are using a computer.

How I Drafted Before	How I Will Draft Now
1. in a notebook	1. on a computer (easier to make changes)
2. carefully, with attention to spelling and grammar	2. letting ideas flow, worrying about spelling and grammar later

Exercise 2 Writing a Draft

Write a first draft of your paper. Use the prewriting notes you created in Exercise 4 of the previous lesson. Refer to the list you just created in this lesson to help guide your drafting process.

Students' drafts will vary. See www.grammarforwriting.com for writing models for each stage of the writing process.

LESSON

1.3

Revising

Few writers get everything right the first time. **Revising** is your chance to make changes to improve your draft.

➡ If possible, set aside your draft for a little while. Then read it aloud to evaluate its strengths and weaknesses. What should you add, delete, replace, or rearrange?

➡ Ask yourself specific questions, such as the ones below, which cover five of the six key **traits of good writing.**

Ideas and Content	• How clear are my ideas? • Where should I add or delete details?
Organization	• How easy is it to follow the order of my ideas? • How well does one sentence connect to the next?
Sentence Fluency	• How do my sentences sound when I read them aloud? Where should I rearrange words? • Which short sentences should be combined?
Word Choice	• Where can I add more precise words? • Which words should I replace?
Voice	• How natural does my writing sound? • How interested do I seem in my topic?

➡ After you've looked over your draft, ask a classmate to read and comment on it. **Peer reviews** give you a chance to receive helpful feedback on your draft. But remember that it's ultimately up to you, the writer, to decide what changes to make.

➡ Mark your revisions directly on your draft. Later you can make a clean copy to hand in.

The passage on the next page shows a revision of the draft from Lesson 1.2.

- How effective are the revisions?
- If you were a peer reviewer, what other changes would you suggest?

WRITING HINT

The sixth writing trait is **conventions,** or correctness in grammar, spelling, usage, punctuation, and mechanics. You'll check for correctness during the next stage of the writing process: editing and proofreading. See **Lesson 1.4.**

Real-World Writing

Note this author's thoughts on revising.

"Revising and cutting take courage and self-confidence. You have to believe that you will write equally brilliant prose again. And you will."

—Gail Carson Levine

Writing Model

Mrs. Belmonti ~~is a woman who~~ has been my neighbor for the past four years. Although ~~She~~ she is eighty years old, she ~~She~~ seems much younger because ~~She~~ she has a crazy sense of humor. Her choice of clothes is ~~crazy and~~ definitely out of the ordinary. For instance, she loves to wear all kinds of ridiculous hats everywhere she goes. A huge purple one with curly orange ribbons is my favorite. She also likes us to tell her ~~crazy~~ silly jokes. ~~My parents hardly ever laugh out loud at jokes.~~ Mrs. Belmonti laughs so hard that ~~she cries.~~ tears stream down her wrinkled cheeks.

Eliminate extra words.

Combine short sentences.

Add details and transition.

Delete unrelated sentence.

Exercise 1 Revising a Paragraph

On a separate sheet of paper, rewrite the paragraph below.

Answers will vary but should improve the paragraph by eliminating extra words and extraneous details, adding transitions, and avoiding repetition. See sample answer in Answer Key at www.grammarforwriting.com.

1. Keep in mind the five traits of good writing listed on the previous page.
2. Use the questions on page 14 to guide your revisions.

[1]In my opinion, I think that vending machines at school are a bad idea. [2]First of all, they would distract students from their classwork. [3]Some kids have no money to spend. [4]Also, imagine the litter that would fill the halls, like empty bags of chips and candy bar wrappers. [5]The kinds of foods

sold in vending machines are unhealthy. [6]Potato chips, soda, and candy bars are unhealthy. [7]It is also unhealthy to avoid exercise. [8]When you want a snack between meals, it shouldn't be unhealthy. [9]Have carrots or an apple. [10]In addition to all of these reasons not to have a vending machine, there is another reason not to have it. [11]Having a vending machine at school is unfair. [12]Not everyone has extra money to buy snacks. [13]Kids get different allowances. [14]Some kids don't get allowances at all. [15]Vote "No" on having a vending machine at Springfield Middle School.

Peer Review Questions

1. Are the ideas in the paper easy to understand?
2. Does the writer include enough details?
3. Are there any details that are not relevant?
4. Does the paper hold the reader's interest?

Exercise 2 Evaluating Your Writing

Reread the draft you wrote for Exercise 3 in Lesson 1.2. Evaluate your draft by completing the sentences below. Answers will vary.

1. The most effective thing about my draft is...

2. What I most need to change is...

3. To make my paper more interesting, I will...

Working Together

Exercise 3 Revising Your Draft

Now trade drafts with a partner. Use the peer review questions on the left to help guide your revising. Meet with your partner to discuss his or her suggestions. Then revise your draft on a separate sheet of paper. Use the writing trait questions from page 14 and your own evaluation from the previous exercise as a guide.

Students' revisions will vary. See www.grammarforwriting.com for writing models for each stage of the writing process.

LESSON 1.4

Editing and Proofreading

The **editing and proofreading** stage provides the opportunity to find and correct errors in the sixth writing trait, **conventions,** which cover grammar, usage, spelling, mechanics, and punctuation.

➡ Edit slowly. Read each sentence carefully, and don't let your eyes skip over even one word or punctuation mark.

➡ Read through your work several times.

➡ To proofread more effectively, create a checklist of common errors. Focus on a different item in the checklist each time you read the draft.

Editing and Proofreading Checklist

- ❑ Have I spelled all words correctly?
- ❑ Did I indent each paragraph?
- ❑ Have I eliminated all fragments and run-on sentences?
- ❑ Have I used commas correctly?
- ❑ Do all subjects and verbs agree?
- ❑ Have I capitalized the names of people and places and the first word of every sentence?
- ❑ Are all verb forms and tenses correct?
- ❑ Does every sentence end with a punctuation mark?

➡ **Proofreading symbols,** like those shown on the next page, can make editing easier. Use them to mark clearly the corrections you need to make in your draft. (See the inside back cover for more proofreading symbols.)

WRITING HINT

Use a computer spell-check program, but don't depend on it to correct every mistake. For example, it cannot tell you that you should have typed *to* instead of *too*.

Symbol	Explanation	Example
ℓ	Delete (remove).	Miguel has seen ~~e~~ the movie.
^	Add.	Did ^the doctor call back?
⊙	Add a period.	Not all poems rhyme⊙
^,	Add a comma.	My birthday is May 4 ^, 1996.
/	Make lowercase.	Leah's /Teacher speaks Japanese.
≡	Capitalize.	Where is the Amazon river? (≡ under r)
∿	Switch order.	The spahgetti was great.
¶	Start a new paragraph.	¶"Absolutely not," he answered.

Notice how one writer used the checklist and proofreading symbols to edit this paragraph.

Writing Model

Although she doesn't like to cook what my mother calls "regular meals," Mrs. Belmonti loves to make desserts. Cookies and cakes are her specialties, and she tops everything with thick layers of brightly colored frosting. When you cook with Mrs. Belmonti, having fun is the top priority.

(Printed with proofreading marks: "de^serts" with "s" added; "Cakes" marked lowercase; "is" deleted and "are" added; "and" added after "specialties,"; "thick with" marked to switch order; "belmonti" marked to capitalize; period added after "priority".)

EXERCISE 1 Making a Proofreading Checklist

Look back through your writing to see which mistakes you make most often. For instance, you may notice a lot of run-on sentences or errors in capitalization. Use the errors you find to create a personalized proofreading checklist on a separate sheet of paper. It will help you avoid those mistakes in the future.

Students' checklists will vary.

Exercise 2 Using Proofreading Symbols

Use the proofreading symbols on page 18 to mark corrections in the paragraph below. Then write a clean copy on a separate sheet of paper.

> ¶ [1]I think having vending machines at schol is a bad idea because they would distract students from their classwork [2]Instead of studying everyone would be thinking about salty and sugary snacks. [3]Also, wrappers and empty bags may create liter. [4]Another argument against vending machines is the nutritional value of the food they sell. [5]Potatoe chips soda and candy are unhealthy for gorwing kids. [6]Finally, having a vending machine at School would be unfair because not everyone has extra money to spend. [7]Vote "No" on having a vending machine at springfield middle school.

WRITING HINT

To ensure that your writing is free of errors, proofread your work one last time after you've made your final copy. At this point, you will be able to catch and correct any mistakes you may have missed.

Exercise 3 Editing and Proofreading Your Writing

Working Together

Return to the revision you created for Exercise 3 on page 16.

1. Edit and proofread your work, using the checklist on page 17 and the checklist you created in Exercise 1. Use proofreading symbols.
2. Trade papers with a partner, and check each other's work for any missed errors.
3. Make a clean copy of your work.

Students' papers will vary. See www.grammarforwriting.com for writing models for each stage of the writing process.

LESSON 1.5

Publishing and Presenting

In the **publishing and presenting** stage of the writing process, you prepare a final copy of your work and share it with others.

Make sure the work you turn in, whether typed or handwritten, is neat and free of errors. Check that you know the exact format your teacher wants. For example, where should your name and the date go?

Consider different ways you could share your finished piece of writing. Try one of the suggestions below, or come up with an idea of your own.

- Submit your work to a school or local newspaper.
- Send it to friends or family in an e-mail.
- Read your work aloud to several classmates. Discuss their reactions and questions.
- Add photos or illustrations, and display your writing in your class or at the school library.
- Share it as part of a formal or informal oral presentation or speech to another class.
- Post it on a blog, or send it to a Web site that publishes student writing.

Remember

When you make a presentation, follow these tips:

- Speak loudly so that everyone can hear you.
- Look at your audience as you speak to them.
- Practice several times beforehand.

Working Together

Exercise Presenting Your Work

Return to the final copy of the piece you created for Exercise 3 on page 19.

1. Trade papers with a partner.
2. Discuss what presentation strategies would work best for each of your pieces. For instance, an anecdote about a trip to the mall might be improved with an illustration. A how-to article might benefit from a diagram.
3. When you are ready to present your work, share it with at least one other person, using one of the ideas listed above.

Students' presentations will vary. See www.grammarforwriting.com for writing models for each stage of the writing process.

ONLINE MODEL
www.grammarforwriting.com

Description

Picture your favorite scene from a movie. What characters, sounds, and sights come to mind? What words would you use to describe the scene to a friend?

In this writer's workshop, you'll learn how to write **description.** When you describe, you use words to create a picture of a person, an animal, a place, an event, or an object. You write about it in a way that makes it interesting for the reader. Description is used all around you.

Your description will focus on a place and should include the following features.

Key Features

- main impression you want to communicate
- clear organization that uses spatial order
- figurative language and vivid imagery
- your feelings about the place
- sensory details

ASSIGNMENT

TASK: Write a two-page **description** about a place where you would love to live. It can be anywhere—another town, a vacation spot, or an imaginary place.

AUDIENCE: your teacher and classmates

PURPOSE: to describe details of the place and your overall impression of it

Prewriting

Pick a Place Before you begin writing, you will need to pick a place to describe. This place should be unusual in some way and something your audience will want to read about.

1. First, brainstorm places where you would want to live. Be imaginative. Jot down real places, made-up ones, or ones from books or movies.

- Mars
- amusement park
- Hawaii
- bottom of the ocean
- Hogwarts School from Harry Potter books

2. Next, select a place you can describe well. Gather details about it. If you need to, look at pictures to jog your memory, or draw a sketch if your place is imaginary.

3. Figure out the main **impression,** or overall feeling, you want to create about the place you chose.

I'd love to live at the bottom of the ocean to explore its mysteries.

Form a Picture Help your audience picture the place you are describing. Paint an image with **sensory details,** which appeal to one or more of the five senses. List them in a chart.

Sight	Sound	Taste	Smell	Touch
strange marine life that glows in the dark	mysterious whale calls	salty sea water	musty smell of sunken ships	rough surface of weird caves

Drafting

Write the Complete Story Now it's time to turn your prewriting ideas into a draft. Figure out what you want to say in the beginning, middle, and end.

Beginning	Middle	End
• Identify the place you chose and your overall impression of it. • Make your introduction exciting so your audience will want to read more.	• Describe every interesting aspect of the place. • Organize your details logically.	• Wrap up your description. • Restate the key reason for choosing your place.

WRITING HINT

The main part of the drafting stage is to write down all of your ideas. You'll get a chance to fix spelling and grammar errors later during the editing and proofreading stage.

Locate It As you draft, organize the details in **spatial order.**

- Present details according to their location in space, such as from top to bottom, left to right, near to far, or front to back.
- Use **transitions,** such as *above, below, across,* and *near,* to help your reader picture the scene.

As you read the model below, notice the use of transitions and sensory details. How effective are they?

Writing Model

[1]The octopuses swimming <u>next to</u> the weird, dark caves tower <u>over</u> me like bright planets. [2]<u>In front</u> of these purple giants, a blue whale glides <u>along</u> the ocean current, feeding on tiny krill. [3]The current trembles under the <u>blue beast's deep call.</u> [4]Behind the whale, strange glow-in-the-dark fish scurry away, leaving only a trail of bubbles. [5]<u>My eyes widen as big as my smile as I try to capture this mysterious scene</u> like a photograph.

Transitions

Sensory details

Writer's feelings

Revising

Use the Revising Questions below to help you decide how to improve your draft. The Writing Model that follows shows the revisions one writer made to part of a draft.

As you revise, keep in mind the traits of good writing. See **Lesson 1.3.**

See the next page for tips on adding figurative language and imagery.

Revising Questions

- ❑ How clear is my use of spatial order?
- ❑ Where can I add figurative language and imagery?
- ❑ How effective is my use of sensory details?
- ❑ How clearly have I expressed my feelings about the place?
- ❑ How clear is the overall impression I have created?

Writing Model

1As I continue to explore the ocean, I bump into the most incredible animals. 2The jellyfish that float beside the sunken ship are ~~big~~ see-through mushrooms. 3They are larger than I read about in science magazines. 4It is fun to watch them ~~swimming~~ slowly wiggle in the water. 5I'm so excited, and I move on quickly to search for more animals. 6~~A~~ In front of the sea mountains, a cave is full of sleek eels, which use their gigantic heads to eat fish larger than themselves. 7~~An~~ To the left of the cave, an anglerfish uses the yellowish light on top of its head to find its prey.

Add imagery.

Add sensory details.

Add transitions.

Clarify spatial order.

Revising

Show, Don't Tell Good writers use words to show, not tell, what they mean. For example, look at the two versions below. Which one is more enjoyable to read?

TELLING I am excited as I find buried treasure.

SHOWING My heart pumps loudly as I discover golden coins on a sunken ship.

Add **figurative language** and **imagery** to show what you mean.

	Definition	Example
Figurative Language	**Metaphors** compare two different things without using the words *like* or *as*.	The octopuses are purple planets, circling overhead.
	Similes compare two different things using the words *like* or *as*.	The octopuses are **like** purple planets, circling overhead.
Imagery	Precise details create a vivid picture in the reader's mind.	Bumpy tentacles stroll back and forth near a volcano.

How effective is the author's description below?

Literary Model

[1]Ocean Park Pier was my playground. [2]All the kids in the neighborhood played ball and skated along the wide cement promenade that bordered the beach from Ocean Park to Venice.

[3]Memories of Ocean Park are warm ones of sunshine, hot days on the beach, building sand castles, playing *Tarzan* and *Jungle Girl*, jumping off lifeguard stands and spraining ankles. [4]Fourth of July was a balmy evening of crowds milling around the pier waiting for fireworks to spray the sky with luminous explosives.

—Excerpt from "A Taste of Snow" by Jeanne Wakatsuki Houston

CONNECTING Writing & Grammar

Use a comma to separate three or more items in a series. See **Lesson 11.2.**

I see squid**,** eels**,** and seaweed.

Editing and Proofreading

Now use the checklist below to edit and proofread your description. Go slowly. Concentrate on one sentence at a time.

Editing and Proofreading Checklist

- ❑ Did I capitalize the first word of each sentence?
- ❑ Have I checked that all words are spelled correctly?
- ❑ Did I indent every paragraph?
- ❑ Did I correctly use commas in a series?

Proofreading Symbols

ⱴ	Delete.
∧	Add.
≡	Capitalize.
#	Add a space.
⊙	Add a period.

Writing Model

[1]In the entire world, noother place is as ~~mysteerius~~ mysterious and exciting as the deep blue ocean. [2]undiscovered marine animals, mountains never explored by humans, and ships lost to the sea make it a a perfect place for discovering a new world [3]I can imagine squids slowly drift by like big lazy birds.

Reflect On Your Writing

- Which descriptive details do you like the most?
- What was the most difficult thing to describe?

Publishing and Presenting

Choose one of these ways to share your description.

- **Present it to your class or family.** Use poster board, and include pictures or keepsakes of the place.
- **Record it.** Work with others to create a video recording of the place. Record pictures and souvenirs. Add music, and use your paper to narrate the video for the class.

Chapter Review

A. Practice Test

In the passage below, there is a question *for each numbered item*. Read the passage carefully, and circle the best answer to each question.

Raising a Guide Dog

Guide dogs provide an invaluable service to people who are blind. They are trusted companions. They (1) protect their owners. You can help improve the quality of life for the blind by volunteering to raise a guide dog puppy. Becoming a puppy-raiser is a big responsibility. It (2) is extremely rewarding. Volunteers take potential guide dogs home with them when the puppies are several weeks old. The puppy-raiser's job is to teach the dog how to behave around people, among other skills (3). When the puppy grows to be about fifteen months old, it leaves the puppy-raiser's home to go

1. What is the best replacement for the underlined section?
A. NO CHANGE
B. trusted companions who
C. trusted loyal reliable companions who
D. trusted. They are loyal. They

2. What is the best replacement for the underlined section?
A. NO CHANGE
B. Becoming a puppy-raiser is a responsibility, it
C. Becoming a puppy-raiser,
D. Although becoming a puppy-raiser is a big responsibility, it

3. How could this part of the sentence be improved?
A. Delete it.
B. Insert a transition.
C. Add specific details.
D. Combine it with the previous sentence.

TEST-TAKING TIP

- Always read *every* answer choice, even if you think you spot the correct answer right away.
- Watch out for answer choices that fix one error but introduce another.

Chapter Review

into formal guide-dog training. This can be difficult because it is difficult [4] for puppy-raisers to give up a puppy. I had a friend who had to give away [5] her dog due to allergies, and she cried for weeks. However, the volunteers are comforted by the fact that the puppies they raised will go on to improve the lives of those who depend on them.

4. What is the best replacement for the underlined section?
A. NO CHANGE
(B.) It can be difficult
C. This can be very difficult because it is difficult
D. This can be difficult because is very hard

5. What change, if any, should be made to this sentence?
A. NO CHANGE
(B.) Eliminate it.
C. Add a transition.
D. Add details.

B. Describing the Writing Process

Suppose you needed to explain the five stages of the writing process to someone who knows nothing about them. On a separate sheet of paper, complete each sentence below. Answers may vary slightly.

1. In the **prewriting** stage, you figure out your purpose and audience and begin to organize your ideas.
2. In the **drafting** stage, you organize your ideas and begin writing your paper.
3. In the **revising** stage, you evaluate your draft and make changes to improve it.
4. In the **editing and proofreading** stage, you find and correct errors in grammar, spelling, usage, mechanics, and punctuation.
5. In the **publishing and presenting** stage, you prepare a final copy of your work and share it with others.

C. Identifying Topics

For each topic idea below, write *B* if the topic is too broad, *N* if it is too narrow, or *S* if it is suitable for a three-page paper. Revise topics you marked *B* or *N*. Revised topics will vary. Sample answers are shown.

B **1.** The History of Dance
The History of Tap Dance

S **2.** How to Tie-Dye

N **3.** The Height of the Washington Monument
How the Washington Monument Was Built

N **4.** What to Feed a Pet Parakeet
How to Care for a Pet Bird

B **5.** Africa and Its People
Popular African Traditions

D. Creating Topics

Write a topic that fits each purpose and audience listed below.

Answers will vary. Sample answers are shown.

1. entertaining story for a kindergarten class
   spaceship landing on school
2. persuasive speech to neighbors
   starting an annual block party
3. entertaining e-mail to a friend
   describing a great movie I saw
4. informational article for the school newspaper
   explaining new rules for school clubs
5. informational how-to article for classmates
   how to make a tree house

E. Reviewing a Description

First, use proofreading symbols to correct any errors in the description below. Then, answer the questions that follow.

Answers will vary. Sample answers are shown.

Proofreading Symbols

Delete.	Add.
Add a period.	Add a comma.
Make lowercase.	Capitalize.
Switch order.	¶ Start a new paragraph.

[1] I was born in a house on whitfield road and lived there until I was Five years. old [2] Most of the homes looked shabby, but the neighborhood park across the street was a paradise filled with trees, wildflowers, and blackberrry bushes. [3] There was a tire swing hanging from the tallest tree, and a brook ran through the woods behind it. [4] The trees were beuatiful in every seasoon.

1. What characteristics of a description does this draft have?
   The draft uses imagery, some spatial order, and descriptive visual details.
2. What is one improvement you would suggest?
   I suggest the writer include more sensory details, use figurative language, and explain his or her feelings about the place.

Chapter Review

CHAPTER 2

Effective Sentences and Word Choice

LESSON 2.1

Correcting Sentence Fragments

A **sentence fragment** is a group of words that is punctuated like a complete sentence but does not express a complete thought.

Sentence Fragment	The world's first skyscrapers. [What about the world's first skyscrapers?]
Complete Sentence	The world's first skyscrapers were built in the 1880s.

➡ A sentence fragment may be missing a subject, a verb, or both.

MISSING A SUBJECT Stands almost 1,500 feet tall.

MISSING A VERB The 1,250-foot Empire State Building in New York.

MISSING A SUBJECT AND A VERB Under construction in China and the Middle East.

➡ Correct a sentence fragment by adding what is missing.

ADD A SUBJECT **The Sears Tower** stands almost 1,500 feet tall.

ADD A VERB The 1,250-foot Empire State Building **is** in New York.

ADD A SUBJECT AND A VERB Several giant **skyscrapers are** under construction in China and the Middle East.

EXERCISE 1 Identifying Sentence Fragments

Label each group of words as a complete sentence or a fragment. Write *sentence* or *fragment* in the blank.

EXAMPLE fragment Our summer vacation to the Grand Canyon.

fragment **1.** The dazzling color of the sky over the canyon.

sentence **2.** We woke up early.

fragment **3.** The long, exhausting trip down to the bottom of the canyon.

fragment **4.** Lots of mules available for campers and their equipment.

fragment **5.** Rented them for a reasonable fee.

fragment **6.** Wouldn't have been able to carry the tents, food, and cooking equipment all by ourselves!

sentence **7.** My brother and I helped.

fragment **8.** Everyone at our campsite, especially my little brother.

fragment **9.** Including toasted marshmallows and s'mores for dessert!

fragment **10.** More stars than ever before.

CONNECTING Writing & Grammar

When you fix a fragment, make sure to use singular verbs for singular subjects.

My **camera captures** images from a long distance.

Use plural verbs for plural subjects.

The **photographs are** clear and vibrant.

For more on subject-verb agreement, see **Chapter 10.**

Exercise 2 Correcting Sentence Fragments

Below are ten sentence fragments.
Answers will vary. Sample answers are shown.

1. Tell what is missing in each: a subject, a verb, or both.
2. Add the missing part(s) to create a complete sentence. Write the corrected sentence on a separate sheet of paper.

EXAMPLE Thousands of tourists each year.

missing a verb – Thousands of tourists visit each year.

1. Should visit the Mount Rushmore National Memorial in South Dakota. missing a subject – You should visit the Mount Rushmore National Memorial in South Dakota.
2. Honors four important people in our country's history.
missing a subject – It honors four important people in our country's history.
3. Portrays the famous faces of George Washington, Thomas Jefferson, Abraham Lincoln, and Theodore Roosevelt.
4. The presidents' faces about sixty feet high.
missing a verb – The presidents' faces are about sixty feet high.
5. Along the half-mile long Presidential Trail, with excellent views of the sculpture through the pine trees.
6. The original carving equipment in the Sculptor's Studio.
missing a verb – The original carving equipment is in the Sculptor's Studio.
7. Each state's flag on the Avenue of Flags.
missing a verb – Each state's flag flies on the Avenue of Flags.

3. missing a subject – The monument portrays the famous faces of George Washington, Thomas Jefferson, Abraham Lincoln, and Theodore Roosevelt.

5. missing a subject and a verb – Visitors can walk along the half-mile-long Presidential Trail, with excellent views of the sculpture through the pine trees.

8. Can bring their own lunches.
missing a subject – Visitors can bring their own lunches.
9. Might like the nearby campgrounds.
missing a subject – You might like the nearby campgrounds.
10. Mount Rushmore, an unforgettable place for the whole family's vacation. missing a subject and a verb – You should visit Mount Rushmore, an unforgettable place for the whole family's vacation.

EXERCISE 3 Editing a Story

Circle each sentence fragment in the paragraph below. Then rewrite the story, adding any missing subjects and verbs.
Edited answers will vary but should include revisions that eliminate the four fragments. See sample answer in Answer Key at www.grammarforwriting.com.

[1]You don't have to travel far to enjoy a good hike. [2]Last summer, my best friend and I went on a different hike each week. [3]Right in our own neighborhood! [4]We explored a different area on each hike. [5]Saw something new on the back roads. [6]Just by paying more attention than usual, we saw many birds, trees, and flowers we had never seen before. [7]Of course, plenty of bugs. [8]Will never forget insect repellent again!

HINT
There are four sentence fragments to correct.

EXERCISE 4 Writing a Story

Working Together

Write a one-paragraph story about a trip you have taken. For example, you can write about a vacation, a visit to family, a shopping experience, or a sporting event.

1. Describe where you went and tell what you did there.
2. When you are finished, ask a partner to help you check the story for fragments.
3. Fix the fragments in your story.

Students' stories will vary, but they should be free of fragments. See sample answer in Answer Key at www.grammarforwriting.com.

LESSON 2.2

Correcting Run-on Sentences

A **run-on sentence** is two or more sentences that have been incorrectly written as one sentence. The sentences are run together with no punctuation or only a comma between them.

Run-on	Mars has ice caps it also has two moons.
Revision	Mars has ice caps**.** **I**t also has two moons.

➡ You can correct a run-on sentence by separating it into two sentences. Each sentence should begin with a capital letter and end with a period, a question mark, or an exclamation point.

Run-on	Saturn is the second largest planet, its rings are spectacular.
Revision	Saturn is the second largest planet**.** **I**ts rings are spectacular.

➡ You can also correct a run-on sentence by using a comma and a **coordinating conjunction,** such as *and, or,* or *but,* to join the two sentences.

CONNECTING Writing & Grammar

When you correct a run-on sentence with a coordinating conjunction between two sentences, be sure to use a comma before the conjunction.

John Glenn was an astronaut**, and** he was also a U.S. senator.

Run-on	Mercury gets extremely hot during the day the temperature can drop to –274 degrees at night.
Revision	Mercury gets extremely hot during the day, **but** the temperature can drop to –274 degrees at night.

Exercise 1 Understanding Run-on Sentences

Suppose a friend shows you the sentence below and says, "I don't understand what's wrong with this sentence. Where is the problem?" Answers will vary. Sample answers are shown.

Most owls hunt at night, they have excellent night vision.

1. Answer your friend's question in two to four sentences.
2. Avoid simply repeating the definition of a run-on.
3. Explain how you would correct the problem.

This sentence is a run-on sentence because it combines two complete sentences with a comma. To fix the run-on, you can either break the sentence into two complete sentences separated by a period, or you can add a coordinating conjunction.

Exercise 2 Identifying Run-on Sentences

Label each of the following items as a run-on sentence (*RO*) or a complete sentence (*CS*).

EXAMPLE RO Many people are afraid of bats, they shouldn't be.

RO **1.** Some people think bats are dirty animals this is not true.

CS **2.** Bats are actually very clean, and they groom themselves as cats do.

RO **3.** You may have heard that bats get tangled in people's hair, this is also untrue.

RO **4.** People are especially afraid of vampire bats they think they will get bitten.

RO **5.** A bat may bite you if you try to catch it, it will act in self-defense.

CS **6.** Just like many other wild animals, bats are afraid of humans.

RO **7.** You should not be scared of a bat, it is probably more afraid of you than the other way around!

RO **8.** Bats actually help people they eat pesky mosquitoes.

CS **9.** Fruit bats drop seeds on the ground, and the seeds help grow more trees.

RO **10.** Some species of bats are endangered, people should protect them.

Working Together

EXERCISE 3 Correcting Run-on Sentences

Work with a partner to correct each run-on sentence in two ways.
Coordinating conjunctions will vary. See Answer Key at www.grammarforwriting.com.

1. Rewrite it as two separate sentences.

2. Rewrite it using a comma and a coordinating conjunction between the two sentences.

Coordinating Conjunctions

and	or
but	so
for	yet
nor	

EXAMPLE Human activities affect black bears' habitats, some bears are endangered.

a. Human activities affect black bears' habitats. Some bears are endangered.

b. Human activities affect black bears' habitats, so some bears are endangered.

1. Black bears can live in many different habitats, they are usually found in forests.

2. Most black bears hibernate in winter they may hibernate for a shorter period of time in warm weather.

3. Some people mistakenly think black bears are vicious, they will kill the bears on sight.

4. People also cut down trees for wood in black bears' habitats, this means the bears are being driven out.

5. We should try to recycle paper and cardboard it is a good way to help conserve the black bears' habitat.

Write What You Think

Choose one statement below, and decide if you agree or disagree with it. Answers will vary. See sample answer in Answer Key at www.grammarforwriting.com.

- Humans should preserve all species of wild animals.
- The needs of humans are more important than the needs of animals.
- It's acceptable to destroy animals' habitats if humans need more land to build homes.

1. On a separate sheet of paper, state your opinion clearly. Write at least four sentences, giving reasons to support your opinion.
2. Check for and fix any run-on sentences.

LESSON 2.3

Eliminating Extra Words

When you write, say what you mean simply and clearly. Revise **wordy sentences** that can confuse readers and make your writing sound awkward.

➡ Eliminate unnecessary repetition. Do not say the same thing twice.

Wordy	Every single day in the months of July and August, my friends and I went swimming at 6 P.M. in the evening.
Revised	**Every day** in **July and August,** my friends and I went swimming at **6 P.M.**

➡ Replace a group of words with one word.

Wordy	Due to the fact that we swam for several hours, we were in a state of exhaustion.
Revised	**Because** we swam for several hours, we were **exhausted.**

➡ Use **active voice** verbs. Revise sentences so that the subject of a sentence performs the action of the verb.

Wordy	The pool was cleaned by the lifeguard. [7 words]
Revised	The **lifeguard cleaned** the pool. [5 words]

Real-World Writing

Some wordy phrases are used so often that we sometimes forget they're wrong. Avoid these common but wordy phrases in your own writing:

at this point in time
best ever
fall down
mix together
never before

Exercise 1 Using Active Voice

Reduce the number of words in each sentence by making each verb active voice. Wording may vary slightly.

EXAMPLE The race was won by the oldest contestant.

The oldest contestant won the race.

1. A half-marathon is organized by our town each year.
Our town organizes a half-marathon each year.

2. The runners are sponsored by townspeople.
Townspeople sponsor the runners.

> **HINT**
> Some sentences have two verbs that should be revised.

3. For three weeks before the race, donations are collected by the runners.
For three weeks before the race, the runners collect the donations.
4. The half-marathon is watched by almost everyone in town.
Almost everyone in town watches the half-marathon.
5. Although an official winner is announced by the judges, everybody wins by raising money for a good cause. Although the judges announce an official winner, everybody wins by raising money for a good cause.
6. This year, water in cups was brought by me to the runners.
This year, I brought water in cups to the runners.
7. The race was run by my sister, and months had been spent by her training for it.
My sister ran the race, and she spent months training for it.
8. She was watched by my mother.
My mother watched her.
9. A special dinner was made at home by my father, and congratulations were given to Liz by all of us.
My father made a special dinner at home, and we all congratulated Liz.
10. It is hoped by me that I will run the race next year.
I hope that I will run the race next year.

Exercise 2 Revising Sentences

Use the three strategies on page 37 to revise the wordy sentences below. Write your sentences on a separate sheet of paper.
Wording may vary slightly.

EXAMPLE In my opinion, I think that the sport of skateboarding is a fun sport.

I think that skateboarding is fun.

1. Some adults don't approve of skateboarding on account of the fact that they think in their minds that it is dangerous.
Some adults don't approve of skateboarding because they think it is dangerous.
2. It is a true fact that skateboarding can cause injuries, but, however, so do many other sports.
It is true that skateboarding can cause injuries, but so do many other sports.
3. There are accidents had by football players just like skateboarders have them, too.
Football players have accidents just like skateboarders do.
4. The key to guarding against accidents is the wearing of the proper and correct equipment.
The key to preventing accidents is wearing the proper equipment.
5. Before you ever step on a skateboard to go skateboarding anywhere, put on kneepads as well as a helmet in addition.
Before you go skateboarding, put on kneepads and a helmet.
6. I told my parents not to worry about my skateboarding, and the reason why there is no need for concern is because I'm a responsible rider. I told my parents not to worry about my skateboarding because I'm a responsible rider.

7. My parents agreed together on the same idea to let me practice in the skateboard park if I always wore a helmet all the time. My parents agreed to let me practice in the skateboard park if I always wore a helmet.
8. I was in a thrilled mood of total and complete excitement the very first time I ever did a jump before without falling. I was thrilled the first time I did a jump without falling.
9. At last after a long time, my parents finally saw once and for all how good I had been becoming at the sport of skateboarding. At last, my parents saw how good I had become at skateboarding.
10. I couldn't have been more surprised when a brand-new skateboard was given to me by them in order so that I could replace my old skateboard! I couldn't have been more surprised when they gave me a new skateboard to replace my old one!

Exercise 3 Revising a Draft

Working Together

Revise this draft to eliminate wordy sentences, but keep all the important details. Then ask a partner to listen as you read your revision aloud. Work together to delete any unnecessary words that remain. Wording may vary slightly. See Answer Key at www.grammarforwriting.com.

[1]It is a fact that the sport of ice-skating goes back thousands of years. [2]The very first ice skates ever found, from about 3,000 B.C., were made of animal bones. [3]In order for the skates to be put on, leather straps were threaded through holes at each end, and then the straps were tied to the feet of the people who wore them. [4]Today, ice skates are made by manufacturers with modern materials, such as nylon, plastic, and steel.

Exercise 4 Improving Your Own Writing

Choose a short report or story you wrote for a class. As you read it aloud, circle any examples of wordiness. Then rewrite your draft to eliminate the wordiness you found.

Answers will vary. If time permits, have students exchange papers and comment on each other's revisions.

LESSON
2.4

Using Precise Words

Using **precise words** makes your writing lively and your meaning clear. Pay special attention to nouns, verbs, and modifiers (adjectives and adverbs) as you write and rewrite.

Original	Despite the bad weather, the man saw the vehicle.
Revised	Despite the **thick fog,** the **police officer spied** the **red convertible.**

Nouns that are specific, instead of general, tell readers exactly what you mean.

General	animal	clothes	plant	furniture
Specific	porcupine	sweatshirts	dandelion	coffee table

Replace dull, overused verbs with ones that are more precise and vivid.

Dull	write	look	said	walk
Vivid	scribble	glare	screamed	scamper

Use precise, colorful adjectives and adverbs to add interest to your style and detail to your descriptions.

Vague	old	big	soft	badly
Precise	wrinkled	seven-foot	fluffy	harshly

CONNECTING Writing & Grammar

Be careful not to confuse adjectives and adverbs. An adjective modifies, or describes, nouns or pronouns. Adverbs modify verbs, adjectives, and other adverbs. See **Lesson 9.1.**

INCORRECT Henry sang quiet.

CORRECT Henry sang **quietly.**
[*Quietly* is an adverb that modifies the verb *sang*.]

Exercise 1 Identifying Precise Words

Read the passage below about the Great Blizzard of 1888.
Students' sentence choices and explanations will vary but should identify precise words and the images they evoke.

1. Underline examples of specific nouns, vivid verbs, and precise adjectives and adverbs.
2. Circle the sentence that gives you the clearest picture of the storm. Be ready to explain why you selected the sentence you did.

Literary Model

[1]Sam struggled and clawed to get free of the snow, but he was in over his head. [2]The more he moved, the more snow fell on top of him. [3]He shrieked for help, but no one heard him above the wind's mighty roar. [4]His boyish romp had turned into a frightening trap in just seconds. [5]Finally, just as his strength was about to give out, a policeman came along and yanked him free.

–Excerpt from *Blizzard!* by Jim Murphy

Real-World Writing

All good writers work hard to pick the word that means exactly what they want to say.

"Wrestling with words gave me my moments of greatest meaning."

–Richard Wright

Exercise 2 Revising Sentences

Replace the underlined words in the following sentences with more precise and effective nouns, verbs, and modifiers. You may add or delete other words, too.
Revised sentences will vary. Sample answers are shown.

EXAMPLE The food tasted good.

The taco sauce tasted spicy.

1. I had a hard day at school, so I was tired when I got home.
   I had a nine-hour day at school, so I was exhausted when I got home.
2. My mom came in, and she said that she'd had a bad day.
   My mom trudged in and complained that she'd had a horrible day.
3. I was happy when my dad said that we were going out.
   I was delighted when my dad announced that we were going out.
4. Dale's Diner is the nicest place in our area.
   Dale's Diner is the fanciest restaurant in our neighborhood.
5. Their dinners are totally awesome because they have a good chef.
   Their dinners are delicious because they have an amazing, well-trained chef.
6. A woman walked us over to our table.
   A friendly hostess led us over to our table.

7. The table had a <u>pretty</u> vase of <u>flowers</u> on it.
The table had a <u>bright red</u> vase of <u>fresh-cut roses</u> on it.
8. We all <u>looked</u> at the menu and <u>talked</u> about which dishes we might <u>like</u>. We all <u>studied</u> the menu and <u>whispered</u> about which dishes we might <u>order</u>.
9. My little sister <u>was sad</u> because she wanted <u>something</u> that wasn't on the menu. My little sister <u>cried</u> because she wanted <u>a chicken sandwich</u> that wasn't on the menu.
10. I <u>said</u> <u>nicely</u> that there were <u>many</u> other <u>things</u> she could order. I <u>explained</u> <u>patiently</u> that there were <u>dozens</u> of other <u>mouth-watering meals</u> she could order.
11. The restaurant was <u>busy</u> that night, so the service was <u>slow</u>.
The restaurant was <u>full of activity</u> that night, so the service was <u>sluggish</u>.
12. <u>They gave</u> us <u>some</u> bread and some <u>other stuff</u> to eat while we waited. <u>The busboys handed</u> us <u>a basket of warm</u> bread and some <u>breadsticks</u> to eat while we waited.
13. The waiter was <u>moving</u> as fast as he could, but it took a <u>long</u> time before he <u>brought</u> our <u>food</u>. The waiter was <u>scrambling</u> as fast as he could, but it took an <u>hour</u> before he <u>served</u> our <u>soups</u>.
14. It was worth the wait because our <u>meal</u> was <u>really great</u>.
It was worth the wait because our <u>pasta</u> was <u>unbelievably fresh</u>.
15. I was <u>hungry</u>, so I <u>ate</u> my <u>dish</u> with <u>enjoyment</u>.
I was <u>starving</u>, so I <u>devoured</u> my <u>spaghetti</u> with <u>delight</u>.

Exercise 3 Writing a Menu

Imagine that you own a restaurant. Using precise words, write your own menu on a separate sheet of paper.
Answers will vary. See sample answer in Answer Key at www.grammarforwriting.com.

1. Describe at least three different foods you serve. Come up with an unusual or funny name for each item.
2. In each description, tell how the food is prepared, what it looks like, or how it tastes. Make your customers want to order it.

Exercise 4 Improving Your Own Writing

Find a story or other creative piece you wrote for a class. Read it aloud, and circle any vague, dull, or overused words. Then rewrite it, adding precise words to improve your writing.
Answers will vary.

Using Sensory Details

Sensory details are what we experience through our five senses—sight, sound, smell, taste, and touch.

Five Senses	
Sight	sparkling blue water, tiny oval stones
Sound	roar of the ocean, bird's high-pitched cry
Smell	burned toast, scent of flowery perfume
Taste	salty water, sour pickles
Touch	powdery sand, smooth cotton

➡ Use sensory words and details to grab your readers' interest and create a clear, vivid picture of your subject.

Notice how the author of the following passage includes sensory details in her description.

Literary Model

1 Lucille led Jake to the kitchen. 2 Randolph was standing at the stove, frowning ferociously and poking at a pan of frying bacon with a long fork, a steaming coffee mug in his other hand. 3 He glowered at them as they came in. 4 A towheaded boy who looked about four years old was sitting on a tall stool at the counter, singing about an itsy-bitsy spider at the top of his lungs. 5 The moment he saw Jake, he stopped singing and stared, his mouth open, his blue eyes wide and round.

—Excerpt from *Surviving the Applewhites* by Stephanie S. Tolan

Smell and taste

Sound

Sight

Reading as a Writer

Sample answers are shown.

1. How well can you picture this scene? Which details are the most effective? I can picture it very well. The most effective details are the boy's reaction to seeing Jake.
2. What other sensory details could the author have added? The author could have added details about the way Jake walked into the kitchen.
3. The author does not tell us how Randolph is feeling. What details show us his mood? The details "frowning ferociously" and "glowered at them" show us Randolph's mood.

Exercise 1 Revising Sentences

Make each sentence more interesting by adding at least one sensory detail as noted in the parentheses. You may add, delete, or rearrange words. Answers will vary. Sample answers are shown.

EXAMPLE The alarm startled Darnell. (sound)

The high-pitched beeping of the alarm startled Darnell.

1. The sun out his window told him he had overslept. (sight) The bright sunlight that shone through his window told him he had overslept.
2. Darnell hurried downstairs to eat breakfast. (taste) Darnell hurried downstairs to devour a delicious breakfast of crispy bacon, scrambled eggs, and fresh fruit.
3. Pedro called out that it was time to get to work. (sound) Pedro shouted crossly that it was time to get to work.
4. When they got to the empty lot, it was hard to imagine it could become a park. (sight) When they got to the abandoned and dirty lot, it was hard to imagine that such a junkyard could become a park.
5. Everybody started picking up trash. (touch) Everybody started quickly grabbing the sticky candy wrappers.
6. When Katie found an old lunch bag, the others held their noses. (smell) When Katie found an old lunch bag that smelled like dead fish, the others held their noses.
7. Darnell put soil on the ground and planted grass seeds. (touch) Darnell put moist soil on the hard ground and planted grass seeds.
8. It was hard work, and soon he was sweating. (touch) It was hard work, and soon his forehead was wet with sweat.
9. They all took a break for lunch. (taste) They all took a break for a tasty lunch of sandwiches and sweet fruit.
10. Josie hammered nails to build a fence around the lot. (sound) Loud pounding shook the park as Josie hammered nails to build a fence around the lot.
11. Katie came each week to water the grass. (sight) Katie came each week to water the tiny blades of green grass and plants.
12. Finally, the flowers were in bloom, and the park was complete. (smell) Finally, the fragrant flowers were in bloom, and the park was complete.
13. The mayor gave a speech at the grand opening. (sound) The mayor gave a booming speech at the grand opening.
14. He handed each volunteer a medal. (sight) He handed each proud volunteer a gleaming silver medal.
15. They had a celebration in the new park. (sound) With rock music blaring, they had a celebration in the new park.

Exercise 2 Brainstorming Sensory Details

Study the picture, and imagine being in this place. In the Web, write words to tell what you would see, hear, smell, touch, and taste. Two examples have been done for you. Answers will vary. Sample answers are shown.

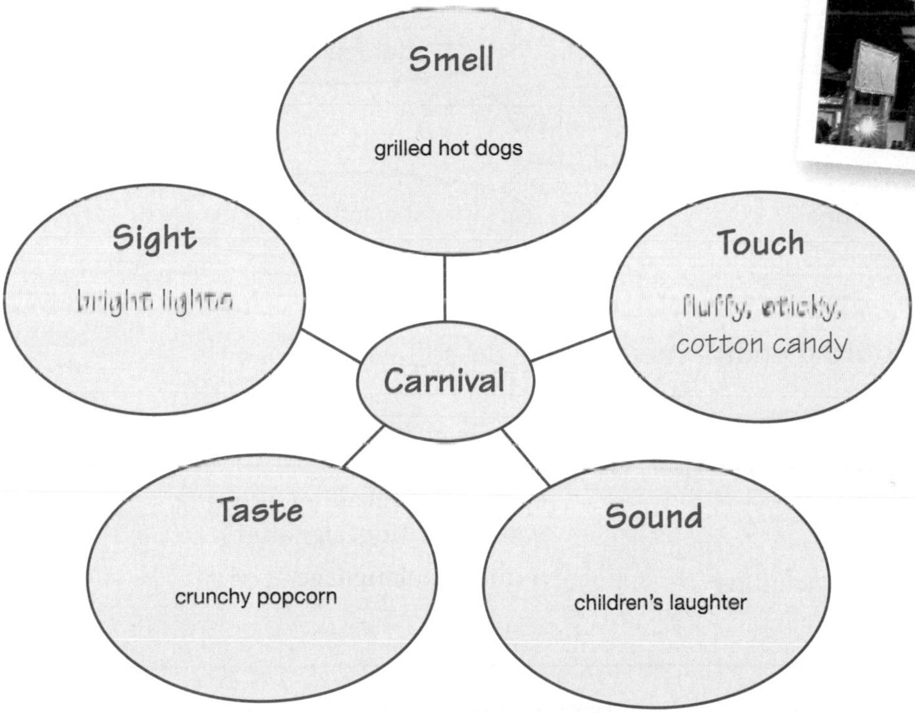

Exercise 3 Writing an Article

Now use the sensory details in your Web to write an article about the scene. Answers will vary but should contain at least one detail for each sense. Sample answer is shown.

1. Write at least five sentences that make the scene come alive for readers.
2. Describe at least one detail for each sense: sight, sound, smell, taste, and touch.

The bright lights on the Ferris wheel and in the stands at the carnival made the night feel like day. The smell of grilled hot dogs attracted people to the food stands. Children's laughter filled the air. The teens giggled as they crunched on hot popcorn. Everyone's eyes sparkled with excitement.

Friendly Letter

When you want to express something to someone you care about, send a **friendly letter.** Friendly letters are little surprises and are more personal than e-mails. The Web lists a few purposes for sending a friendly letter. What other reasons can you think of?

When you write a friendly letter, include the following.

Key Features

- clear organization
- friendly tone
- specific details, including sensory details
- five parts (heading, greeting, body, closing, signature)
- informal language

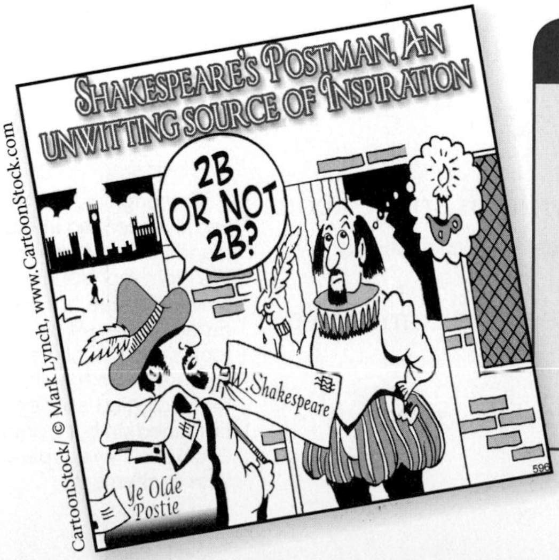

CartoonStock/ © Mark Lynch, www.CartoonStock.com

ASSIGNMENT

TASK: Write a one-page **friendly letter.**

GOAL: to thank someone

TARGET: someone who did something for you

SPECIAL INSTRUCTIONS: Write at least two body paragraphs. Include details about what the person did.

Make a Plan First, decide whom you are going to thank. Then, spend some time thinking about what you want to say. Make a list of specific details to include in your letter.

1. Jot down three or four specific details about what the person did for you and why it was special.
2. Describe how the action made you feel, such as thrilled, surprised, or relieved.

<u>What the Person Did</u>

- visited me over spring vacation
- explored the new city with me
- showed me that we're still friends

<u>How It Made Me Feel</u>

- happy
- less lonely

Stay Focused Next, organize the details in your list. Clear **organization** of your paragraphs will make your letter easy to follow.

1. Decide which details to include in each paragraph. For example:

PARAGRAPH 1	what the person did
PARAGRAPH 2	how the action made you feel

2. To unify your paragraphs, cross out details that don't stick to the topic. For instance, if you're thanking your aunt for a gift she gave you, don't include details about a gift from another person.

For help with paragraph unity, see **Lesson 4.3.**

Keep It Interesting As you write, imagine that you're talking to the person you're writing to.

WRITING HINT

Sensory details appeal to the five senses—sight, sound, smell, taste, and touch. See **Lesson 2.5.**

The smooth bow felt like silk. **[touch]**

1. Be yourself. Keep your **tone,** or attitude, friendly.
2. Use specific details, such as **sensory details,** to make your letter interesting and entertaining.

   VAGUE I was excited to receive the gift.

   SPECIFIC When I got the fuzzy red sweater, I chuckled and darted to my room to put it on.

3. Use **informal language** such as contractions, slang, abbreviations, and short sentences.

Formal Language	Informal Language
I am writing to inform you	I'm dropping a note to say
It gave me great pleasure	I was psyched
Thank you kindly	Thanks so much

Point out to students that not all friendly letters need a heading, but they always should include a date.

Follow the Format Include the parts of a friendly letter.

Heading: your address and the date →
211 Curtis St.
Dayton, OH 34343
April 2, 2009

Greeting: the beginning of the letter ← Dear Rick,

Body: one or more paragraphs that make up the main part ← What's up? Thanks for visiting during spring break. It was awesome to hang out and explore the new city.

Closing: a phrase that ends your letter ← Talk to you soon,

Signature: the signing of your name ← Jake

Review Your Letter Use the checklist to make sure your letter is correct. The model below shows one writer's letter.

WRITING CHECKLIST

Did you…

- ✔ use clear organization?
- ✔ include specific and sensory details?
- ✔ use informal language and a friendly tone?
- ✔ include all five parts of a friendly letter?
- ✔ include two body paragraphs?
- ✔ add commas in the heading, greeting, and closing?

CONNECTING Writing & Grammar

Add commas in three parts of a friendly letter.

Heading: Add a comma after the city and between the date and year.

Greeting: Add a comma after your greeting.

Closing: Add a comma after the closing.

211 Curtis St.
Dayton, OH 34343
April 2, 2009

Dear Rick,

[1]What's up? [2]Thanks for visiting during spring break. [3]It was awesome to hang out and explore the new city.

[4]The arcade we discovered is amazing. [5]I still can't believe that it has over two hundred video games, miniature golf, and bumper cars. [6]The friends we made at the bowling alley are hilarious.

[7]I was sad when I first moved here, but now that you showed me these cool places and we met new people, I feel better about the move. [8]Now we have two cities to hang out in.

[9]I'll see you over summer break. [10]We're visiting my Aunt Carmen for two weeks. [11]Let's get together with Steve and Mike.

Talk to you soon,
Jake

All five parts of a friendly letter

Friendly tone and informal language

Specific details

CHAPTER
2

Chapter Review

A. Practice Test

Read each sentence below carefully. If you find an error, choose the underlined part that must be changed to make the sentence correct. Fill in the circle for the corresponding letter. If there is no error, fill in circle *E*.

EXAMPLE

Ⓐ Ⓑ Ⓒ Ⓓ Ⓔ I went to an amazing (A) concert last week, now (B) I want to learn (C) how to play the piano (D). No error (E)

Ⓐ Ⓑ Ⓒ Ⓓ Ⓔ **1.** My (A) dad said that he would (B) arrange for (C) piano lessons to be given to me by Mr. Ramos (D). No error (E)

Ⓐ Ⓑ Ⓒ Ⓓ Ⓔ **2.** We don't have (A) enough room (B) in our house for (C) a piano. A keyboard instead (D). No error (E)

Ⓐ Ⓑ Ⓒ Ⓓ Ⓔ **3.** I met (A) my teacher (B) on the day of (C) May 17th (D). No error (E)

Ⓐ Ⓑ Ⓒ Ⓓ Ⓔ **4.** Reading (A) music takes practice you (B) have to learn (C) the symbols for notes and rhythm (D). No error (E)

TEST-TAKING TIP

To identify sentence errors, follow these steps:

1. Read the whole sentence, and look at each underlined part.
2. Cross out the underlined parts you know are correct.
3. Identify the part that contains the error. If there is no error, mark *E*.

Chapter Review

ⒶⒷⒸⒹ● **5.** My teacher has been playing since he was my age.
A B C
He's terrific. No error
D E

●ⒷⒸⒹⒺ **6.** My keyboard has a great sound it also has a volume
A B
switch, which lets me practice quietly if the baby is
C D
asleep. No error
E

ⒶⒷⒸ●Ⓔ **7.** I like to play all types of music, but I have one favorite
A B C
piece. "Für Elise" by Beethoven. No error
D E

ⒶⒷ●ⒹⒺ **8.** My recital was in the afternoon yesterday
A B C D
afternoon. No error
E

ⒶⒷⒸⒹ● **9.** I was nervous, but as soon as I began to play, my hands
A B
knew exactly what to do. No error
C D E

Ⓐ●ⒸⒹⒺ **10.** I will keep practicing one day I will play as well as my
A B C
teacher does. No error
D E

B. Choosing Precise Words

Underline the word or phrase in parentheses that is most precise.

1. I enjoy (painting, making) all kinds of (artwork, landscapes).

2. To create a rainy effect, I (hold, grip) the brush so the paint (goes, drizzles) onto the canvas.

3. I prefer (light, pastel) paints to (other, red) tones.

4. My art teacher (said, proclaimed) that my work was (unique, good).

Chapter Review

5. If I practice (regularly, some), I may become a (big, respected) artist someday.

6. I began (doing, sketching) a new piece (yesterday, previously).

7. It will be a (picture, portrait) of my (brothers, family).

8. It is (annoying, bad) because they keep (laughing, messing around).

9. I promised I would give them a (gift, new book) if they (were good, sat still).

10. I will (keep working on, finish) the portrait (tomorrow, in the near future).

11. The art (event, contest) is (next week, soon).

12. Many (artists, people) will be (registering, there).

13. Visitors will (go, crowd) into the small (building, museum).

14. Which (one, painting) best shows my (style, use of color)?

15. I will (go with, submit) the painting of my (nice, energetic) brothers.

C. Writing Sensory Details

On a separate sheet of paper, write a sentence that includes a sensory detail that appeals to each sense listed below.

Answers will vary. Sample answers are shown.

1. sight
   The excited gray dog pulled on its leash.
2. smell
   The park smelled of fresh flowers.
3. touch
   Children tightly grabbed the hard monkey bars.
4. sound
   Dogs angrily barked at cooing pigeons.
5. taste
   We took a break and snacked on sweet, tangy oranges.

D. Revising a Friendly Letter

Carefully read the friendly letter below.

1. Rewrite it, correcting any fragments or run-ons.
2. Eliminate wordy sentences.
3. Add any parts of the letter that are missing or incorrect.
4. Write your revised letter on a separate sheet of paper.
5. Answer the questions that follow.

Students' rewrites will vary but should contain no fragments, run-ons, or wordy sentences. Students should add a date, greeting, and closing. See sample answer in Answer Key at www.grammarforwriting.com. Sample answers to the questions are shown.

100 East Spring Street
Ridgefield, NJ 56021

Aunt Casey,

[1]I'm writing to invite you to come to my school to see our production of The Wizard of Oz. [2]It's on Friday, April 2. [3]The play starts at 7 P.M. on that Friday evening. [4]It's in the auditorium.

[5]I am very excited and eager because I have a big part! [6]The Wicked Witch of the West. [7]It's a lot of fun to play the character, you should hear my evil cackle! [8]I've been practicing all month I really am looking forward to it. [9]My costume is so cool!

[10]A big party is being organized by my parents after the play, and I hope you can make it. [11]There will be lots of good food.

Leslie

- What features of a good friendly letter does this draft have?

The draft has clear organization, a friendly tone, and informal language. The evil cackle is a good sensory detail.

- What is one suggestion you would give to the writer about how to improve the letter?

I'd suggest the author include a few more specific details about the play, her part, and the party afterwards.

Chapter Review

CHAPTER 3

Sentence Variety and Structure

LESSON 3.1

Kinds of Sentences

Different kinds of sentences have different purposes.

A **declarative sentence** makes a statement. It ends with a period.

During the Middle Ages, a knight was a soldier on horseback.

An **imperative sentence** gives a command or makes a request. Imperative sentences usually end with a period.

Please describe the weapons a knight used.

The subject of an imperative sentence is *you,* even if *you* doesn't appear in the sentence. *You* is called the **understood subject.**

(You) Show me a picture of a knight.

An **interrogative sentence** asks a question and ends with a question mark.

How did boys train to become knights?

An **exclamatory sentence** shows strong feelings. Exclamatory sentences end with an exclamation point.

Maya's report about the Middle Ages was fantastic!

For more on end punctuation, see **Lesson 11.1.**

Exercise 1 Classifying Sentences

Add the correct punctuation mark to each sentence below. Label it as *declarative, imperative, interrogative,* or *exclamatory.*

EXAMPLE interrogative Will you help me paint my bedroom ?

declarative **1.** I bought two cans of paint, two brushes, and a long-handled roller so we can reach the ceiling .

interrogative **2.** Could you help me move the furniture, too ?

interrogative **3.** Don't you think this shade of blue is absolutely incredible ?

imperative **4.** Please help me cover the bed with a drop cloth .

exclamatory **5.** Hey, that paint is about to spill !

exclamatory 6. Yikes, my father would ground me for a month !

interrogative 7. I don't even particularly like that color, but I guess Will does, doesn't he ?

exclamatory 8. Wow, the paint I chose looks incredible !

interrogative 9. Should we stop painting for an hour and take a break for lunch ?

imperative 10. Let me cook something special to thank you .

Working Together

Exercise 2 Writing a Silly Script

On a separate sheet of paper, add eight or more sentences to continue this conversation.

Answers will vary but should include at least two of each of the four types of sentences.

1. Use each kind of sentence listed on page 55 at least twice to create a script.
2. Read your script aloud with a partner, using your voices to express emotions.

MS. PRIM N. PROPER: Why on earth are you wearing those ridiculous shoes?

MR. SILLY SHOES: I haven't the faintest idea what you mean.

Exercise 3 Finding Examples

Look for the four kinds of sentences in a book you are reading.

Answers will vary.

1. On a separate sheet of paper, write down two examples of each of the four kinds of sentences. Label them.
2. If you cannot find examples of a particular kind of sentence, explain why. Why might the author not need to use certain kinds of sentences?

LESSON 3.2

Sentence Variety

You can make your writing more lively by paying attention to **sentence variety.**

See **Lesson 3.1** to review the four kinds of sentences: declarative, imperative, interrogative, and exclamatory.

➡ Mix different kinds of sentences in a paragraph. An occasional question, command, or exclamation can help keep your writing from sounding monotonous.

ORIGINAL Many people take part in marathons. It takes a lot of strength and endurance to run more than twenty-six miles, and it also requires determination. It takes a long time to get in shape.

DIFFERENT KINDS OF SENTENCES Have you ever thought of taking part in a marathon? It takes a lot of strength and endurance to run more than twenty-six miles, and it also requires determination. Start getting in shape today!

➡ Avoid starting each sentence with the same word or phrase. Use a variety of sentence beginnings to make your writing flow smoothly.

ORIGINAL Runners may race on a track, a city street, or a forest trail. Runners often wear specially designed shoes to avoid injury. Runners sometimes select shoes with spikes to prevent falls.

DIFFERENT BEGINNINGS **Runners** may race on a track, a city street, or a forest trail. **Wearing specially designed shoes** helps them avoid injury. **To prevent falls,** runners sometimes select shoes with spikes.

➡ Vary the length of your sentences. Mixing long and short sentences creates an appealing rhythm and keeps readers interested.

As you read the following excerpt from a novel, notice the range of sentence lengths.

Literary Model

Short sentence between two long ones

[1]If you listen to everybody who claims to have seen Jeffrey-Maniac Magee that first day, there must have been ten thousand people and a parade of fire trucks waiting for him at the town limits. [2]Don't believe it. [3]A couple of people truly remember, and here's what they saw: a scraggly little kid jogging toward them, the soles of both sneakers hanging by their hinges and flopping open like dog tongues each time they came up from the pavement.

—Excerpt from *Maniac Magee* by Jerry Spinelli

Reading as a Writer Answers will vary. Sample answers are shown.

1. Why might the author have made sentence 2 so short?
2. Think about how you could rewrite sentence 3 into two separate sentences. Why might the author want such a long sentence here?
3. How well has the author used different kinds of sentences and sentence beginnings?

1. The short sentence emphasizes the idea and grabs a reader's attention.
2. Since the author just used a short sentence, he may have wanted to add a long sentence to avoid choppiness. One of the many ways to divide the sentence is: "A couple of people truly remember, and they saw a scraggly little kid jogging toward them. The soles of both sneakers hung by their hinges and flopped open like dog tongues each time they came up from the pavement."
3. The author varied the sentences well. He used different beginnings, one command, and two statements.

Exercise 1 Revising Sentences

On a separate sheet of paper, rewrite each group of sentences below to add sentence variety. Revised paragraphs will vary. See sample answers in Answer Key at www.grammarforwriting.com.

1. In your revisions, use different kinds of sentences, varied beginnings, and a range of sentence lengths.
2. You can add, delete, change, or rearrange words and add details. Remember to indent your paragraphs.

EXAMPLE Fruit is an important part of a healthy diet. Fruit provides your body with the vitamins it needs. Fruit is a delicious snack.

If you think you can stay healthy without fruit in your diet, think again. Your body needs the vitamins that fruit provides. So put down that candy bar. Eat a juicy orange instead!

1. Eating from the five food groups is important. Choose foods from the five food groups every day. Each food group has different nutrients.

2. Pasta is made of grain. Cereal is also made of grain. Grains have carbohydrates. Carbohydrates provide energy.

3. Dairy products contain protein. Dairy products provide calcium to strengthen bones. Dairy products include milk, cheese, and yogurt.

4. Did you know that many people do not eat vegetables? How are their bodies affected? Why don't more people like vegetables? What about the rainbow of colors that vegetables come in? Doesn't this make them fun to eat?

5. Meat is a source of protein. It is not the only one. Beans have protein. Tofu has protein. Soy has protein. Nuts have protein. Vegetarians can still eat plenty of protein.

EXERCISE 2 Writing a Paragraph

Write a paragraph using information from the notes below. Use at least two kinds of sentences, and vary the lengths and beginnings of your sentences.

Students' paragraphs will vary. See sample answer in Answer Key at www.grammarforwriting.com.

- CPR: cardiopulmonary resuscitation
- can revive person who has stopped breathing
- mouth-to-mouth: rescuer blowing air into victim's mouth, forcing air into lungs
- chest compressions: rescuer pressing hands on victim's chest to get oxygen to brain and move blood out of heart if it has stopped beating
- repeat 2 breaths + 30 chest compressions

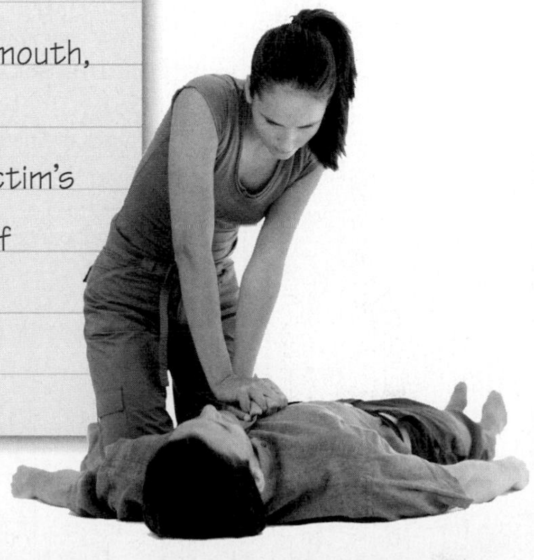

LESSON 3.3

Kinds of Clauses

A **clause** is a group of words that contains a subject and a verb. Writers use two kinds of clauses.

➡ An **independent** (or **main**) **clause** expresses a complete thought and can stand by itself as a sentence. Every sentence has at least one independent clause.

ONE INDEPENDENT CLAUSE	Frogs and toads are amphibians.
TWO INDEPENDENT CLAUSES	They can live on land, and they can live in water.

➡ A **subordinate** (or **dependent**) **clause** does not express a complete thought. It cannot stand alone as a sentence.

because they are cold-blooded	**which** have soft, moist skin

➡ A subordinate clause by itself is a **sentence fragment.** Join a subordinate clause with at least one independent clause to make a complete sentence.

SENTENCE FRAGMENT	When baby frogs and toads hatch.
COMPLETE SENTENCE	When baby frogs and toads hatch, they are called tadpoles.

INDEPENDENT CLAUSE   SUBORDINATE CLAUSE

Some Words That Begin Subordinate Clauses

after	if
because	when
before	which

For more on recognizing and correcting sentence fragments, see **Lesson 2.1.**

Exercise 1 Identifying Clauses

Label each underlined clause as *independent* or *subordinate.*

subordinate **1.** Mark Twain, whose given name was Samuel Clemens, was born in 1835.

independent **2.** In 1865 he wrote "Jim Smiley and His Jumping Frog," and it was published in a newspaper.

independent **3.** Twain also worked as a riverboat pilot, but the boats stopped sailing when the Civil War broke out.

subordinate **4.** Before he chose the name "Mark Twain," he wrote stories under the name "Thomas Jefferson Snodgrass."

subordinate **5.** The phrase "mark twain," which was used on riverboats, is an old nautical term meaning "two fathoms deep."

Exercise 2 Writing Sentences

Write five sentences by adding the item in parentheses. Underline the independent clause(s) in each new sentence.

Students' sentences will vary, but each independent clause should be underlined. Sample answers are shown.

EXAMPLE I like to read. (At the beginning, add a subordinate clause that begins with *when*.)

When I get home from school, I like to read.

1. I go to the library every week. (At the end, add a subordinate clause that begins with *if*.)
   I go to the library every week if I have time.
2. Last week, I finished reading *Then Again, Maybe I Won't*. (At the end, add an independent clause that begins with *and*.)
   Last week, I finished reading *Then Again, Maybe I Won't*, and I am ready for a new book.
3. I liked the new book. (At the end, add a subordinate clause that begins with *because*.)
   I liked the new book because it was very funny.
4. when I read (At the beginning, add an independent clause.)
   I sit on my couch when I read.
5. I would like to write stories. (At the beginning, add a subordinate clause that begins with *after* or *when*.)
   When I am older, I would like to write stories.

Exercise 3 Fixing Sentence Fragments

Circle the two subordinate clauses that are punctuated as if they are complete sentences. Fix them by adding or connecting an independent clause to each.

Students' independent clauses will vary, but they should fix the two circled sentence fragments correctly. See sample answers in Answer Key at www.grammarforwriting.com.

[1]Shel Silverstein's poetry is known for its zany rhymes and wildly imaginative topics. [2]Because the characters are outrageous. [3]Adding to the fun are Silverstein's quirky line drawings. [4]Which are sure to tickle the funnybones of generations to come.

LESSON 3.4

Simple, Compound, and Complex Sentences

Sentences may be classified according to the number and kind of clauses they have.

A **simple sentence** contains one independent clause and no subordinate clauses. It may include a compound subject, a compound verb, or both. (See Lesson 6.4.)

Simple Sentences	Vultures are the largest birds of prey. They soar high in the sky and look for dead or dying animals to eat.

WRITING HINT

Too many sentences of one type in a row can sound boring. Using a variety of simple, compound, and complex sentences makes your writing more interesting.

A **compound sentence** contains at least two independent clauses and no subordinate clauses. The clauses are often joined with a comma and a coordinating conjunction, such as *and, or, but, so, for, nor,* and *yet.*

Compound Sentences	Vultures have excellent eyesight, **and** their sense of smell is superb. Most nest on cliffs or in trees, **but** some lay their eggs on the ground.

A **complex sentence** contains one independent clause and one or more subordinate clauses. The subordinate clauses can go at the beginning, in the middle, or at the end.

Complex Sentences	The California condor, **which is a vulture,** is the largest land bird. **When its wings are fully spread,** they extend more than ten feet.

EXERCISE 1 Writing Sentences

Write an original sentence that fits each guideline below.
Answers will vary. Sample answers are shown.

EXAMPLE a simple sentence with a compound verb

My sister runs and plays in our backyard.

1. a compound sentence with two independent clauses joined by *but*
   The team played well, but it lost.
2. a complex sentence with one subordinate clause at the beginning
   When I answered the phone, I sneezed.
3. a simple sentence with a compound subject
   Andy or David is in the car.
4. a complex sentence with one subordinate clause at the end
   We will arrive before noon unless our plane is delayed.
5. a compound sentence with three independent clauses
   Tyrus swept the floor, Tony washed the windows, and Candi scrubbed the sink.

Exercise 2 Analyzing a Model

The author of the passage below used a variety of sentences to make her story interesting to read. For each numbered sentence, do the following:

1. Write the number of independent clauses.
2. Circle any subordinate clauses.
3. Label the sentence as *simple, compound,* or *complex.*

Literary Model

[1]Mrs. Small slept or at least kept her eyes closed.

[2]Thomas was thinking about the new house in Ohio.

[3]The house was a relic with secret passages and rooms.

[4]He and his family were leaving an old house and folks who were mostly relatives.

[5]He had known the old house and the old people forever.

[6]All around were heavy patches of mist, and there was a steady rain.

—Excerpt from *The House of Dies Drear* by Virginia Hamilton

[1]one independent clause, simple sentence

[2]one independent clause, simple sentence

[3]one independent clause, simple sentence

[4]one independent clause, complex sentence

[5]one independent clause, simple sentence

[6]two independent clauses, compound sentence

Working Together

Exercise 3 Revising a Paragraph

Rewrite the paragraph below. Combine some simple sentences to create at least one compound and one complex sentence. Switch papers with a partner, and discuss any differences in your revisions. Answers will vary but should contain at least one compound and one complex sentence. See sample answer in Answer Key at www.grammarforwriting.com.

[1]Many families have traditions around the winter holidays. [2]Some families display menorahs and light candles to celebrate Hanukkah. [3]Kwanzaa is another holiday with lighted candles. [4]The Kwanzaa celebration uses a kinara. [5]To celebrate Christmas, families often decorate a tree with lights and ornaments. [6]Las Posadas is a Mexican and Mexican-American holiday. [7]Children sometimes carry candles. [8]They walk through the neighborhood and visit different families' homes. [9]Many winter celebrations involve lights and candles. [10]This is a nice way for families to brighten up cold, dark winter nights.

WRITING HINT

To combine two simple sentences, use a comma and a conjunction, such as *and, but,* or *or.* See **Lesson 3.5.**

ORIGINAL

I celebrate Kwanzaa. It's my favorite holiday.

COMBINED

I celebrate Kwanzaa**, and** it's my favorite holiday.

Write What You Think

On a separate sheet of paper, write a short paragraph to answer the questions below. Back up your opinion with at least two reasons. In your paragraph, include at least one simple sentence, one compound sentence, and one complex sentence.

Students today need to balance home life and extracurricular activities with schoolwork. Are students today given too much homework? Why or why not?

Answers will vary but should include at least one of each type of sentence. See sample answer in Answer Key at www.grammarforwriting.com.

LESSON 3.5

Combining Sentences

Using only short sentences can make your writing sound simple and dull. Notice how **combining sentences** makes the passage below shorter, smoother, and more interesting to read.

ORIGINAL Archaeologists study history. They analyze things people have made. They also analyze things people have built. Items might include coins, tools, and houses. Archaeologists also examine tombs.

COMBINED Archaeologists study history and analyze the things people have made and built. Items might include coins, tools, houses, and tombs.

➡ You can combine sentences by using a **compound subject** or a **compound verb.** Look for two sentences that have the same subject but different verbs or that have the same verb but different subjects.

For more on compound subjects and verbs, see **Lesson 6.4.**

ORIGINAL In 1922 Howard Carter went to Egypt. Howard Carter began digging in the Valley of the Kings.

COMBINED In 1922 Howard Carter **went** to Egypt and **began** digging in the Valley of the Kings. [compound verb]

ORIGINAL King Tut's tomb was discovered. His burial chamber was discovered, too.

COMBINED King Tut's **tomb** and burial **chamber** were discovered. [compound subject]

➡ Sometimes you may want to create a **compound sentence** to combine two closely related sentences. Use a comma and a coordinating conjunction, such as *and, or,* or *but.*

ORIGINAL Some archaeological sites are easy to find. Others are hidden beneath ground.

COMBINED Some archaeological sites are easy to find**, but** others are hidden beneath ground.

Remember

Combining short sentences often makes your writing seem more interesting and sophisticated. However, authors may use a short simple sentence to draw the reader in. Refer to the literary model in **Lesson 3.2** for an example.

Another way to combine short sentences is to take a **key word** from one sentence and insert it into another sentence. Sometimes you will need to change the form of the key word before you can insert it.

ORIGINAL Ancient Egyptian artists designed gold jewelry. They were skillful.

COMBINED **Skillful** ancient Egyptian artists designed gold jewelry.

COMBINED Ancient Egyptian artists **skillfully** designed gold jewelry.

Exercise 1 Combining Sentences

Use one of the techniques described in this lesson to combine each pair of sentences. Use each technique at least once.

Answers will vary but should combine sentences correctly. Sample answers are shown.

EXAMPLE New technology is ground-breaking. It allows people to control live television programs.

Ground-breaking new technology allows people to control live television programs.

1. Digital video recorders let viewers pause a live program. They also allow viewers to rewind live programs.
Digital video recorders allow viewers to pause and rewind a live program.
2. DVRs record TV shows when you're not home. Videocassette recorders also have this ability.
DVRs and videocassette recorders record TV shows when you're not home.
3. You can record with a DVR at the touch of a button. With a VCR, more steps are involved. You can record with a DVR at the touch of a button, but with a VCR, more steps are involved.
4. With a DVR, you can rewind a frame to catch something you missed. This is quick and convenient. With a DVR, you can quickly and conveniently rewind a frame to catch something you missed.
5. If the phone rings, you can pause the program. You can also step out of the room.
If the phone rings, you can pause the program and step out of the room.
6. A DVR can record one program. Meanwhile, you can watch a different program.
You can set a DVR to record one program, but you can watch a different one.
7. Most DVRs allow you to record the whole series of a show. They allow you to search through the program guide for a favorite show, too. Most DVRs allow you to record the whole series of a show, and they allow you to search through the program guide for a favorite show, too.

8. You can save programs to watch later. You can fast-forward through the commercials.
   You can save programs to watch later and fast forward through the commercials.
9. The DVR is more technologically advanced than a VCR. It is modern.
   The modern DVR is more technologically advanced than a VCR.
10. Most people love their DVRs. Most people who own them can't imagine life without them.
    Most people love their DVRs and can't imagine life without them.

HINT

You may add, delete, or change words as necessary.

EXERCISE 2 Revising an Advertisement

On a separate sheet of paper, rewrite the advertisement below by using the techniques in this lesson to combine sentences.

Students' rewrites will vary. See sample answer in Answer Key at www.grammarforwriting.com.

Buy the All-New Hi-Phone!

[1]The new Hi-Phone is amazing. [2]It is the latest in cell phone technology. [3]It allows you to download videos. [4]It also allows you to download music. [5]You can send text messages. [6]You can send them to anyone in your network. [7]They are free. [8]Some people like to talk a lot. [9]Other people like to talk less. [10]The Hi-Phone gives you flexibility. [11]The Hi-Phone calling plan gives you flexibility, too. [12]Buy a Hi-Phone. [13]Say "Hi" to someone today!

EXERCISE 3 Writing an Advertisement

On a separate sheet of paper, write an advertisement for a real product or one you make up.

Students' advertisements will vary but should be at least five sentences long and contain at least one compound sentence. See sample answer in Answer Key at www.grammarforwriting.com.

1. Make your ad at least five sentences long.
2. Use the methods you learned in this lesson to avoid having too many short sentences in a row.
3. Use at least one compound sentence in your ad.

ONLINE MODEL
www.grammarforwriting.com

Autobiographical Incident

Think of the first time you performed in a play or gave a speech. What happened, and how did you feel? How would you retell this event to friends? What details would you include to relive the moment with them?

An **autobiographical incident** is a true story about an event that happened in the life of the writer. In this workshop, you will learn how to write about a short incident from your life that had a big impact on you, such as:

- the toughest day of your life
- the best trip you ever took
- your most embarrassing moment

Your autobiographical incident should have the following features.

Key Features

- short, memorable experience
- first-person point of view, using such pronouns as *I, me, we, us*
- chronological order
- sensory details and dialogue
- your feelings and what you learned from the experience

ASSIGNMENT

TASK: Think about a time you discovered you liked a person, place, or hobby that you didn't like at first. Write a two- to three-page **autobiographical incident** about your experience.

AUDIENCE: your teachers, classmates, friends, and family

PURPOSE: to tell the story of a meaningful event in your life

Prewriting

Choose an Important Event Before you begin writing, you will need to choose an important event. Try one of these techniques.

1. **Brainstorm** Create a list of things it took you a while to like.

- playing the violin
- acting in a play
- going camping
- babysitting my brother
- going shopping
- visiting my cousins

2. **Freewrite** List your topic at the top of the page. Then write down whatever comes to mind related to this topic. Try not to worry about organization or misspellings. Just write!

   Next, use the Topic Checklist on the right to help pick your topic. If you don't have a good answer to each question, go back and pick another topic, or continue to brainstorm.

Jog Your Memory Then make a chart to record key facts, such as who was involved, what you didn't like, why you didn't like it, and how you came to like it. Remember that your audience wasn't there, so you need to include all of these important details.

Who	What	When	Where	Why	How
my dad, our dogs, and me	camping	last August	Lake Caribou	thought it was boring	made me feel in touch with nature

TOPIC CHECKLIST

- ✔ Is the incident short enough to write about in detail?
- ✔ How clear are my feelings about the experience?
- ✔ How well do I remember the incident?

Drafting

Tell the Whole Story As you draft, think about what you will say in the beginning, middle, and end of your essay.

Beginning	Middle	End
• Write an introduction that catches your reader's interest. • Identify what you didn't like, and give key background information.	• Explain the events that caused you to change your mind. • Include details and dialogue.	Briefly state why you changed your mind and what you learned.

As you draft, use **chronological order.** Organize events from first to last, in the order they occurred. Use words such as *first, then,* and *before* to signal the order.

Open Up and Connect Use these tips to keep the focus on yourself and draw your reader into the story. How effective is the model below?

- Since *you* are telling the story, use **first-person point of view** and pronouns such as *I* and *we*.
- Include important conversations, or **dialogue,** and use **sensory details** that appeal to the five senses (sight, sound, smell, touch, and taste).

Real-World Writing

As you draft, keep your reader in mind.

"It's not enough to merely put down information about your life; the trick is to fashion your memories into an engaging story."

—Ralph Fletcher

First-person point of view

Sensory details

Writer's change

Dialogue

[1]As I hesitantly climbed into the canoe, my heart pounded, and my neck and arms itched under the stiff life jacket. [2]But as we quietly paddled out under the twinkling night sky, I felt overwhelmed by the number of stars and the way the water hummed with each stroke of our paddles. [3]Suddenly, nature was no longer a boring place. [4]"I am a part of this," I whispered.

Revising

Use the Revising Questions below to improve your draft. Ask a classmate to review it. Note the suggestions one peer reviewer made about the draft below.

Revising Questions

- ❑ How effectively have I used first-person point of view?
- ❑ How clear is the chronological order?
- ❑ Where should I add or delete sensory details?
- ❑ Where can I add dialogue to liven up the story?
- ❑ How clearly did I express my feelings?

As you revise, keep in mind the traits of good writing. See **Lesson 1.3.**

After the fire burned out,
^[1]I walked to the edge of our campsite. [2]The sky was filled with stars, and the moon was only a thin crescent. [3]It was a very cold night, but the chilly air no longer annoyed me. [4]Even the ^(slimy) bugs were less irritating. [5]All I could see were the stars, the ^(sparkling) river, and the variety of animals around me. [6]I finally wanted to explore nature more, but we were leaving the next day. [7]Then I heard it. [8]A tiny voice asking, "Who?" hiccupped above me. [9]"Who? Who? Who?" [10]I looked up and saw an owl gazing at me^
Its friendly gaze surprised me, and I smiled in return.

Make the order clearer.

Make more sentences descriptive like the second sentence.

Describe how you felt when you saw the owl.

Revising

CONNECTING Writing & Grammar

Add a comma before the conjunction in a compound sentence. See **Lesson 11.2.**

The deer leaped**,** **and** it disappeared.

Keep Your Sentences Interesting

Try these tips:

1. **Mix it up.** Start each sentence with a different word, and use a mix of short and long sentences. (See Lesson 3.2.)
2. **Combine sentences.** Combine two short sentences with a conjunction, such as *and* or *but.* (See Lesson 3.5.)

CHOPPY I was tired. I still went for a walk.

SMOOTH I was tired**, but** still I went for a walk.

Read the passage, and answer the questions below.

Literary Model

[1]At recess, my group was ready. [2]They were my backup singers and moral support. [3]Robert Lindsay introduced me as Elvis, and the class burst out laughing. [4]Miss Ehlis stood in the back of the room with her arms crossed, smiling. [5]My hands were cold and clammy. [6]The record started and I began to lip-synch the longest song of my life. [7]"Treat me like a fool. Treat me mean and cruel, but love me . . ." [8]Everyone shouted and clapped, drowning out the music. [9]Robert Lindsay raised the volume, and the class raised their own volume. [10]Finally Miss Ehlis told everyone to quiet down. [11]She asked me to start over. [12]I felt more at ease and began the song again. [13]My group swayed and clapped to the rhythm of the song. [14]When it was over, everyone cheered and clapped, including Miss Ehlis. [15]Some yelled out, "That was cool, Frankie!" [16]From that day on, I was an Elvis fan.

—Excerpt from *Breaking Through* by Francisco Jiménez

Reading as a Writer

Answers will vary. Sample answers are shown.

1. How effective is the author's use of sentence variety?
2. Why might the author have made sentence 5 short?

1. The author's use of sentence variety is very effective. He starts sentences in different ways and uses sentences of different lengths.
2. The author may have made sentence 5 short to emphasize that he was nervous.

Editing and Proofreading

Now use the checklist below to correct your essay.

Editing and Proofreading Checklist

- ❑ Have I checked that all words are spelled correctly?
- ❑ Did I avoid run-on sentences and fragments?
- ❑ Do compound sentences have a comma before a conjunction?
- ❑ Are any words missing or run together?

Writing Model

was hunched

[1]My dad ^ over the fire pit. [2]The sun dipped beneath the top of the trees ^, and I could see that his hands were covered in scratches. [3]This was the frist time I felt sad about leaving. [4]I didn't give this place a chance. [5]Next time I will ⊙

Publishing and Presenting

Choose one of these ways to share your story.

- **Add it to your portfolio.** Keep a writing portfolio of your best pieces of writing throughout the school year. Your portfolio will help you track your growth as a writer.
- **Start an autobiography.** Put your essay in a notebook with other autobiographical incidents. Share them with your family.

CONNECTING Writing & Grammar

To fix a fragment, add the missing subject or verb. See **Lesson 2.1.**

ORIGINAL Hiked up the mountain. The stream by the camp.

REVISED **We** hiked up the mountain. [A subject was added.]

The stream **Is** by the camp. [A verb was added.]

Proofreading Symbols

ℓ	Delete.
^	Add.
⊙	Add a period.
∿	Switch.
^,	Add a comma.

Reflect On Your Writing

- What new thoughts or memories came to mind as you wrote?
- What did you learn about autobiographical writing?

CHAPTER 3 Chapter Review

A. Practice Test

Read each sentence below carefully. Decide which answer choice best replaces the underlined part, and fill in the circle of the corresponding letter. If you think the underlined part is correct as is, fill in the circle for choice *A*.

EXAMPLE

Ⓐ Ⓑ Ⓒ Ⓓ Jackie Robinson was famous for playing baseball, as well as for being a civil rights activist.
(A) baseball, as well as for being a civil rights activist.
(B) baseball, as well as for being a civil rights activist!
(C) baseball, as well as for being a civil rights activist?
(D) baseball. As well as for being a civil rights activist.

Ⓐ Ⓑ Ⓒ Ⓓ **1.** When Robinson began playing baseball. African-Americans and whites played in different leagues.
(A) baseball. African-Americans and whites
(B) baseball, African-Americans and whites
(C) baseball, African-Americans, and whites
(D) baseball. African-Americans and whites,

Ⓐ Ⓑ Ⓒ Ⓓ **2.** When Robinson joined the Dodgers, fans and teammates objected to having an African-American in the major leagues.
(A) Dodgers, fans and teammates
(B) Dodgers. Fans and teammates,
(C) Dodgers, fans, and teammates,
(D) Dodgers! Fans and teammates

TEST-TAKING TIP

1. Read each item and *all* answer choices.
2. Cross out choices you know are wrong and choices that introduce new errors.
3. Fill in the letter of the choice that best completes the sentence. If the underlined part is correct as written, choose choice *A*.

ⒶⒷⒸ● 3. The crowds heckled Robinson. The crowds insulted Robinson. The crowds jeered at him when he got up to bat, but he never let it affect his game.

(A) heckled Robinson. The crowds insulted Robinson. The crowds jeered at him
(B) heckled Robinson, insulted Robinson, and jeered at Robinson
(C) heckled Robinson. They insulted Robinson. They jeered at him
(D) heckled, insulted, and jeered at Robinson

ⒶⒷ●Ⓓ 4. Despite the prejudice that surrounded him. Robinson was named Rookie of the Year. This was in 1947.

(A) him. Robinson was named Rookie of the Year. This was in 1947.
(B) him, Robinson was named Rookie of the Year. This was in 1947.
(C) him, Robinson was named Rookie of the Year in 1947.
(D) him. Robinson was named the Rookie of the Year. The year was 1947.

Ⓐ●ⒸⒹ 5. With that kind of bravery, is it any wonder that so many baseball fans consider him to be the most important player in the history of the sport.

(A) player in the history of the sport.
(B) player in the history of the sport?
(C) player. In the history of the sport.
(D) player in the history of the sport,

B. Revising Sentences

On a separate sheet of paper, change each sentence below to the type of sentence indicated in parentheses. You may add, delete, or change words.

Answers will vary. Sample answers are shown.

1. I'd like to know whether I should see the movie. (interrogative)
   Should I see the movie?
2. The ad was very well done. (exclamatory)
   The ad was unbelievably well done!
3. Did you read the reviews in the newspapers? (declarative)
   There were reviews in the newspapers.
4. I don't know if you noticed, but the reviews were terrible! (interrogative)
   Did you notice that the reviews were terrible?
5. I'd like to hear your opinion of the movie's pros and cons. (imperative)
   Tell me your opinion of the movie's pros and cons.

C. Matching Sentences

Read each numbered sentence and match it with the correct description. Write the letter of the description on the line.

d **1.** I wanted to enter the talent contest, but I wasn't sure.

b **2.** While most kids at my school enjoy hip-hop music, I like jazz standards.

a **3.** My best friend and I enjoy the unusual rhythms of jazz.

e **4.** My favorite song, which is called "Summertime," was written by a famous composer named George Gershwin.

c **5.** I finally entered a contest and won!

a. simple sentence with a compound subject

b. complex sentence with a subordinate clause at the beginning

c. simple sentence with a compound verb

d. compound sentence with two independent clauses

e. complex sentence with a subordinate clause in the middle

D. Identifying Clauses

Read the paragraph below. Underline each independent clause. Draw a circle around each subordinate clause.

1 In medieval times, lords and ladies often lived in castles. 2 The castle served as a home for the family, but it also served as a fortress to protect them from enemy invasions. 3 Many castles had moats, which were water-filled ditches designed to keep enemies from entering. 4 If an enemy was captured, he was often imprisoned in a tower. 5 The most secure part of the castle was also its highest point, and this was called the keep.

E. Revising an Autobiographical Incident

On a separate sheet of paper, revise this student's paragraph describing an autobiographical incident. Follow the directions below to make the writing more interesting. You may add, delete, and rearrange words.

Answers will vary but should meet the criteria indicated in the directions. See sample answer in Answer Key at www.grammarforwriting.com.

1. Begin sentences in different ways.
2. Use different kinds of sentences and a variety of sentence lengths.
3. Combine sentences to include at least one compound sentence and one complex sentence.

[1]My best friend Josie and I were having trouble in math class. [2]We were nervous about the upcoming quiz. [3]Josie happened to get to class early the day before the quiz. [4]Josie saw a printout of the quiz on Mr. Bennett's desk. [5]Josie grabbed it without thinking. [6]Josie stuffed it in her backpack. [7]Josie ran to my locker. [8]I was putting away my books. [9]Josie grabbed my shoulder. [10]Josie seemed pale and upset. [11]Josie explained what she had just done. [12]Josie stared at me. [13]I stared back. [14]We were silent. [15]We were both tempted to look at the test. [16]We decided to throw the printout away without looking at it. [17]We learned something about ourselves that day. [18]We wanted to earn our grades fairly whether they were good or bad.

CHAPTER 4

Effective Paragraphs

LESSON 4.1

Paragraphs and Their Parts

A **paragraph** is a group of related sentences that develop a topic or **main idea.** Some paragraphs stand by themselves, but most are parts of longer pieces of writing.

➡ Writers use four main types of paragraphs. The kind you write depends on your purpose.

Types of Paragraphs

Narrative	tells a story or recounts a series of events
Descriptive	describes a person, place, or thing
Expository	gives information, such as facts and ideas
Persuasive	convinces readers to agree with an opinion and sometimes take an action

➡ Paragraphs have no set rules for length or organization. However, many effective paragraphs (especially expository and persuasive paragraphs) include a topic sentence and supporting sentences.

1. Use a **topic sentence** to state your main idea or purpose. A strong topic sentence at the beginning of a paragraph introduces readers to the topic, focuses them on your point, and makes them want to read on.
2. The main part of your paragraph explains or supports the main idea. These **supporting sentences,** also called the **body,** can include facts, examples, quotations, and other details.

See **Lesson 4.2** for more about supporting details.

Notice the parts of the following expository paragraph from a biography of Abraham Lincoln.

Topic sentence states the main idea.

Supporting sentences explain why Lincoln was not a common man.

Literary Model

[1]Lincoln may have seemed like a common man, but he wasn't. [2]His friends agreed that he was one of the most ambitious people they had ever known. [3]Lincoln struggled hard to rise above his log-cabin origins, and he was proud of his achievements. [4]By the time he ran for president he was a wealthy man, earning a large income from his law practice and his many investments. [5]As for the nickname Abe, he hated it. [6]No one who knew him well ever called him Abe to his face. [7]They addressed him as Lincoln or Mr. Lincoln.

—Excerpt from *Lincoln: A Photobiography* by Russell Freedman

➡ Sometimes writers choose to end their paragraphs with a **concluding sentence,** also called a **clincher.** Concluding sentences often restate the main idea in a new way and tie the supporting sentences together. What might be a good concluding sentence for the paragraph about Lincoln?

EXERCISE 1 Analyzing Paragraphs

Remember

The topic sentence is not always at the beginning of a paragraph. It can sometimes be in the middle or at the end.

Label each paragraph below as narrative, descriptive, expository, or persuasive. Underline the topic sentence. If the paragraph has a concluding sentence, circle it.

expository

[1]If you were a bottle-nosed dolphin, you'd spend the first few days of your life listening to your mother whistle! [2]That's because a mother dolphin needs to teach her calf how to identify her own special call. [3]Dolphins communicate with one another mainly through sound. [4]In addition to whistles, they produce squeals, clicks, and chirps to send each other messages.

[1]You should help save endangered sea turtles by respecting their habitat. [2]After a day at the beach, you should leave the shoreline just as you found it. [3]Of course, it's important never to leave litter behind. [4]Also, you must always knock down any sandcastles you may have built. [5]These types of constructions can block baby turtles' path into the water. [6]Remember, the beach belongs to everyone—humans and animals alike.

persuasive

[1]The giant panda is the only animal in the bear family with its distinctive black-and-white coloring. [2]Pandas have white faces with black ears, and black circles around their eyes. [3]Their pupils are slit-shaped, like those of a cat. [4]Pandas also have separate "thumbs" on their front paws, allowing them to grasp bamboo stems, which make up a major part of their diet. [5]These are just a few of the features that distinguish the giant panda from other bears.

descriptive or expository

EXERCISE 2 Writing a Paragraph

On a separate sheet of paper, complete the sentence below. Use it as a topic sentence for an expository paragraph that includes at least five supporting sentences. Decide whether the topic sentence should be at the beginning, in the middle, or at the end. Answers will vary. See sample answer in Answer Key at www.grammarforwriting.com.

TOPIC SENTENCE My favorite animal is ___________.

LESSON 4.2

Main Idea and Supporting Details

As you write a paragraph, ask yourself, "What is the main idea I want to get across?"

The **topic** is what the paragraph is about. The **main idea** is what the writer says *about* the topic. You may decide to state your main idea directly in a **topic sentence.**

Topic	the Sonoran Desert
Topic Sentence	The Sonoran Desert in Arizona presents some of the most breathtaking sights in America.

Many writers use a topic sentence to begin a paragraph, but topic sentences can go in the middle or at the end, too. Not every paragraph needs a topic sentence, however. Sometimes you may want to imply, or suggest, rather than directly state your main idea, as seen in the expository paragraph below.

The main idea is that the Grand Canyon is huge.

Writing Model

[1]The Grand Canyon is almost three hundred miles long. [2]At its widest point, it stretches eighteen miles wide. [3]It is incredibly deep in spots, measuring about one mile from the rocky bottom to the tops of the steep cliffs.

Be sure to provide enough **supporting details** to explain or develop your main idea. Depending on your purpose, you may want to choose facts, examples, sensory details, or quotations to help readers understand your ideas.

Each of the different kinds of details in the chart below supports the following main idea:

> Rafting down the Colorado River can be the most thrilling ride of your life.

Kind	Definition	Example
Facts	statements that can be proved true	The currents are strong in parts of the 1,450-mile-long Colorado River.
Examples	specific cases or instances	Our raft almost flipped over three times.
Sensory Details	words that appeal to the five senses	Tim's hands gripped the smooth paddle tightly until the icy water sloshed into the raft.
Quotations	spoken or written words from an expert or authority	According to our guide, Dr. Lin, "The Colorado is a wet and wild rafting experience."

EXERCISE 1 Writing Topic Sentences

Read each set of sentences. Decide the author's main idea. Then write a strong topic sentence for each expository paragraph.

Answers will vary. Sample answers are shown.

EXAMPLE Getting exercise burns calories, which helps keep bodies fit. It also builds the foundation for strong muscles as bodies get older.

Topic sentence: Kids need exercise to stay healthy.

1. The cerebrum part of your brain controls your voluntary muscles, and your memory is stored there, too. Without the cerebrum, you couldn't think, walk, or play a sport.
The cerebrum is an essential part of the brain.

2. Make sure your computer monitor is placed about twenty inches away from your face, so you do not have to strain your eyes. You should also give your eyes a break by stepping away from the computer every thirty minutes.
Working on a computer for extended periods of time can harm your eyes.

3. Being prone to sleepwalking may run in families. It can also happen if you're sick or have a fever. Stress and not getting enough sleep may be other underlying causes.
Sleepwalking is a condition caused by various factors.

4. Peanuts and nuts are often found in foods from breakfast cereals to chili. People with the allergy should also beware of sweets, such as ice cream and chocolate candies.
People with an allergy to nuts need to beware of everyday foods that contain nuts.

CONNECTING Writing & Grammar

When you include a quotation as a supporting detail, remember to use quotation marks to start and end it.

She screamed, **"**How fast are we going?**"**

5. Some braces are clear, and others are made to match your tooth color. Some are even placed behind the teeth, where they can't be seen at all.
Some new kinds of braces are virtually unnoticeable.

HINT

You may use the Internet or a classroom encyclopedia to find facts. You may interview a teacher to get a quotation.

Exercise 2 Adding Supporting Details

For each main idea listed add the supporting sentences indicated in the parentheses. Write your expository paragraphs on a separate sheet of paper.
Answers will vary. See sample answers in Answer Key at www.grammarforwriting.com.

EXAMPLE Many of kids' physical traits are inherited from their parents. (three examples)

My hair is the same shade of red as that of my mother. I get my long legs from my father's side of the family. My brother has freckles, similar to both of our parents.

1. Talking about bad feelings can help you resolve them in a healthy way. (one quotation and one example)
2. Several symptoms indicate the possibility of an oncoming flu virus. (three sensory details)
3. Many schools have pushed back the starting time of classes to cater to students' needs. (one example and one quotation)

Exercise 3 Writing from Notes

Use the notes below to write a strong paragraph with a topic sentence at the beginning.
Answers will vary. See sample answer in Answer Key at www.grammarforwriting.com.

- incisors—wide, thin teeth at front of mouth that cut, tear, and hold food
- canines—pointy teeth next to incisors that cut and tear food
- molars—behind other teeth, teeth with ridges that break up, cut, and grind food

LESSON
4.3

Paragraph Unity

In an effective paragraph, all the sentences should relate to a single topic.

➡ A paragraph has **unity** when its sentences work together to support one main idea.

LACKS UNITY — Scientists are not sure why record numbers of honeybees began dying suddenly in 2006. Bees live in large groups, or colonies. Some researchers felt a new virus was the cause. Others blamed chemicals spread near the hives. A lot of marine life also died that year. [The underlined sentences do not relate.]

REVISED — Scientists are not sure why record numbers of honeybees began dying in 2006. Some researchers felt a new virus was the cause. Others blamed chemicals spread near the hives. [Each sentence here supports the main idea.]

➡ Stating your main idea in a **topic sentence** can help you write a unified paragraph. Be sure that all other sentences clearly relate to that idea, as in the revised example above.

For more about topic sentences, see **Lesson 4.2.**

STEP BY STEP

To check for and fix problems with unity:

1. Identify your topic sentence and the main idea you included.
2. Ask yourself, "Do all the sentences and ideas relate to or support my main idea? Do any sentences wander off the topic?"
3. Take out any sentences and ideas that don't belong.

EXERCISE Improving Paragraph Unity

Read the paragraphs below. On a separate sheet of paper, revise each paragraph by deleting any details or sentences that don't relate to the main idea.

[1]The Metropolitan Museum of Art, located in New York City, has a collection of Impressionist works that are well worth a visit. [2]You'll see paintings by Renoir, Monet, and Manet and get a chance to examine the brushstrokes up close. [3]~~Claude Monet was born on November 14, 1840, in Paris, France.~~ [4]Canvases by Degas and Matisse are also part of the museum's permanent collection.

[1]Erwin E. Smith, a photographer known for his images of cowboy life, was born in North Texas in 1886. [2]Growing up, he wanted to be both a cowboy and an artist. [3]~~Cowboy culture has continued to be popular over the years.~~ [4]Wanting to know more about his subjects, Smith spent time actually working as a cowboy. [5]He honored the lives of these men with his dramatic photos of roundups and other ranch scenes. [6]~~Smith attended the School of the Boston Museum of Fine Arts, where he studied with a well-known sculptor.~~ [7]Smith's work celebrated cowboy life, but also showed its harsh side.

Write What You Think

Read the persuasive writing prompt below. On a separate sheet of paper, write one paragraph stating your opinion. Check your paragraph for unity. Eliminate unrelated details if necessary.

Should the government fund art education in public schools? Why or why not? Answers will vary. See sample answer in Answer Key at www.grammarforwriting.com.

Organizing Paragraphs

An effective paragraph needs not only clearly stated ideas, but also an easy-to-follow **organization.**

➡ Arrange the information in your paragraphs in a way that makes sense. Writing that is not well organized will frustrate readers. For instance, the sidebar shows one reader's reaction to the draft below.

[1]Musicians in an orchestra sit in special sections. [2]Woodwind (such as oboe and clarinet) players sit in the middle. [3]Percussionists (such as drummers) sit at the back. [4]At the front sit the violin players. [5]The brass section (such as trumpet and trombones) sits in the middle. [6]Cello players sit in front.

The sentences jump around a lot. It's hard for me to picture who sits where.

Below is a revised version. Notice how much easier it is to follow. Grouping related ideas together and changing the order of several sentences help the reader understand the information better.

Writing Model

[1]Musicians in an orchestra sit in special sections. [2]At the front sit the string (such as violin and cello) players. [3]The woodwind (such as oboe and clarinet) players and the brass (such as trumpet and trombone) players sit in the middle. [4]Percussionists (such as drummers) sit at the back.

➡ If possible, use one of several common **patterns of organization** to help your readers follow your ideas.

Organization	Function
Chronological Order	presents details or events in the order in which they occur (what happens first, second, and so on)
Spatial Order	describes details according to their location (such as top to bottom, near to far, or left to right)
Order of Importance	arranges details or reasons from the least important ones to the most important ones—or the reverse
Logical Order	groups related details (such as facts, similarities, or examples) together in a clear way that is easy for the reader to follow

➡ The order you choose depends on your topic and writing purpose. For instance, use chronological order to tell a story, and use logical order to explain key facts about a topic in the news.

Exercise 1 Choosing an Organizational Pattern

Read each writing purpose below. Tell which organizational pattern you would use to write a paragraph, and why.
Reasoning will vary.

EXAMPLE to explain what happened in the last two minutes of an overtime basketball game

I would use chronological order because I want to build up tension and show the score changes until the last second.

1. to describe an unusual object in your home or school
spatial order
2. to show the similarities and differences between tennis and ping-pong logical order
3. to summarize the principal's recent talk on how to improve school spirit logical order or order of importance

4. to describe a store's location spatial order

5. to summarize the plot of a story chronological order

Exercise 2 Writing Paragraphs

Reread the writing purposes in Exercise 1, and choose three. On a separate sheet of paper, write one paragraph for each purpose. Organize your paragraph using the method you selected. You may use your imagination to make up details.

Students' paragraphs will vary. See sample answer in Answer Key at www.grammarforwriting.com.

Exercise 3 Improving Organization

Working Together

Working with a partner, read the jumbled set of instructions for recycling below.

Answers will vary. See sample answer in Answer Key at www.grammarforwriting.com.

1. Improve the organization by rearranging the sentences into chronological order. Add any missing information.

2. Rewrite your paragraph on a separate sheet of paper.

[1]Recycling is easy to do. [2]Take the time to remove any labels from containers, and take off the caps from all bottles. [3]Keep paper with paper, plastic with plastic, and so on. [4]Use the proper bins provided by your community, and familiarize yourself with local recycling guidelines. [5]Separate what you want to recycle by material. [6]Rinse all cans and plastic containers. [7]Finally, recycle larger or more dangerous items, such as computers and devices that contain mercury, at designated locations. [8]Keep aluminum with aluminum.

Writing Hint

To connect one sentence to the next, add transitions, such as *first, next, then,* and *finally*. See **Lesson 4.5.**

LESSON 4.5

Using Transitions

An effective paragraph has **coherence,** meaning each sentence flows smoothly and logically to the next.

➡ Use **transitions** to tie one sentence to another and show the connections between your ideas. Transitions are sometimes called "signal words," because they signal the order being used in paragraphs.

ORIGINAL Last Saturday night during the storm, strong winds hit the area. Many trees were uprooted and damaged. Several maple trees by the hospital fell on cars.

REVISED Last Saturday night during the storm, strong winds hit the area. **As a result,** many trees were uprooted or damaged. **For example,** several maple trees by the hospital fell on cars.

➡ Choose transitional words and phrases that fit your purpose and make your organization clear.

Common Transitions

To show **time**	after, before, during, finally, later, until
To show **location**	above, behind, in front of, inside
To show **cause and effect**	as a result, because, due to, since, so
To show **examples**	for example, for instance, in addition
To show **similarities and differences**	also, but, on the other hand, too, yet

Notice how the following paragraph uses transitions to link sentences together.

TEST-TAKING TIP

Some test questions give you a passage and ask you to add a transition between two sentences. Ask yourself, "How are the sentences logically connected?" For an example, see question 3 on page 97.

Literary Model

[1]Even though it was cold, I took off the jacket <u>during</u> lunch and played kickball in a thin shirt, my arms feeling like braille from goose bumps. [2]But when I returned to class I slipped the jacket on and shivered <u>until</u> I was warm. [3]I sat on my hands, heating them up, <u>while</u> my teeth chattered like a cup of crooked dice. [4]<u>Finally</u> warm, I slid out of the jacket but a few minutes later put it back on when the fire bell rang.

—Excerpt from "The Jacket" by Gary Soto

Transitions that show time

Reading as a Writer Sample answers are shown.

1. Besides the ones underlined, what other transitional words or phrases can you find?
2. Why might the author have used so many transitions?
3. How does the author connect sentences 1 and 2? Why?

1. *even though, but, when, a few minutes later*
2. The author uses transitions to show how the narrator keeps taking off and putting on the jacket, perhaps to show the narrator's connection to the jacket.
3. The author uses the transition *but* to connect the sentences and show a change in the narrator's actions.

EXERCISE 1 Adding Transitions

Rewrite each set of sentences below. Add one or more transitions, as indicated in parentheses, to improve coherence.

Revised sentences will vary. See sample answers in Answer Key at www.grammarforwriting.com.

EXAMPLE Some kids in my neighborhood like to hang out at the mall. The same kids hang out at the diner. Other kids spend their time studying at the library. (similarities and differences)

Some kids in my neighborhood like to hang out at the mall. They also hang out at the diner. Some kids, on the other hand, spend their time studying at the library.

HINT

You may add or delete words and combine or change the order of sentences.

1. The drama club meets in the auditorium. The drama club meets in the last row of seats. The marching band meets in the first row of seats. (location)
2. Tuesday is my busiest day of the week. I go to school. I have my violin lesson. I walk the neighbor's dog. I come home. I help make dinner. I do my homework. (time)

3. Parents should let kids make some of their own choices. They can let kids choose their own extracurricular activities. They can let them choose their own clothes. (examples)

4. One lane was closed on the road to school this morning. There was lots of traffic. Half of our class was late to school. We had to reschedule the spelling test. (cause and effect)

5. Some of my friends collect stamps. Others collect baseball cards. I collect sea glass. My friends can buy things to add to their collections. I have to rely on nature. (similarities and differences)

Exercise 2 Rewriting an Editorial

Rewrite the editorial below on a separate piece of paper. Improve coherence by adding transitions and combining sentences as needed.

Answers will vary. See sample answer in Answer Key at www.grammarforwriting.com.

[1]Teenagers need to spend more time giving back to the community. [2]There are lots of opportunities for doing volunteer work in our area. [3]Teens can collect food and clothing for the local shelter. [4]They can help cook meals at the soup kitchen. [5]Most teenagers have at least an hour per week of free time. [6]Teens who spend that time helping others can make a real difference in our community. [7]These teens will feel better about themselves. [8]Volunteering can help boost self-esteem. [9]It benefits the volunteers as much as it benefits the people they serve.

Working Together

Exercise 3 Writing a Description

See **Lesson 2.4** for help with using precise words and details.

In one paragraph, describe your room as if you were standing at the door. Add transitions that help readers follow along, and include at least five specific details. Then, ask a classmate to draw a sketch based on your description. How well could your classmate picture your room?

Answers will vary. See sample answer in Answer Key at www.grammarforwriting.com.

Opinion Paragraph

You probably have opinions about music, movies, food, sports, and almost everything else. **Opinions** are beliefs that cannot be proved either true or false. While there are no right or wrong opinions, some are more convincing than others because they are specific and can be backed up by strong evidence.

Weak Opinions	Opinions with Reasons
Popcorn is gross.	I dislike popcorn because it sticks in my teeth and is often too salty.
Sports are fun.	Young people should play sports because sports promote overall fitness and health.

An **opinion paragraph** is a type of persuasive writing. Remember to include the following.

Key Features

- clearly stated opinion
- an argument organized in logical order
- strong supporting details and evidence
- moderate tone

ASSIGNMENT

TASK: Write an **opinion paragraph** about a rule you want to see changed at school.

GOAL: to persuade people to take action

TARGET: your teachers and classmates

SPECIAL INSTRUCTIONS: Include at least two types of details to support your opinion.

WRITING HINT

As you write your draft, keep a reasonable **tone,** or attitude. Be polite. You don't need to insult someone just to prove your point. In fact, an annoyed or angry tone may signal to readers that you don't have enough evidence to back up your opinion.

What's Your Point? First, choose a topic to write about. To pick a good topic, ask yourself these questions:

- Which rules at my school would I really like to change?
- Why do I feel this way?
- How could I convince others to share my opinion?

Create a list of your opinions similar to the one below.

- Food should be allowed in study hall.
- Students should not be assigned homework on Fridays.
- Lunch periods are too short.

Since you are only writing one paragraph, pick a topic that is narrow and focused. For example, instead of writing about all the rules regulating cell phone use in school, focus on one rule.

Sell Your Point To win your readers over, gather strong **evidence.**

- **Facts** Facts are statements that can be proved true or false. For example, "Dogs are mammals" is a fact because it can be proved true. "Dogs are fun pets" is an opinion because it cannot be proved either true or false.
- **Examples** Specific events and details illustrate the point that you are trying to make.
- **Quotations** Spoken or written opinions of experts in the field will make your argument more convincing.

For more help with organizing paragraphs, see **Lesson 4.4.**

As you write, use **logical order** to organize your evidence. Group related details together in a clear way that is easy for your audience to follow.

Keep It Clear Make sure your argument is easy to follow. Remember to include a **topic sentence** that states the main idea, a body that lists the **supporting details,** and a **concluding sentence** that restates the main idea. See the models below.

Main Idea	Students should be given longer lunch periods.
Supporting Details	1. unhealthy to have short lunches because kids eat junk food, which is quicker to eat 2. hard to finish lunch in only 25 minutes 3. can study during longer lunch periods
Concluding Sentence	There can be no question that the short lunch periods at Carol Middle School hurt students' diets and their academics.

CONNECTING Writing & Grammar

Capitalize all proper nouns, which name specific people, places, things, ideas, or events. See **Lesson 12.1.**

I attend **U**nity **J**unior **H**igh **S**chool.

[1]Students should be given longer lunch periods for several reasons. [2]First, students would eat healthier meals if they had more time. [3]Since lunches are so short, students tend to eat junk food, which is quicker to eat. [4]Also, longer lunches would give students time to eat slowly, which doctors recommend. [5]Right now, students have only twenty-five minutes to find a table, unpack their lunch, eat, and throw away trash. [6]Finally, longer lunch periods would allow students time to study. [7]There can be no question that the short lunch periods at Carol Middle School hurt students' diets and their academics.

Clear opinion

Three supporting details

Concluding sentence

WRITING CHECKLIST

Did you...

- ✔ clearly state your opinion?
- ✔ include at least two types of supporting details?
- ✔ organize your paragraph in logical order and use a reasonable tone?

Chapter Review

A. Practice Test

Read the draft and questions below carefully. The questions ask you to choose the best revision for sentences or parts of the draft. Fill in the corresponding circle for your answer choice.

(1) Born in a rough neighborhood of New Orleans in 1901, Louis Armstrong began working at the age of seven. **(2)** He dropped out of school in the third grade. **(3)** He was taken to live at a group home for boys. **(4)** Louis mastered the bugle and the cornet. **(5)** When he was released at age 13, he earned money by selling newspapers and occasionally playing at jazz clubs. **(6)** Other musicians took notice of Armstrong's talent and helped him begin his career. **(7)** He was also known for wearing colorful outfits. **(8)** He earned fifty dollars a week performing on steamboats, which was a lot in those times. **(9)** Armstrong eventually switched from playing the cornet to the trumpet and began recording music as a professional. **(10)** His talent for "scat" singing—improvising with nonsense syllables and using the voice as an instrument—gave his music a unique sound and made him internationally famous.

TEST-TAKING TIP

When answering a question concerning the "best" way to do something, think of a possible answer before you even read the answer choices.

Ⓐ●ⒸⒹⒺ **1.** Which topic sentence best states the paragraph's main idea?
(A) Louis Armstrong was born into a poor family.
(B) Louis Armstrong, who came from humble beginnings, developed his musical talent over the course of his life.
(C) Louis Armstrong showed a keen interest in music.
(D) Louis Armstrong's early life was difficult.
(E) Louis Armstrong was a famous jazz musician.

ⒶⒷ●ⒹⒺ **2.** Which transition should be added to the beginning of sentence 3?
(A) On the other hand,
(B) For instance,
(C) Then,
(D) In contrast,
(E) No revision is needed.

ⒶⒷⒸ●Ⓔ **3.** Which transition should be added to the beginning of sentence 4?
(A) In addition,
(B) However,
(C) Finally,
(D) While at the home,
(E) As a result,

ⒶⒷ●ⒹⒺ **4.** Which of the following sentences could be removed from the paragraph to improve unity?
(A) sentence 5
(B) sentence 6
(C) sentence 7
(D) sentence 8
(E) sentence 9

Ⓐ●ⒸⒹⒺ **5.** Which of the following makes the best concluding sentence for the paragraph?
(A) Armstrong died in 1971.
(B) Through his recordings, Armstrong's music continues to thrill jazz-lovers all over the world.
(C) Therefore, Armstrong was a great man and a great musician.
(D) If you've never heard jazz music, you don't know what you're missing.
(E) This is why Armstrong's music is so great.

Chapter Review

Chapter Review

B. Matching Topic Sentences to Paragraphs

Read each topic sentence in the first column. Decide what type of paragraph and organization fits best with each one. Write the letter of the correct choice in the space provided.

__e__ **1.** Before you adopt a puppy, you should know the top ten facts about dog ownership.

__d__ **2.** The street where I grew up was one of the most beautiful I've ever known.

__c__ **3.** Leslie Carroll deserves your vote as student council president.

__b__ **4.** Though koalas look like little bears, several key differences set them apart.

__a__ **5.** My first day at sleep-away camp was a bit overwhelming.

a. narrative paragraph with chronological order organization

b. expository paragraph with logical order organization

c. persuasive paragraph with order of importance organization

d. descriptive paragraph with spatial order organization

e. expository paragraph with order of importance organization

C. Identifying Transitions

In each paragraph below, underline the transition word(s) or phrase(s). In the space provided, label the transition(s) *T* for time, *L* for location, *CE* for cause and effect, *E* for example, or *SD* for similarities and differences. Only one kind of transition is used in each paragraph.

__SD__ **1.** The debate team and the book club discuss differences of opinion, but the book club's discussions are more informal. The book club enjoys exploring differences of opinion. However, the debate team crushes differences of opinion.

__T__ **2.** The book club is meeting after school on Tuesday. After a two-week exploration of one book, the members will focus on poetry. At the end of the month, the book club will attend a poetry reading at a local café.

__L__ **3.** We're meeting in front of the new public library. The library is on the corner of Lake and Crain, next to the mall. We'll be sitting on the benches to the left of the entrance.

E **4.** We've read many autobiographies this year, such as *The Diary of Anne Frank*. We also read contemporary fiction, such as *The House on Mango Street*. In addition, we read a great poetry collection by Langston Hughes.

CE **5.** Make sure to read Chapter Three because we will be discussing it at the next meeting. Take notes since we will split up into small groups to present our feedback. Due to a shorter meeting period, keep your notes brief but specific.

D. Revising an Opinion Paragraph

Rewrite the following paragraph on a separate sheet of paper.
Answers will vary but should eliminate sentences 2, 5, and 7. Answers should include at least one supporting sentence of each type. See sample answer in Answer Key at www.grammarforwriting.com.

1. Underline the main idea of the paragraph.
2. Delete three sentences that disrupt paragraph unity.
3. Improve the organization by moving sentences and adding transitions as needed.
4. Add at least one fact, one example, and one sensory detail.
5. Add a concluding sentence.

[1]Many people believe that the country is the best place to raise a family, but life in the city can benefit kids in many ways. [2]Last year, my best friend's family moved to a house in the country. [3]Cities are crowded, but there are lots more things for kids to do. [4]In addition, kids are exposed to many different cultures in a big city. [5]My friend doesn't like living in the country nearly as much as she liked living in the city. [6]In the city, there is always an event to attend, a museum to visit, a movie theater to go to, and so on. [7]However, city life can be dangerous in a lot of ways and often causes kids to grow up too fast.

Chapter Review

CHAPTER 5

Writing an Essay

LESSON 5.1

Parts of an Essay

In school you will be asked to write different kinds of **essays,** or compositions. Essays are pieces of writing composed of several paragraphs.

➡ Paragraphs and essays often share similar features because each expresses and explains a main idea.

Paragraph		Essay
Topic Sentence	tells the main idea	**Introductory Paragraph**
Supporting Sentence **Supporting Sentence** **Supporting Sentence**	develops the main idea	**Body Paragraph** **Body Paragraph** **Body Paragraph**
Concluding Sentence	restates the main idea	**Concluding Paragraph**

➡ Essays have three basic parts, or sections: an introduction, a body, and a conclusion.

Introduction	states the main idea and captures the readers' attention
Body	supports and explains the main idea with facts, examples, sensory details, quotations, and so on
Conclusion	sums up the writer's main point and brings the essay to a close

➡ The introduction and conclusion are often composed of just one paragraph each. In contrast, the body usually includes three or more paragraphs.

Exercise Recognizing Parts of an Essay

Read the short essay that follows.

1. Break it into the three parts of an essay, and label each part.
2. Mark a ¶ to signal each new paragraph.
3. Underline the main idea in the introduction and conclusion.

introduction

[1]Imagine a world with no doctors, no science, no democracy, no theater, and no fables. [2]That's what life would be like if not for the ancient Greeks. [3]Many of the ideas we use today, including areas of medicine, government, and art are rooted in ancient Greece.¶[4]We take for granted the idea that illness has a logical explanation that relates to the human body. [5]But Hippocrates, an ancient Greek physician, was the first person to make this discovery. [6]He is still known as the "Father of Medicine."¶[7]Our system of government also comes from ancient Greece. [8]The word democracy is from the Greek demokratia, which means, "rule by the people." [9]If it weren't for the Greeks, we wouldn't vote for our leaders as we do today.¶[10]The Greeks also gave us many art forms. [11]For example, Aesop invented the fable, and many credit Thespis with the invention of dramatic acting.¶[12]So the next time you get a checkup, vote for class president, or applaud for a play, you'll know whom to thank. [13]Without the contributions of the ancient Greeks, life today just wouldn't be the same.

body

conclusion

Write What You Think

Answer the question below by writing a short essay on a separate sheet of paper. Include three short paragraphs: an introduction, a body, and a conclusion. Answers will vary. See sample answer in Answer Key at www.grammarforwriting.com.

Think of the contributions an ancient people made. For example, the Egyptians made the first 365-day calendar and developed mathematics. The Chinese invented gunpowder and the compass. How do these contributions influence your life today, regarding food, school, travel, or music?

LESSON
5.2

Thesis Statements

The introduction of most good essays includes a **thesis statement.** A thesis statement is one or two sentences that clearly state the main idea of an essay.

EXAMPLE Playing with other children is an important part of children's lives, since it builds necessary skills, such as sharing, listening, and communicating.

➡ The thesis statement of an essay is similar to the topic sentence of a paragraph. Just as all of the sentences in a paragraph should support the topic sentence, all paragraphs in an essay should support the thesis statement.

➡ To write a thesis statement, ask yourself, "What is my 'big idea' or the main point I want to make about my topic?" Be sure that your thesis statement is a complete sentence and that it is neither too broad nor too narrow. Remember that the rest of your paper should explain and support this idea.

WEAK Being an only child.
[This is not a complete sentence. It only announces a topic.]

WEAK Some people like being an only child.
[This is true, but it is a broad statement of fact.]

STRONG Being an only child has three important advantages.
[The focus on three advantages narrows the topic and gives readers an idea of what to expect in the essay.]

Exercise 1 Identifying Thesis Statements

Read both introductory paragraphs that follow.

1. Underline each thesis statement. Remember, the thesis statement is not always the first sentence.
2. Circle the weaker of the two thesis statements.
3. On a separate sheet of paper, explain what makes the thesis statement weak and how it might be improved.

Answers will vary but should note that the circled thesis statement in the first paragraph is a broad statement of fact and does not make a clear point about the topic. A suggestion for improvement might be to include and support an opinion, such as "During the winter, Springfield is one of the best cities for winter sports."

[1]Some people enjoy living in Springfield in the winter. [2]Though the temperatures may dip below freezing, residents enjoy the sparkling white scenery. [3]Residents ski during the winter, and groups of tourists visit the area during that time. [4]Children enjoy riding sleds down hills and building snowmen.

[1]Are you looking for a new sweater? [2]Stop by the clothing shops on Waverly Street. [3]Do you need a birthday gift for your best friend? [4]Try Judy's Toy Store on Evergreen Lane. [5]On Main Street, you'll find everything from antiques to sporting goods. [6]Springfield's impressive downtown shopping district offers something for every shopper.

Working Together

EXERCISE 2 Writing Thesis Statements

Choose three of the five suggested topics and purposes from the list below. For each, write a strong thesis statement that you could support in a two-page paper. Then, compare and discuss your ideas with a partner. Answers will vary. Sample answers are shown.

EXAMPLE persuasive essay about the environment

Carpooling is an easy and effective way to fight air pollution.

1. expository essay that explains the life of a sports hero

2. persuasive essay that makes an argument about Internet access at school

3. descriptive essay about a friend

4. narrative essay about an unusual trip

5. expository essay that gives information about computers

1. Venus Williams's challenging childhood helped make her one of the best tennis stars today.
2. Internet access at school should be limited to students who want to do research for class assignments.
3. Kenan is one of the nicest persons I know.
4. The weird weather and the strange hotel made our trip to Nashville an unusual experience.
5. While e-mail is a common form of communication today, there are several key advantages and disadvantages of e-mail.

LESSON 5.3

Body Paragraphs

The **body paragraphs** of an essay come after the introduction. They provide the information readers need to understand the essay's main idea, or **thesis statement.**

In many of the essays that you write for school, the body contains at least three paragraphs. Each one should have **unity,** meaning each should focus on a single idea, often stated directly in the **topic sentence.**

Writing Model

[1]<u>The Sahara Desert in Africa has a dry climate with an extremely wide range of temperatures.</u> [2]During the day, the temperature can rise to above 130 degrees in the hot sun. [3]During the night, however, temperatures can fall to freezing.

The topic sentence directly states the paragraph's main idea.

Remember

Avoid trying to pack too much information into one body paragraph. An overly long paragraph can overwhelm and confuse readers.

Pay special attention to the organization of your body paragraphs. To give your essay **coherence,** arrange paragraphs (and the sentences within each one) in a clear order. Use **transitions** to link paragraphs and sentences smoothly.

Writing Model

[1]<u>Thousands of years ago</u>, West Africa was a hard place to reach. [2]<u>Because</u> no one knew how to sail against the winds, travel from Europe or Asia was difficult. [3]Crossing the Sahara Desert was <u>also</u> dangerous.

[4]<u>However</u>, travel to and from North Africa was much easier. [5]North Africans had lots of contact with other cultures <u>as a result</u>. [6]<u>For example</u>, traders from other countries visited often.

Include transitions to connect sentences and paragraphs.

Working Together

Exercise 1 Revising Body Paragraphs

Work with a partner to revise the passage below.
Sample answers are shown.

1. Mark a ¶ where a new paragraph should begin.
2. Add a transition to link the first paragraph to the second.
3. Finally, add a topic sentence to the end of the second paragraph.

See the lessons in **Chapter 4** for more tips about writing strong paragraphs.

[1]Before adopting a dog, you need to consider the responsibility involved. [2]A dog can be a wonderful pet and a best friend, as long as you have plenty of time to devote to its care. [3]Dogs need exercise, so be prepared to go for walks outside several times a day. ¶ [4]~~C~~ On the other hand, cats do not need to be walked outside. [5]You might choose to adopt a cat if you'd rather have an indoor pet. [6]But keep in mind if cats don't get enough playtime, they may become bored and unhappy. Before you adopt a cat, make sure you have the time to give it the attention it needs.

Exercise 2 Analyzing Body Paragraphs

In a magazine or newspaper, find an article, and choose three body paragraphs. On a separate sheet of paper, answer the questions below about the passage. Answers will vary.

1. What is each body paragraph about?
2. How does the writer connect one paragraph to the next?
3. How effective are the paragraphs? Support your opinion by referring to specific examples in the paragraphs.

Exercise 2 Revising Conclusions

Revise and rewrite each conclusion on a separate sheet of paper, using the strategies from this lesson. You may use the Internet or an encyclopedia to find facts as needed.

Students' revised conclusions will vary. See sample answers in Answer Key at www.grammarforwriting.com.

a. [1]As you can see, no one knows for sure why the dinosaurs died out. [2]Researchers are still looking for answers. [3]There are even some scientists who believe a supernova, or exploding star, was the cause.

b. [1]As mentioned above, "cold-blooded" animals have a body temperature that changes according to the temperature outside. [2]Many animals are cold-blooded, but people aren't.

Exercise 3 Reviewing Introductions and Conclusions

Working Together

Exchange previously written papers with a classmate. As you read through his or her work, ask yourself the questions below. Then discuss your answers with your partner. If you don't have papers available, pick an article from a classroom magazine to review together. Answers will vary.

1. How clear is the thesis statement, and how effective is the introduction?
2. How effective is the conclusion? What is a different way to end the paper?

ONLINE MODEL
www.grammarforwriting.com

Persuasive Essay

What do a movie review, book review, editorial, pop-up ad, and TV commercial have in common? They're all types of persuasive writing, or writing that tries to influence your opinion.

Movie Review	Book Review	Editorial
The movie's special effects were incredible...	If you want excitement, you must read this book...	The condition of the city's only park is a disgrace...

The purpose of a **persuasive essay** is to convince readers to adopt an opinion or take a specific action. In this workshop, you'll learn how to write a persuasive essay. Be sure to include these features in it.

Key Features

- strong thesis statement that states a clear viewpoint, or position
- convincing reasons and evidence
- clear organization
- strong introduction and conclusion
- reasonable tone
- counterargument and response to counterargument

ASSIGNMENT

TASK: Write a two- to three-page **persuasive essay** about a change you want to see in your community.

AUDIENCE: your mayor, local officials, and neighbors

PURPOSE: to persuade community members to make the change you propose

Prewriting

Pick a Hot Topic Choose a topic you'll want to write about and your audience will want to read about. Follow these tips for researching possible topics:

1. Close your eyes. Imagine that you are in a helicopter looking down at your neighborhood. What's missing? What would make your town or block better? Make a list.
2. Think about places and events in the communities where your friends or relatives live. Which thing would you like to see most in your own community? Why?
3. Review the editorial page of local newspapers to see issues residents are concerned about. Interview your parents and neighbors. Jot down the issues you feel strongly about, too.

Use the Topic Checklist to pick the issue that matters most to you. If you don't have a good answer for each question, go back and pick another topic.

TOPIC CHECKLIST

- ✔ How strong is my opinion about this topic?
- ✔ How well does the topic fit the length of the paper? Do I need to narrow it or make it broader?
- ✔ Why should people care about it?
- ✔ How much evidence do I have to support my opinion?

Be Bold Opinions are everywhere—on television, on the Internet, and in our everyday conversations. But not all opinions are equal. In your **thesis statement,** make sure to include an opinion that is clear and well supported. Avoid thesis statements that don't say much or simply present a fact.

WEAK There are lots of problems with our community's recreation center.

STRONG Due to its lack of resources, our recreation center does not provide the kinds of kid-friendly services our community needs.

WEAK Our recreation center was built in 1965.

STRONG Because our recreation center is over forty years old, it lacks many facilities our community needs. It's time to renovate the Oakwood Recreation Center.

A thesis statement clearly states the main idea of an essay. See **Lesson 5.2.**

Prewriting

Make Your Opinion Count Once you have chosen the topic of your essay, you will need to provide two or more reasons to support your thesis statement. Support your reasons with a variety of **evidence.**

Evidence	Definition
Examples	specific cases or instances
Facts	statements that can be proved true
Quotations	spoken or written words from an expert or authority

Organize your reasons and evidence in an Argument Organizer.

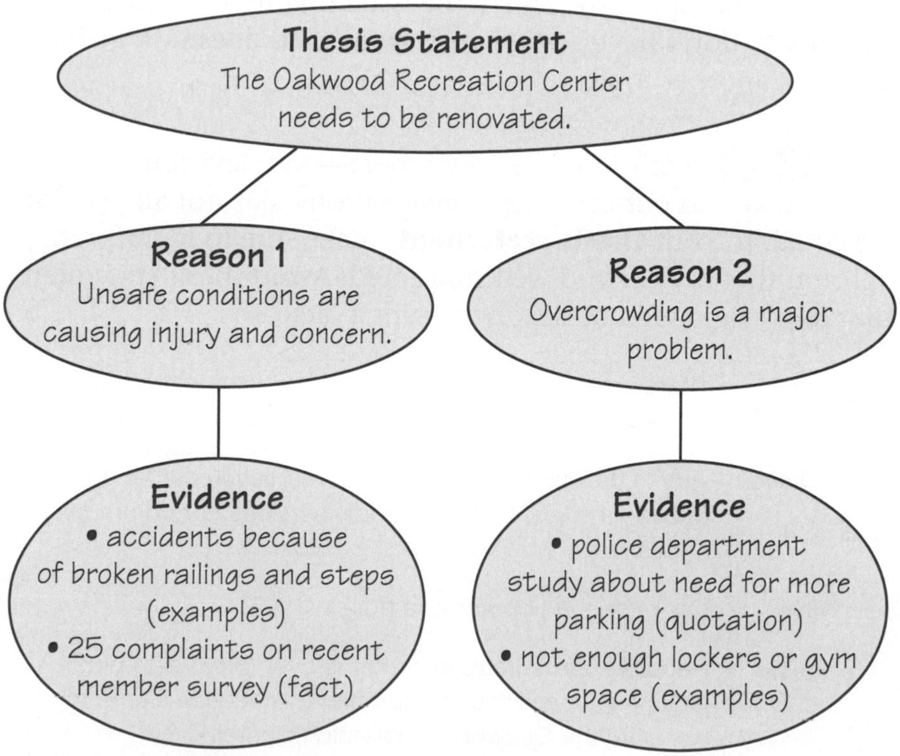

WRITING HINT

Avoid using circular arguments, which use opinions as evidence.

CIRCULAR The recreation center **needs repairs** because it is in **poor condition.**

CLEAR THESIS The recreation center needs repairs because the roof leaks, the pool pump is broken, and the equipment room is flooded.

WRITING HINT

As you gather evidence, consider your readers. How much do they already know about the topic? What reasons would make them take action?

Drafting

Include the Key Parts As you draft, start organizing your details into the three parts of an essay.

1. **Introduction** Grab your readers' attention, and include your thesis statement in the introduction.
2. **Body** Organize all of your reasons and evidence. Arrange your ideas and details in order of importance, from strongest to weakest, or weakest to strongest.
3. **Conclusion** Wrap up your essay by restating your thesis or leaving your audience with something more to think about.

For more on writing an introduction, body, and conclusion, see **Lessons 5.3** and **5.4.**

Defend Yourself Try to anticipate **counterarguments,** or the arguments that could be used against you. Present the counterargument fairly, and use a reasonable, polite **tone** in your response to it.

HARSH It's dumb to ignore the renovations the center needs.

REASONABLE The renovations the center needs are crucial. Ignoring them would be a huge mistake.

[1]Some have argued that our community needs a tax cut more than a renovated community center. [2]However, the money needed for the renovations to our recreation center would cost each resident only one dollar. [3]This is less than the cost of a cup of coffee. [4]How is a cup of coffee more valuable than a functioning pool, a gym for basketball and volleyball, and common areas where seniors can meet and socialize?

Counterargument

Response to counterargument

Reasonable tone

Revising

As you revise, keep in mind the traits of good writing. See **Lesson 1.3.**

After you have completed your draft, the next step is to revise. Slowly reread your essay several times. Each time you reread, focus on a different Revising Question. The model below shows one writer's revisions to the introduction.

WRITING HINT

Revising on a computer allows you to easily delete, move, or add details in the exact location you want.

However, read a printout first. You'll be more likely to spot errors and ways to improve your draft.

Revising Questions

- ❑ How clear and strong is my thesis statement?
- ❑ Where can I add more convincing reasons and evidence?
- ❑ How clear is my organization?
- ❑ How strong are my introductory and concluding paragraphs?
- ❑ How well have I maintained a reasonable tone?
- ❑ How well have I addressed counterarguments?

Begin with questions to grab the readers' attention.

Maintain a reasonable tone.

Include a strong thesis statement.

[1]What makes a strong community? [2]Is it the people or the community's resources? [3]I think it is both. [4]I believe our community is strong, but it deserves more. [5]At one time, the Oakwood Recreation Center offered many things: a pool for fun and fitness, a gymnasium, and common areas for events. [6]Now the center ~~is disgusting~~ is in disrepair**. [7]We must take steps to improve this valuable resource** ^ The Oakwood Recreation Center needs to be renovated.

Revising

Start Strong Review your introduction to check that it's interesting. You can start in one of these ways:

- a fascinating or unusual fact
- a quotation
- a controversy
- a scenario, or brief scene

For more help with introductions, see **Lesson 5.4.**

Read the introduction below, and answer the questions that follow.

Literary Model

[1]Much attention today is being given to the waters that are already polluted. [2]Billions of dollars are being spent to return them to good health. [3]These efforts deserve your wholehearted support. [4]But there is something of equal importance that you should do—give your attention to waters that are still clean.

—Excerpt from *Our Poisoned Waters* by Edward F. Dolan

Reading as a Writer Answers will vary. Sample answers are shown.

1. How does the author capture the readers' attention?
   The author makes the reader think about clean waters, not just polluted ones.
2. How effective is the introduction?
   It is effective because it opens readers' eyes to a new idea. The thesis statement is clear.

Clarify the Order Reread your draft to check the organization of the body of your essay.

1. Make sure that your reasons and evidence appear in order of importance, either from the least important details to the most important ones, or vice versa.
2. Move any details that are out of order.
3. Make your organization clear by adding transitions, such as *first, second, next, another reason,* and so on.

CONNECTING Writing & Grammar

Watch out for these frequently confused words.

they're: contraction for "they are"

They're swimming.

there: adverb that points out location or introduces a sentence

There is one pool.

Editing and Proofreading

Read your draft several times, each time checking for a different item on the Editing and Proofreading Checklist.

Editing and Proofreading Checklist

- ❑ Have I misspelled any words or used any words incorrectly?
- ❑ Did I correct run-on sentences and fragments?
- ❑ Have I left out or run together any words?

Proofreading Symbols

∧	Add.
⊙	Add a period.
≡	Capitalize.
#	Add space.

[1]Without ap[p]ropriate facilities for fitness and fun, our community will become more unhealthy and less social. [2][There] ~~They're~~ can[#]be no doubt that renovating and modernizing the oakwood[≡] Recreation Center would be of long-term benefit [to] our community[⊙]

Reflect On Your Writing

- Which arguments were the most difficult to express?
- In what ways have you improved your abilities as a persuasive writer?

Publishing and Presenting

Choose one of these ways to share your persuasive essay.

- **Present it.** At your next community meeting, read your essay. Be sure to practice your presentation beforehand.
- **Blog it.** Add your essay to your blog or a community blog. Invite friends, family, or community members to start a discussion about the changes you have suggested.

Chapter Review

A. Practice Test

In the passage below, there is a question *for each numbered item*. Read the passage carefully, and circle the best answer to each question.

Books Versus Movies

Books and movies are two very different forms of entertainment.[1] It can be exciting to hear that your favorite book is being turned into a film you can't wait[2] to see the characters and situations brought to life. However,[3] all too often the film ends up being a disappointment. The director's vision of the characters may not match the one in the reader's imagination, and this can be jarring to fans of the book, the time[4] constraints of film may disappoint readers. Key events and characters may need to be eliminated to fit into a two-hour movie format. Reading a book is more stimulating to the brain.[5] Movies do have some advantages over books, however.[6]

1. What is the main problem with the essay's thesis statement?

A. NO CHANGE
B. It is a broad statement of fact.
C. It is missing.
D. It is too narrow.

2. What is the best replacement for the underlined part?

A. NO CHANGE
B. a film. When you can't wait
C. a film because you can't wait
D. a film. Because you can't wait

3. What is the best replacement for this part?

A. NO CHANGE
B. brought to life, however,
C. brought to life. For example,
D. Begin a new paragraph between *life* and *However*.

4. What is the best replacement for this part?

A. NO CHANGE
B. fans of the book because the time
C. fans of the book. In addition, the time
D. fans of the book, the time

For one, going to the movies is a social activity. Seeing a movie is also a good option if you're in the mood for a story but are pressed for time. [7]

As a result, you get the best of both worlds [8] when a wonderful book is made into a wonderful movie. This combination may be rare, but it's not unheard of. *The Wizard of Oz*, for instance, was a delightfully imaginative book by L. Frank Baum.

It later became a movie that many consider to be a classic. Some specific elements of the book were changed, but the general spirit of the text was preserved. [9]

The key is to balance reading books and watching movies. If you read a lot but never go to the movies, you're missing out on some valuable films, and vice versa. It's like following a healthy diet. [10]

5. What is the best replacement for this part?
A. NO CHANGE
B. Reading a book is fun.
C. Read a new book every week.
D. Eliminate it.

6. How can this sentence be improved?
A. NO CHANGE
B. Move it to the beginning of the next paragraph.
C. Take out *however.*
D. Add a transition before *Movies.*

7. Where in the essay does this sentence belong?
A. in the introduction
B. in the conclusion
C. in the body
D. in the thesis

8. What is the best replacement for this part?
A. NO CHANGE
B. Of course, you get the best of both worlds
C. The best of both
D. Eliminate it.

9. What is the main problem with this section of the essay?
A. It needs a transition.
B. It disrupts the essay's unity.
C. It contradicts the thesis.
D. It should be part of the previous paragraph.

10. How can this sentence be improved?
A. NO CHANGE
B. Eliminate it.
C. Include a prediction.
D. Add an example.

B. Creating Thesis Statements

For each topic below, create a strong thesis statement that you could support in a two- to three-page paper.

Answers will vary. See sample answer in Answer Key at www.grammarforwriting.com.

1. going to school in the summer
2. winning a championship
3. growing up in the city
4. advertisements on television
5. allowing cell phones in school

C. Revising a Persuasive Essay

Read the persuasive essay below. On a separate sheet of paper, revise the draft to include the elements below.

Revisions will vary. See sample answer in Answer Key at www.grammarforwriting.com.

1. a clear, strong thesis
2. an attention-grabbing introduction
3. a well-organized body with logical paragraph breaks
4. a reasonable response to the counterargument
5. a strong conclusion that restates your thesis in a new way

[1]Some people think Internet censorship is okay. [2]I think it's probably a bad idea. [3]There are several reasons, which I will explain here. [4]First of all, the First Amendment guarantees all American citizens freedom of speech. [5]This means we can say whatever we want, even if other people don't agree. [6]I may not like it when my friends say certain things, but I don't have the right to shut them up! [7]That reminds me of an argument I got into recently. [8]Second of all, not everyone agrees about what is appropriate and what is not. [9]Third, if we let the government censor the Internet, what's next? [10]The government might decide to tell us what political views we're allowed to have, what books we're allowed to read, and so on. [11]Also, if parents are so worried about what their kids might see, why don't they just watch their kids while they're online? [12]That's what I think, anyway.

CHAPTER 6

Parts of a Sentence

LESSON 6.1

Complete Subjects and Predicates

A **sentence** is a word group that expresses a complete thought. Every sentence has two main parts, a subject and a predicate.

The **subject** is the person or thing that performs the action of the sentence. The **predicate** is the part of the sentence that tells something about the subject. It includes the **verb,** or the word that expresses the action.

The **complete subject** includes all the words that describe the subject. The **complete predicate** includes all the words that tell what the subject does, has, or is.

Complete Subject	Complete Predicate
My favorite comic strip	is "Peanuts" by Charles Schulz.
Charles Schulz	drew "Peanuts" for almost 50 years.
The cartoonist	was brilliant.
His drawings of Charlie Brown and his friends	appear in many newspapers today.

If you cover the column on the left above, you'll see that the predicates don't make sense by themselves. The same thing happens if you cover the right column. Subjects don't make sense alone either.

STEP BY STEP

Here are steps for finding the complete subject and complete predicate in a sentence:

Many comic strips make me laugh.

1. To find the complete subject, ask yourself *who* or *what* does, has, or is something. *What* makes me laugh? *many comic strips*
2. To find the complete predicate, ask yourself what the subject *does, has,* or *is*. What do many comic strips *do? make me laugh*

WRITING HINT

Make sure each sentence is complete and has a subject and a predicate. Remember that a sentence fragment is a group of words punctuated as a complete sentence but missing a subject, a predicate, or both.

FRAGMENT "Peanuts" by Charles Schulz.

COMPLETE A legendary comic strip is "Peanuts" by Charles Schulz.

For more about fixing fragments, see **Lesson 2.1.**

ONLINE PRACTICE
www.grammarforwriting.com

HINT

Remember that the complete subject and the complete predicate may be one word or many words.

Artists paint.

Many established artists paint portraits for a living.

EXERCISE 1 Finding Subjects and Predicates

Underline the complete subjects in the following sentences once. Underline the complete predicates twice.

EXAMPLE Georgia O'Keeffe is a famous artist.

1. Georgia O'Keeffe was born on a farm in 1887.
2. Her parents and teachers recognized her talent.
3. She studied art in Chicago and in New York.
4. Her first successful paintings portrayed colorful flowers.
5. She painted for many years in New Mexico.

Working Together

EXERCISE 2 Reading a Paragraph

With a partner, find the complete subjects and complete predicates in the article below. Share your answers with the class.

[1]Different cultures throughout history have painted murals, or large paintings that cover entire walls or ceilings. [2]The ancient Romans portrayed important events in their murals. [3]Michelangelo, an Italian, painted religious murals on the ceilings of chapels. [4]Mexican artist Diego Rivera expressed his political beliefs in his murals. [5]African-American muralist John Biggers incorporated African symbols, history, and legends.

Georgia O'Keeffe

EXERCISE 3 Writing Sentences

Use the photo to the left to write five sentences. Use a variety of complete subjects and complete predicates. Underline the complete subjects once and the complete predicates twice.

Answers will vary. Students should include a variety of subjects and predicates.
See sample answer in Answer Key at www.grammarforwriting.com.

LESSON 6.2

Simple Subjects and Predicates

A **simple subject** is the key word or group of words in the complete subject. The complete subject is made up of the simple subject and words that describe, or modify, it.

Many food **stores** sell organic food. [*Many food stores* is the complete subject. *Stores* is the simple subject.]

A **simple predicate** is always a **verb** or **verb phrase.** A verb phrase has a main verb and one or more helping verbs. The complete predicate is made up of the simple predicate and all the words that describe it or complete its meaning.

A government inspector **enforces** strict rules. [The verb *enforces* is the simple predicate. *Enforces strict rules* is the complete predicate.]

In most sentences, the simple subject comes before the simple predicate.

Canned wild **salmon makes** a good school lunch.

In a question, the subject often comes after part or all of the simple predicate.

Is the organic **cereal** tasty? Do **you** like it?

Note: In this book, the term *verb* refers to the simple predicate, and *subject* refers to the simple subject unless otherwise noted.

Remember

A **verb** is a word or words that express action or a state of being. See **Lesson 8.1.**

Some Common Helping Verbs

am	has
are	have
be	is
been	may
being	might
can	must
do	was
does	were
had	would

Exercise 1 Finding Simple Subjects and Predicates

Underline each simple subject once and each simple predicate twice. **Remember:** The simple predicate is a verb or verb phrase.

1. Good health results from good habits.
2. Diet is one crucial factor.
3. Daily meals should include generous servings of vegetables.
4. Nutritionists recommend a diet with foods from all food groups.

ONLINE PRACTICE
www.grammarforwriting.com

5. Protein builds strong bones and muscles.
6. A regular exercise routine promotes good health.
7. Exercising relieves stress.
8. Do you exercise regularly?
9. Some good activities are hiking and running.
10. Swimming regularly keeps your body fit.

Exercise 2 Writing Sentences

Start with the notes below. Add a simple subject or a simple predicate to write a sentence. Write *SS* for simple subject or *SP* for simple predicate to show what you added.
Answers will vary. Sample answers are shown.

1. milk—an important dairy product
   Milk is an important dairy product. (SP)
2. provides energy
   Fruit provides energy. (SS)
3. has a lot of sugar
   Juice has a lot of sugar. (SS)
4. experts—daily physical activity
   Experts suggest daily physical activity. (SP)
5. can skate on a frozen pond for exercise
   You can skate on a frozen pond for exercise. (SS)
6. an orange—a good source of vitamin C
   An orange is a good source of vitamin C. (SP)
7. helps the immune system
   Vitamin C helps the immune system. (SS)
8. a balanced diet—necessary for good health
   A balanced diet is necessary for good health. (SP)
9. is an easy and fun activity
   Jumping rope is an easy and fun activity. (SS)
10. nuts, eggs, and meat—protein
   Nuts, eggs, and meat contain protein. (SP)

CONNECTING Writing & Grammar

Remember that a singular subject takes a singular verb, and a plural subject takes a plural verb. See **Lesson 10.1.**

SINGULAR Marco **plays** basketball.

PLURAL His sisters **play** volleyball.

Write What You Think

On a separate sheet of paper, write at least five sentences to answer the question below. When you are finished, underline all simple subjects once and all simple predicates twice.

In what ways do you take care of your health? Explain and give examples.
Answers will vary. See sample answer in Answer Key at www.grammarforwriting.com.

Hard-to-Find Subjects

LESSON 6.3

In some sentences, the subject may be hard to find. You need to find the subject so you can choose the correct verb to go with it. Note the following clues for finding a subject.

In a question, the subject often comes *after* the verb instead of before it. A good way to find the subject is to change the question into a statement. Then ask *who* or *what* the sentence is all about.

> Were Tuskegee Airmen in World War II?
> [Statement: Tuskegee Airmen were in World War II. *Who* is the sentence about? *Tuskegee Airmen*]

> Does the article discuss equality?
> [Statement: The article discusses equality. *What* is the sentence about? *article*]

In a command, the subject is *you*. It is called the **understood subject** because it is not stated in the sentence.

> Read this book about African-American soldiers.
> [*You* read this book about African-American soldiers.]

In **inverted sentences**, the subject comes after the verb. Inverted sentences often begin with *there* or *here*. *There* and *here* are never the subject of a sentence.

> There is a museum in Tuskegee.
> [*Museum* is the subject, not *there*.]

> Here are photographs of soldiers.
> [*Photographs* is the subject, not *here*.]

The subject is never part of a prepositional phrase. For more about prepositional phrases, see Lesson 9.4.

> The photographs of the Tuskegee Airmen are fascinating.
> [*Photographs* is the subject, not *Tuskegee Airmen*.]

> Men from cities across the United States became pilots.
> [*Men* is the subject, not *cities* or *United States*.]

Remember

A subject may include more than one word.

New York City was home for some Tuskegee Airmen.

Today, **Aviation Career Education** sponsors camps for teens.

ONLINE PRACTICE
www.grammarforwriting.com

EXERCISE 1 Identifying Subjects

Underline the subject in each sentence. Write *you* if the subject is understood.

EXAMPLE Pay attention to the museum exhibit. (*you*)

HINT

One sentence in the passage has a **compound subject,** or two subjects that share the same verb.

There were three **cars** and two **buses.**

1. What do you know about World War II?
2. Was your grandfather in the army or navy?
3. Does your grandmother remember the war?
4. Here is an exhibit of family life during the war.
5. Throughout America, families of soldiers waited for their return.
6. Look at this poster of a popular war slogan. (you)
7. Americans recall D-Day on June 6, 1944.
8. Watch the short documentary in this exhibit. (you)
9. Can you or Greg recall the name of the general?
10. There were thousands of injured veterans.

Poster featuring member of the 99th Pursuit Squadron

EXERCISE 2 Finding Subjects in Literature

Underline the subjects in the passage.

Literary Model

[1]On the morning of January 27, members of the 99th were patrolling the skies near Anzio. [2]The Allies had just landed in Italy. [3]Below them were ships along the Mediterranean coastline and thousands of troops on shore. [4]The 99th was protecting the coastal area from enemy aircraft.

—Excerpt from *The Red Tails: World War II's Tuskegee Airmen* by Steven L. Jones

LESSON 6.4

Compound Subjects and Verbs

In a sentence with a **compound subject,** two or more subjects **(s)** share the same verb. A connecting word like *and* or *or* is used to join the separate subjects.

Size (s) and **usefulness** (s) are reasons for the MP3's popularity.

In a sentence with a **compound verb,** two or more verbs **(v)** share the same subject. A connecting word like *and* or *or* is used to join the separate verbs.

MP3 players **fit** (v) in a pocket and **hold** (v) thousands of songs.

Compound Subject	Compound Verb
You and your **friends** can make calls with cell phones.	You **can make** calls and **send** e-mails with some cell phones.
A **smartphone** or a **cell phone** fits in a pocket.	Some cell phones **display** photos or **communicate** with a computer.

You can combine sentences using compound subjects and compound verbs. Combining sentences is a good way to eliminate short, choppy sentences from your writing.

Short Sentences	Combined Sentences
Smartphones send e-mail. **Smartphones** receive e-mail.	**Smartphones** send and receive e-mail.
Laptops work with smartphones. **Desktops** work with smartphones.	**Laptops** and **desktops** work with smartphones.

Remember

Verbs must agree with their subjects in number. A compound subject joined by *and* needs a plural verb.

The **pitcher and catcher practice** today.

The verb agrees with the closest subject when a compound subject is joined by *or*. See **Lesson 10.3.**

The pitcher or base **runners were** at fault.

The base runners or **pitcher was** at fault.

Exercise 1 Combining Sentences

Combine the sentences by using a compound subject or a compound verb. Underline the subjects once and the verbs twice. Sample answers are shown.

EXAMPLE The smartphone sends e-mails. It plays music.

The smartphone sends e-mails and plays music.

ONLINE PRACTICE
www.grammarforwriting.com

HINT
Drop or add words if necessary.

1. Water can damage a cell phone. So does extreme heat.
   Water or extreme heat can damage a cell phone.
2. With a cell phone, some people make calls. They watch TV.
   With a cell phone, some people make calls and watch TV.
3. Cell phones work inside and outside your home. So do many wireless computers.
   Cell phones and many wireless computers work inside and outside your home.
4. Smaller computers are developed every year. Fancier phones are developed every year, too.
   Smaller computers and fancier phones are developed every year.
5. Cell phone codes identify the phone's owner. They tell the service company's name.
   Cell phone codes identify the phone's owner and tell the service company's name.

Exercise 2 Improving a Paragraph

Rewrite the public service message below by combining some sentences. Use compound subjects and compound verbs.
Answers will vary. See sample answer in Answer Key at www.grammarforwriting.com.

[1]A movie theater is a public place. [2]A library is a public place. [3]Crying babies used to be the number one problem in public places, but now it is cell phones. [4]A ringing phone can be annoying. [5]A loud conversation can be annoying, too. [6]Please do your part. [7]Please turn your cell phone off before you enter a public place. [8]You can check for messages later.

Working Together

Exercise 3 Writing an Ad

Work with a partner to write an ad announcing the introduction of a new smartphone.

1. Tell about its features, such as playing games and music.
2. Include five compound subjects and compound verbs. Underline the compound subjects once and the compound verbs twice.

   Answers will vary. Remind students to use compound subjects and compound verbs in their ads. See sample answer in Answer Key at www.grammarforwriting.com.

LESSON 6.5

Direct Objects

Some sentences with **action verbs** have a direct object. A **direct object (DO)** is a noun or pronoun that tells *who* or *what* receives the action of the verb.

➡ To identify the direct object, first find the action verb. Then ask the question *whom?* or *what?* after the verb.

Juan and I cleaned the **basement.** (DO: basement)
[Cleaned *what?* Answer: *basement*]

Our friends helped **us.** (DO: us)
[Helped *whom?* Answer: *us*]

We painted the **ceiling.** (DO: ceiling)
[Painted *what?* Answer: *ceiling*]

➡ A direct object may be a compound of two or more objects.

We spread **newspapers** and **rags** on the floor. (DO: newspapers; DO: rags)
[Spread *what?* Answer: *newspapers* and *rags*]

I called his **mother** and his **father.** (DO: mother; DO: father)
[Called *whom?* Answer: *mother* and *father*]

➡ Sentences with more than one action verb may have a direct object after each action verb.

Juan's father liked the red **walls,** but his mother preferred the old **color.** (DO: walls; DO: color)
[Liked *what?* Answer: *walls*. Preferred *what?* Answer: *color*]

We congratulated **ourselves** and grabbed our **coats.** (DO: ourselves; DO: coats)
[Congratulated *whom?* Answer: *ourselves*. Grabbed *what?* Answer: *coats*]

For more about action verbs, see **Lesson 8.1.**

Remember

A direct object only answers *what* or *whom* after the verb. It does not tell *how*, *when*, or *where*. No direct objects appear in these sentences.

I painted **carefully.** [how]

We began at **noon.** [when]

Paint dripped **here.** [where]

EXERCISE 1 Identifying Direct Objects

Underline each direct object in the sentences below. Remember that a sentence may have more than one direct object.

1. All mammals and plants use <u>oxygen</u>.

2. Warm-blooded animals make their own <u>heat</u>.

3. Scientists classify <u>animals</u> in many ways.

4. Vertebrates have backbones, but invertebrates do not.
5. Plant-eating insects can damage crops and trees.
6. Some birds, such as the toucan, eat fruit or insects.
7. Bats and whales can detect very high or very low sounds.
8. Kangaroos eat mostly grasses.
9. Spiders often trap insects in elaborate webs, and scorpions catch their prey with their pincers.
10. I should ask my teacher for more information.
11. Chimpanzees use stones and sticks as tools.
12. Snakes can shed their skin.
13. An animal's bones protect its heart and other organs.
14. Many animals protect themselves by changing color.
15. Some dolphins have learned sign language.
16. In some areas, pollution seriously endangers animals.
17. Wildlife protection groups need money.
18. I made a donation recently.
19. Please tell your friends about the Wildlife Fund.
20. Mrs. Wong knows ways to help at the local zoo.

Exercise 2 Using Direct Objects

Think about activities you have done in the last week.

1. On a separate sheet of paper, write five sentences about those things.
2. Use an action verb and a direct object in each sentence.
3. Circle the action verb, and underline the direct object.

EXAMPLE I watched a television show about sharks.

Answers will vary. Sample answers are shown.

1. I read an article about the rainforest.
2. I saw a movie with my best friend.
3. I played baseball with my brothers.
4. My parents took me to a family barbeque.
5. My class attended a play.

LESSON 6.6

Subject Complements

A **subject complement (sc)** is a word or group of words that follows a linking verb and tells something about the subject of a sentence. **Linking verbs** connect, or "link," the subject to a word in the predicate.

Mr. Perez is a great **coach**.

He seems **nice**.

My teammates are **nervous** about the game.

There are two main kinds of subject complements: predicate nominatives and predicate adjectives. A **predicate nominative** is a noun or pronoun that identifies the subject. A **predicate adjective** is an adjective that describes the subject.

Predicate Nominative	Our opponents are the **Tigers.** [The noun *Tigers* tells who the *opponents* are.] The new players are **Rob** and **I.** [The noun *Rob* and the pronoun *I* tell who the *players* are.]
Predicate Adjective	Coach Perez feels **confident** about the game. [The adjective *confident* tells what *Coach Perez* is like.] Liz appears **calm.** [The adjective *calm* tells what *Liz* is like.]

Both predicate nominatives (**PN**) and predicate adjectives (**PA**) may be compound.

Our team captains are **Vic Dreesen** and **Lee Chen.**
[The nouns *Vic Dreesen* and *Lee Chen* identify the subject, *captains*.]

The fans in the bleachers became **quiet** and **nervous.**
[The adjectives *quiet* and *nervous* describe the subject, *fans*.]

Common Linking Verbs

am	look
appear	seem
are	smell
become	sound
feel	taste
grow	was
is	were

For more about linking verbs, see **Lesson 8.1.**

ONLINE PRACTICE

www.grammarforwriting.com

EXERCISE 1 Identifying Subject Complements

Underline and label each subject complement in the sentences below. Write *PN* for predicate nominative or *PA* for predicate adjective.

EXAMPLE Watching baseball games is interesting (PA).

1. The Chicago Cubs is a baseball team (PN).
2. The team's home is Wrigley Field (PN).
3. The two baseball teams from New York are the Yankees (PN) and the Mets (PN).
4. I became a Yankee fan (PN) two years ago.
5. Before that, baseball seemed dull (PA) to me.
6. Now the most loyal Yankee fans are my dad (PN) and I (PN).
7. Basketball was my favorite sport (PN).
8. Most basketball players look unbelievably tall (PA) and strong (PA).
9. Few young players become superstars (PN) like Michael Jordan.
10. Luck, hard work, and talent are important (PA) to success.

EXERCISE 2 Using Subject Complements

On a separate sheet of paper, write a sentence using each of the kinds of complements listed below. Underline the complement(s) in each sentence.

Answers will vary. Sample answers are shown.

EXAMPLE a predicate nominative after the verb *is*

My grandfather is a teacher.

1. a predicate adjective
   My grandfather's students were grateful to have him as a teacher.
2. a compound predicate adjective
   My grandfather was smart and hilarious.
3. a predicate nominative after the verb *were*
   His students were hard workers.
4. a compound predicate nominative
   He was a great teacher and a caring friend.
5. a compound predicate adjective after the verb *feel*
   I feel proud and happy to be his granddaughter.

Story

Stories are everywhere—in television shows and commercials, in books and magazines, and in songs and movies. Everyone enjoys a good **story,** because it transports us to a different place and lets us experience new and unusual people and things. Most stories have several basic elements.

Characters	Characters are the people described in a story. Their quoted conversations are dialogue.
Plot	The plot is the series of events that make up the story. It usually includes a conflict, or central problem.
Setting	The setting is the time and place in which the action occurs.
Theme	The theme is the story's overall message about life.

When you write your story, remember to include the following.

Key Features

- characters and theme
- exciting beginning, middle, end
- consistent point of view
- setting
- plot that revolves around a conflict
- dialogue

ASSIGNMENT

TASK: Write a two- to three-page **story** that includes a lot of action.

GOAL: to entertain

TARGET: your classmates

SPECIAL INSTRUCTIONS: Include at least two characters.

Spark an Idea First, figure out a basic idea on which you can base your story. You may brainstorm an idea by completing a sentence starter, like the ones below. Be creative in your responses.

If children ruled the world, then…
If humans lived in space, then…
If the year were 2210, then…
If people were trapped in a storm in the middle of nowhere, then they could use survival tips they have heard about.

Pick Your Players Next, choose the characters of your story. There are several types of characters.

- **Main characters** play the major roles in the story and are the focus of most of the action.
- **Minor characters** play supporting roles, helping to move the plot along.

Create Character Maps to help you determine details about your characters.

Character Map

What Character Says and Does
travels alone for first time

How Character Looks
tall for an 11-year-old, lanky, brown hair

Character's Name
Ramiro

What Character Thinks or Feels
excited and nervous

What Others Think About Him or Her
can tell he is worried

WRITING HINT

During prewriting, choose the **setting,** or the time and place where the story will occur.

Real-World Writing

Note how this author drafts her stories.

"In my first drafts, I usually tell what the characters see and hear as well as how they feel. Later revisions often include what the characters taste, smell, and touch."
—Peg Kehret

What's the Crisis? Next, choose the **conflict,** or problem, that your main character will confront in the story.

1. In an **internal conflict,** the main character struggles with him- or herself. For example, the character may struggle with a negative personality trait or a decision that is difficult to make.
2. **External conflicts** are outside the main character. External conflicts can be between two characters or between a character and an outside force, such as climbing a mountain.

> **WRITING HINT**
> As you choose a conflict, think about the **theme,** or the message you want your readers to get from the story.

Set Up the Story Now create a **plot,** the series of events that make up the story. Use **dialogue,** the quoted speech of characters, to add details and interest.

1. The **beginning** of your story should introduce the characters and setting. Open with a bang to keep your readers interested. Be sure to show or hint at the conflict.
2. The **middle** should feel like climbing up the hill in a roller coaster. Tension should build until you reach the **climax,** or turning point of the story.
3. The **end** of the story should resolve the main conflict.

Use a Story Map to plan your story before you begin writing.

Story Map

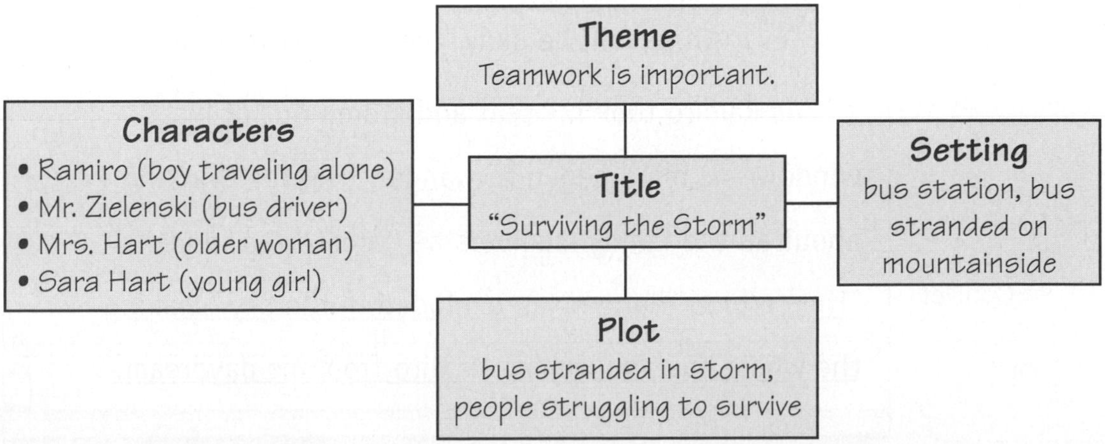

CONNECTING Writing & Grammar

Stories can sound flat when short sentences repeat words. To keep your sentences interesting, use compound subjects and verbs to combine sentences. See **Lesson 6.4.**

ORIGINAL **Ramiro** shivered. **Sara** shivered.

COMBINED **Ramiro and Sara** shivered.

Check Your Draft Use the checklist to check your draft.

WRITING CHECKLIST

Did you...

- ✔ include two or more characters and dialogue?
- ✔ include an action-filled beginning, middle, and end?
- ✔ establish a clear plot, conflict, theme, and setting?
- ✔ check for errors in spelling and fragments?

Writing Model

[1]As Ramiro climbed aboard, he looked around the bus. [2]"I bet nobody's traveling because the weather is so bad," he thought. [3]The only other people on the bus, besides the driver, were a middle-aged woman and a little girl. [4]They watched Ramiro stroll down the aisle with his big green duffle bag.

Characters introduced

[5]"Mommy, it's starting to rain," said the little girl.

[6]"Everything will be okay," her mother replied.

Dialogue

[7]As Ramiro took his seat and stared out of his window, his mind began to wander. [8]He was thinking about all the family members he hadn't seen in years. [9]Then a loud thunderclap exploded in the sky, shaking the whole bus and waking Ramiro from his daydream.

Conflict

Chapter Review

A. Practice Test

Read the draft and questions below carefully. The questions ask you to identify parts of sentences. Fill in the corresponding circle for your answer choice.

(1) The practice of setting clocks forward in the spring began around the time of World War I. **(2)** The sun rises earlier in the spring and summer. **(3)** Daylight Saving Time works by giving people an extra hour of light in the evening. **(4)** The sun rises later in the autumn and winter, so we turn the clocks back. **(5)** In this way, parents and children don't start their day in the dark. **(6)** Daylight Saving Time saves energy by providing more natural light, thereby reducing the need for lamps, heat, and other energy sources. **(7)** Not all states use Daylight Saving Time, however. **(8)** People in Hawaii and Arizona never change their clocks. **(9)** In the rest of the United States, Daylight Saving Time begins on the second Sunday in March and ends on the first Sunday in November.

Ⓐ Ⓑ Ⓒ Ⓓ ● **1.** Which of the following is the simple subject of sentence 1?
(A) clocks
(B) spring
(C) World War I
(D) setting
(E) practice

Ⓐ Ⓑ Ⓒ ● Ⓔ **2.** Which of the following is the complete predicate of sentence 3?
(A) giving people
(B) giving
(C) works by giving
(D) works by giving people an extra hour of light in the evening
(E) giving people an extra hour of light in the evening

● Ⓑ Ⓒ Ⓓ Ⓔ **3.** Which of the following is true of sentence 5?
(A) It contains a compound subject.
(B) It contains a compound verb.
(C) The subject complement is *their day*.
(D) The direct object is *the dark*.
(E) It is a fragment.

Ⓐ Ⓑ Ⓒ ● Ⓔ **4.** Which of the following is true of sentence 6?
(A) It is a command.
(B) The simple subject is *energy*.
(C) It contains a compound subject.
(D) The simple predicate is *saves*.
(E) It is a fragment.

Ⓐ Ⓑ ● Ⓓ Ⓔ **5.** In sentence 8, which of the following is the direct object?
(A) parts of Indiana
(B) Hawaii
(C) clocks
(D) Hawaii and Arizona
(E) change

B. Identifying Subjects and Verbs

Read each sentence below. Underline the subject(s) once and the verb(s) twice. If the subject is *you* (understood), write *you* in the margin.

1. Are you and your brother going to the museum?
2. Please go to the museum with me. you
3. There is an amazing exhibit of robotic technology.
4. Visitors from all over flooded the exhibit on the first day.
5. Did you hear about it on the news?
6. Here is an extra ticket.
7. Take a camera and notebook. you
8. Most people take the bus or train to the museum.

9. Can you see or hear the train coming?

10. What did Ernie think of the exhibit?

C. Writing Complete Subjects and Predicates

For each item below, add the missing complete subject or predicate. Include at least one verb phrase. Then underline the simple subject once and the simple predicate twice. Change capital letters and punctuation as needed. Answers will vary. Sample answers are shown.

1. My lucky sneakers. My lucky sneakers are red.
2. Goes to dance class every Thursday. My older sister goes to dance class every Thursday.
3. Plays on the basketball team. My best friend plays on the basketball team.
4. Most kids at school. Most kids at school like pizza a lot.
5. Bert and Tessa's parents. Bert and Tessa's parents have traveled to Mexico.

D. Analyzing and Extending a Story

Read the story below.

Students' stories will vary. A sample answer is shown.

1. Label the parts of each sentence: *S* for subjects and *V* for verbs.
2. Write *PN* for predicate nominatives, *PA* for predicate adjectives, and *DO* for direct objects.
3. Write three to four sentences telling what happens next in the story. Include at least one compound subject and one compound verb.

S V
[1]Beth was walking down the hallway at school.
S V DO S S V PN
[2]She saw Marnie. [3]Beth and Marnie were best friends.
S V V
[4]Marnie was talking and laughing with a group of new
S V DO S V
friends. [5]Then, Marnie made a joke about Beth. [6]Beth was
PA S V V V DO
shocked. [7]She had always admired and trusted Marnie.
V S PA S
[8]Was their friendship real? [9]At that moment, Marnie
V V DO
turned and noticed Beth.

Marnie blushed and looked surprised to see Beth. Beth pulled her aside and explained how upset she was. Marnie's cheeks and eyes were red. She felt sorry and apologized to Beth.

CHAPTER 7

Nouns and Pronouns

LESSON 7.1

Nouns

Parts of speech, such as nouns, verbs, and adjectives, identify how words work in a sentence. A **noun** names a person, place, thing, or idea.

PERSON THING IDEA PLACE
Emily read a **book** about **honor** in **Japan.**

A noun can be a single word, or it can be two or more words used together.

A **common noun** names any person, place, thing, or idea. A **proper noun** names a specific person, place, thing, or idea. Begin a proper noun with a capital letter, and capitalize each important word.

COMMON NOUN	PROPER NOUN
character	Harry Potter
team	Boston Red Sox
river	Nile River
city	Philadelphia
country	Kenya
bridge	Golden Gate Bridge
holiday	Memorial Day
language	Spanish
university	University of Washington

Remember

Remember that words can be different parts of speech in different sentences.

Fall is my favorite season. [noun]

Leaves **fall** from the trees. [verb]

The **park** looks beautiful. [noun]

Let's **park** near the entrance. [verb]

EXERCISE 1 Identifying Nouns

Underline the nouns in each of the following sentences. Label each noun *C* for common noun or *P* for proper noun.

P C
EXAMPLE I read about Amelia Earhart in class.

P C
1. Amelia Earhart was a famous pilot.

P P
2. Earhart flew a shaky and noisy Lockheed Electra.

ONLINE PRACTICE
www.grammarforwriting.com

Amelia Earhart

3. Her navigator (C) for a flight (C) around the world (C) was Fred Noonan (P).
4. Earhart (P), Noonan (P), and their plane (C) disappeared without a trace.
5. Their fate (C) remains a puzzle (C) to historians (C).

Exercise 2 Using Nouns in Sentences

On a separate sheet of paper, write one sentence about each topic below. Underline the common nouns you used. Circle the proper nouns.

Answers will vary. See sample answers in Answer Key at www.grammarforwriting.com.

EXAMPLE airplanes

(Orville) and (Wilbur Wright) made history at (Kitty Hawk), (North Carolina.)

1. hiking
2. deserts
3. rafting
4. skiing
5. a holiday in a city
6. a trip to a new place
7. camping
8. driving
9. skateboarding
10. skating

WRITING HINT

Using proper nouns helps make your writing more specific and concrete. Notice the difference between these two sentences.

COMMON NOUNS The **boys** went to the **city** to see the **team** play.

PROPER NOUNS **Sam** and **Patrick** went to **Denver** to see the **Rockies** play.

Exercise 3 Writing an Encyclopedia Article

On a separate sheet of paper, write an article for a children's encyclopedia. Answers will vary. Have students exchange papers and check whether all common and proper nouns were properly identified and labeled. See sample answer in Answer Key at www.grammarforwriting.com.

1. Pick an interesting event or person you've read about.
2. Write four to five sentences about your topic.
3. Include common and proper nouns in each sentence.
4. When you have finished, underline all the common nouns. Circle the proper nouns.

Pronouns

LESSON 7.2

Pronouns (P) are words that are used in place of nouns. The word the pronoun replaces is called its **antecedent (A).**

The **concert** [A] was incredible, but **it** [P] was too short.

Ian enjoys **dances** [A] and goes to **them** [P] often.

Some pronouns have more than one antecedent.

Maria [A] and **Laura** [A] enjoy jazz, and **they** [P] attend many concerts.

Luis [A] is a guitarist. **Emma** [A] sings. **They** [P] are in a band.

While there are many different types of pronouns (see lists on the right), the ones used most are **personal pronouns,** such as *I*, *you*, and *it*.

Can **you** go to the concert with **me**?

Possessive pronouns are personal pronouns that show ownership or possession. Some possessive pronouns go before nouns, and some are used alone.

His father could not come to the concert.

The idea for the costumes was **hers.**

Remember that possessive pronouns never have an apostrophe.

The band played **its** greatest hits. [not *it's*]

Indefinite pronouns refer to nonspecific persons or things. They may have no clear antecedents.

Everyone is invited to the show.

Both of the families had children.

Exercise 1 Identifying Pronouns

Underline the four personal pronouns in the paragraph. Use a double line under the eight possessive pronouns.

EXAMPLE He called his friend back on the phone.

Personal Pronouns

he	she
her	them
him	they
I	us
it	we
me	you

Possessive Pronouns

her	our
hers	ours
his	their
its	theirs
mine	your
my	yours

Some Indefinite Pronouns

anybody	neither
anyone	no one
both	nobody
each	one
everybody	several
everyone	somebody
few	someone
many	

ONLINE PRACTICE
www.grammarforwriting.com

Literary Model

[1]Our family, the Taos, lived in a compound with more than fifty rooms, all surrounded by a wall. [2]Grandfather was head of the family, and he had two sons, Big Uncle and my father. [3]Both of them lived there with their wives and children and their own servants. [4]Each family had a set of rooms grouped around a courtyard. [5]Although I spent most of the time in our own rooms with my parents, my two elder sisters, and my little brother, I often visited other courtyards.

—Excerpt from *Ties That Bind, Ties That Break* by Lensey Namioka

Exercise 2 Using Pronouns

Add the missing personal, possessive, or indefinite pronoun in each blank. Answers will vary. Sample answers are shown.

1. Everyone in my class needed to watch a TV program about Kofi Annan, the former secretary-general of the United Nations.
2. Marco, ___my___ younger cousin, came for an overnight visit.
3. Marco wasn't excited, but _he_ agreed to try watching it.
4. The program explained Annan's accomplishments, and _it_ also showed him accepting the Nobel Peace Prize.
5. Marco said, "_You_ were right. This program is interesting."

Exercise 3 Writing a Description

Write at least five sentences about the person you admire most. Underline personal pronouns once and possessive pronouns twice. Circle any indefinite pronouns.

Answers will vary, but students should use a variety of pronouns discussed in the lesson. See sample answer in Answer Key at www.grammarforwriting.com.

Subject and Object Pronouns

A **subject pronoun** is a pronoun used as the subject of a sentence or a clause.

> **She** is clearly the finest diver. [not *her*]

A subject pronoun is also used as a subject complement following a linking verb. It replaces a noun that renames the subject. When a subject pronoun functions this way, it is called a **predicate nominative.**

For more on subject complements and predicate nominatives, see **Lesson 6.6.**

> The winners are Katie and **she.** [not *her*]

Subject Pronouns	I, we, you, he, she, it, they

An **object pronoun** is a pronoun used as an object. It may be a direct object. A **direct object** answers the question *whom?* or *what?* following an action verb.

> Coach Ramos encouraged **her.** [not *she*]
>
> The coach helped others, and he advised **them** well. [not *they*]

For more on direct objects and objects of prepositions, see **Lessons 6.5** and **9.4.**

In addition, use an **object pronoun** as the object of a preposition, such as *after, at, between, for, to,* and *with.*

> The coach glanced at **us** during the diving event. [not *we*]
>
> My classmates were cheering for **me.** [not *I*]
>
> Competition for first place is between you and **me.** [not *I*]

Object Pronouns	me, us, you, him, her, it, them

Pronouns in compound subjects and objects often cause problems. To avoid making a mistake, try each part separately, and see how the sentence sounds. You probably wouldn't say, "Him burst out in applause" in the first sentence below or "with I" in the second sentence.

> (My mom and) ~~him~~ *he* burst out in applause.
>
> Pablo is going to the swim meet with (Kyle and) ~~I~~ *me*.

ONLINE PRACTICE
www.grammarforwriting.com

WRITING HINT

Is it *us students or we students*? It all depends. How are the words used in the sentence? If the words are a subject or subject complement, use *we students.*

We students try to do well.

If the words are a direct object or the object of a preposition, use *us students.*

Success is up to **us** students.

To figure out which word to use, drop the noun: *We try to do well. Success is up to us.*

Exercise 1 Choosing the Correct Pronoun

Circle the correct pronoun(s) in each sentence.

EXAMPLE Jim and (I, me) are brothers.

1. My best friends are Jerry and (him, he).
2. Sibling rivalry is a problem for some, but not for my brother and (me, I).
3. (We, Us) get along well and have some friends in common.
4. (Him and me, He and I) have our own interests, too.
5. Our parents encourage (us, we) to learn from each other.

Exercise 2 Editing a Paragraph

As you read the paragraph below, circle the five errors in subject or object pronouns. Write the correct pronouns in the margin.

[1]Bart is on vacation. [2]Him and his family are sitting on a quiet, sandy beach on a hot summer day. [3]The ocean is calm. [4]It barely makes a sound. [5]Next to he, his dad builds a sand castle. [6]Next to him is Tonya. [7]Her is Bart's sister. [8]She begged to come along with Bart and he. [9]Suddenly, Bart hears a shout. [10]He sees his brother Sam running toward the ocean and shouting, "Last one of we in buys lemonade for everyone." [11]They all take off running. [12]No one wants to be last.

He
him
She
him
us

Exercise 3 Writing a Paragraph

Think about an enjoyable day you had with your family, and write about it in a paragraph. Use at least three subject pronouns and two object pronouns to refer to people, places, and things. Underline the subject pronouns once and the object pronouns twice. Answers will vary. Remind students that subject pronouns are used as subjects and as subject complements. Object pronouns are used as direct objects and objects of prepositions. See sample answer in Answer Key at www.grammarforwriting.com.

Pronoun Agreement

LESSON 7.4

➡ Each pronoun you use should agree with its **antecedent,** the word to which the pronoun refers.

> **Tasha** finished **her** history project early. [singular antecedent and singular pronoun]
>
> The other **students** were making **their** posters. [plural antecedent and plural pronoun]

➡ When two or more antecedents are joined by *and,* use a plural pronoun.

> **Mrs. O'Hara** and **Mr. Santos** took **their** classes to the gym.

When two or more singular antecedents are joined by *or* or *nor,* use a singular pronoun.

> Either **Tasha** or **Nicole** will present **her** speech first.

➡ Pay special attention to pronoun agreement in sentences with **indefinite pronouns.** As the lists on the right show, some indefinite pronouns are always singular, and some are always plural. (See Lessons 7.2 and 10.4.)

> SINGULAR **Neither** of the boys rushed **his** presentation.
>
> PLURAL **Many** of the students ended **their** speeches well.

When the antecedent of a singular indefinite pronoun includes both males and females, use *his or her,* or rewrite the sentence.

> INCORRECT **Everyone** should gather **their** materials.
>
> CORRECT **Everyone** should gather **his or her** materials.
>
> CORRECT **All students** should gather **their** materials.

➡ Depending on the word they refer to, the indefinite pronouns *all, any, most,* and *some* can be singular or plural.

> SINGULAR **Some** of the <u>cake</u> was left in **its** box.
>
> PLURAL **Some** of the <u>students</u> ate **their** lunches.

Some Singular Indefinite Pronouns

anybody	neither
anyone	nobody
each	no one
either	one
everybody	somebody
everyone	someone

Plural Indefinite Pronouns

both	many
few	several

WRITING HINT

Avoid confusing pronoun references. Replace a pronoun whose antecedent is unclear with a noun or noun phrase.

UNCLEAR Mrs. O'Hara asked Tasha if she could take a photo. [Does *she* refer to Mrs. O'Hara or Tasha?]

CLEAR Mrs. O'Hara asked Tasha if **Tasha** could take a photo.

ONLINE PRACTICE

www.grammarforwriting.com

EXERCISE Choosing Correct Pronouns

Circle the pronoun in parentheses that agrees with its antecedent. **Hint:** First, find and underline the antecedent(s).

EXAMPLE My sisters and brothers like (his or her, their) rooms.

1. Both of the girls have (her, their) desks by the window.
2. Each of the boys wants to paint (his, their) closet doors.
3. Neither of my brothers cares about making (his, their) bed.
4. Did either Sue or Emily say (she, they) left her phone here?
5. Everyone worked on (his or her, their) chore.
6. Few stop (his or her, their) work to start a conversation.
7. Many of my friends don't know the names of people in (his, their) neighborhood.
8. Either Derrick or Kevin volunteers (his, their) time to plan a yearly block party.
9. Some of my aunts bring flowers to the families who move into (her, their) apartment building.
10. Everybody should try to know (his, his or her) neighbors.

Write What You Think

Answers will vary. See sample answer in Answer Key at www.grammarforwriting.com.

On a separate sheet of paper, write at least five sentences that explain your answer to the question below.

Suppose you were asked to put three things in a time capsule to show what life is like in your community today. What three things would you choose? Why?

1. Make sure that all pronouns agree with their antecedents.
2. Use at least one singular indefinite pronoun.

WRITER'S WORKSHOP

ONLINE MODEL
www.grammarforwriting.com

How-to Essay

Have you ever made cookies or assembled a bicycle or a toy? If so, you have probably read a how-to essay. **How-to essays** describe the steps and supplies needed to do or make something. Among the many different kinds of how-to writing are instructions, recipes, and technical manuals.

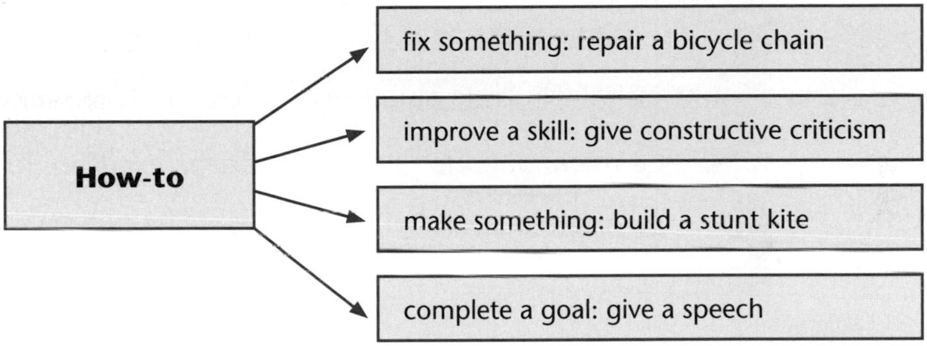

In this workshop, you will learn how to write a how-to essay. Your how-to essay should have the following features.

Key Features

- an interesting introduction
- clear, specific task
- easy-to-follow steps
- chronological order with transitions, such as *first, next,* and *then*
- specific details
- materials needed

ASSIGNMENT

TASK: Write a three-page **how-to essay.**

AUDIENCE: someone who has never made what you are describing

PURPOSE: to explain how to make something

Prewriting

Pick an Interesting Topic What unique things can you make? Create a list. Consider your audience when you make your list. Why might others enjoy making or doing the things on your list? Would others find them too difficult? Too easy?

Things I Like to Make	Why Others Would Like It
• gelatin fruit squares	• fun, healthy recipe
• volcano model	• easy, exciting, fun
• origami swan	• good decoration or gift

From your list, choose the topic that fits these criteria:

- You are very familiar with the process.
- You think your audience will enjoy making it.
- The process is not too complicated to explain.

Think About Your Audience Unlike you, your audience has never made the thing you are describing. You must present readers with *all* of the information they will need to complete the steps. Before you begin writing, make a plan.

- **List materials.** Create a list of all of the materials your readers will need.
- **Picture the process.** Mentally go through all of the steps in the process you are going to describe.
- **Clarify terms.** List and define any terms your audience might not know.
- **Do research.** Double-check recipes, go online, or visit the library if any step is not clear in your mind.

Drafting

Put Everything in Order The order in which you present the information in a how-to essay is just as important as the information itself. Use **chronological order.** Put the steps in order from first to last.

1. Use Process Notes to organize the steps. Begin by listing all of the materials in the order they will be used.
2. As you draft, use **transitions,** such as *first* and *next,* to help your readers follow the order.

Some Transitions for Chronological Order

after	later
afterwards	next
before	second
finally	then

Materials	Step 1	Step 2	Step 3	Step 4
empty bottle tinfoil baking soda glitter empty bowl funnel white vinegar red food coloring dishwashing detergent	Shape tinfoil into cone around empty bottle.	Pour enough baking soda into empty bottle to cover bottom. Add a dash of glitter.	In empty bowl, mix 1/4 cup of white vinegar, two drops of dish detergent, and a dash of food coloring.	Empty vinegar mixture into bottle, using funnel. Stand back and enjoy.

Make the Steps Clear When you write about something you know well, you may forget to mention key details that your readers need to know. As you draft, always put yourself in your readers' shoes. Ask yourself questions such as these:

1. **What's missing?** Look at your Process Notes, and check if any materials or steps are missing. Make sure not to take the small steps for granted. Explain the process step by step.

Drafting

2. **What's unclear?** Make sure you describe complicated or easily misunderstood steps in the simplest way possible. Add a diagram or picture to help clarify the step.

3. **What errors are common or possible?** Point out mistakes you've made in the past or errors that can cause a problem. For example, what might happen if two or more steps were completed out of order?

Note the changes one writer made to clarify the steps.

Add transitions.

Put steps in correct order to avoid confusion.

Warn about possible errors.

First,
[1]~~P~~inch one edge of a sheet of tinfoil around the top of the bottle. [2]Secure the sheet at the top with a rubber band, if necessary. [3]Make sure the bottle you are going to use is clean and dry. [4]Then, shape the tinfoil so that it resembles a cone. [5]The tinfoil should extend to the bottom of the bottle.
Make sure that the bottle is steady. If it is not, the bottle could fall over as it erupts.

Write a Complete Essay
Include three parts.

1. Write an **introduction** that grabs your readers' attention. Begin with a question, such as "Have you ever wanted to see a volcano erupt?" Or, add sensory description, such as "The powerful lava shoots up and over the sides of the volcano."

2. Write a **body** that clearly explains each step in the process. Describe each step in the order it is performed. Use paragraphs and transition words to emphasize this step-by-step organization.

3. In your **conclusion,** suggest ways your readers can expand on the project they have just completed.

Revising

Next, use the Revising Questions to improve your draft.

Revising Questions

- ❑ How strong is my introduction?
- ❑ Where can I add transitions to clarify the order?
- ❑ Which steps can I clarify or make more specific?

As you revise, keep in mind the traits of good writing. See **Lesson 1.3.**

[1]Pour enough baking soda into the bottle to cover the bottom. ^Next, add glitter.^ [2]Then, shake the bottle slightly to mix the baking soda and glitter. [3]Set the bottle aside. [4]~~Add glitter.~~

[5]Add one cup of white vinegar to a clean mixing bowl. [6]^Then,^ ~~A~~add several drops of red and orange food coloring to the vinegar. [7]Mix the vinegar and food coloring together so that the color is even. [8]^Finally,^ ~~A~~add one or two drops of liquid dish detergent.

[9]Now, place the funnel into the mouth of the foil-wrapped bottle. [10]Slowly pour the vinegar mixture into the bottle. [11]Don't pour too much at once. ^If you do, the volcano will erupt all over your clothes.^

Put steps in correct order.

Add transitions.

Explain what will happen if a step isn't followed correctly.

Editing and Proofreading

Use the Editing and Proofreading Checklist below, each time looking for a different item. The model introduction shows the corrections one student made.

Proofreading Symbols

- ^ Add.
- ⊙ Add a period.
- ℘ Delete.
- / Make lowercase.
- # Add space.

Editing and Proofreading Checklist

- ❑ Are all words spelled correctly?
- ❑ Did I capitalize the first word of each sentence?
- ❑ Do all pronouns and their antecedents agree in number?
- ❑ Have I used subject and object pronouns correctly?

[1]Lava blasts into the air! [2]It pours over the sides of~~f~~ the volcano. [3]Everyone takes a step back from where ^he or she is ~~they are~~ standing. [4]Is this class exploring a volcanic island? [5]Actually, the teacher and students are sitting in their classroom on a regular school day. [6]You can build your own volcano for a class assignment. [7]The lava won't be real, of course, but the volcanic eruption is incredible to ~~be~~ watch. [8]Your classmates will be amazed, and your teacher will be impressed. [9]Or, you can make the volcano at home on a rainy day. [10]Wherever you decide to make ^it ~~them~~, the best part of this experiment is that it's simple to^#do⊙

Editing and Proofreading

CONNECTING Writing & Grammar

Check Pronoun Agreement As you edit and proofread your draft, check that your pronouns **agree** with their antecedents in number. If the noun is singular, use a singular pronoun.

INCORRECT	My grandparents know how to make a baking soda and vinegar volcano. He has lots of great tricks!
CORRECT	My grandparents know how to make a baking soda and vinegar volcano. They have lots of great tricks!

For more help with pronoun agreement, see **Lesson 7.4.**

In this example, the antecedent, *grandparents,* is plural, so the pronoun must be plural, too.

INCORRECT	Do not allow a young person to make the volcano alone. They might get hurt.
CORRECT	Do not allow a young person to make the volcano alone. He or she might get hurt.

In this example, the antecedent, *person,* is singular, so the pronoun *they* is incorrect. Because the gender of this young person is not stated, using *he or she* is best.

Publishing and Presenting

Finally, choose a way to share your how-to essay.

- **Give your how-to essay to a friend.** Have him or her read the essay and do a demonstration for your class.
- **Post your essay on the Internet.** Include photographs and diagrams. See if others can use your essay to complete the task you describe. Get permission from a teacher or parent before posting online.
- **Invite two younger people to read your essay.** See if they can complete the tasks you have described. Have them follow the steps at home and report back on their successes and failures.

Reflect On Your Writing

- What part of your essay do you think is most effective?
- What steps were hardest to describe?

CHAPTER 7

Chapter Review

A. Practice Test

Read each sentence below carefully. If you find an error, choose the underlined part that must be changed to make the sentence correct. Fill in the circle for the corresponding letter. If there is no error, fill in circle *E*.

EXAMPLE

Ⓐ Ⓑ ● Ⓓ Ⓔ   Birth order theory states that (A) children (B) develop certain traits depending on whether them (C) were (D) born first, last, or in the middle. No error (E)

Ⓐ ● Ⓒ Ⓓ Ⓔ   **1.** Parents expect a lot from an oldest child (A), and he (B) often expect him (C) or her (D) to set an example. No error (E)

Ⓐ Ⓑ Ⓒ ● Ⓔ   **2.** An (A) older brother may struggle to do things (B) perfectly because he (C) wants to please their (D) parents. No error (E)

Ⓐ ● Ⓒ Ⓓ Ⓔ   **3.** A daughter born in the middle may want to stand out from her (A) siblings, so they (B) will find her (C) own (D) interests. No error (E)

TEST-TAKING TIP

1. Read the *entire* sentence.
2. Rule out the parts you know are correct. Remember, some sentences may not have an error.

Ⓐ Ⓑ Ⓒ Ⓓ ● **4.** Youngest children may become spoiled if they are used
A B C
to getting everything they want. No error
D E

Ⓐ Ⓑ Ⓒ ● Ⓔ **5.** Only children may like to be the center of attention,
A B
because children who have no siblings don't have to
C
share the spotlight with they. No error
D E

Ⓐ Ⓑ ● Ⓓ Ⓔ **6.** If a child is the only girl in a family of boys, her may try
A B C
to outdo her brothers. No error
D E

● Ⓑ Ⓒ Ⓓ Ⓔ **7.** If a boy grows up in a family of all girls, him and his
A B
father might compete with each other, according to this
C D
theory. No error
E

Ⓐ Ⓑ Ⓒ Ⓓ ● **8.** Some of the children who fall in the middle of a very
A B
large family may feel that they are not unique. No error
C D E

Ⓐ Ⓑ ● Ⓓ Ⓔ **9.** Many have doubts about whether he or she believe birth
A B C
order theory is true. No error
D E

● Ⓑ Ⓒ Ⓓ Ⓔ **10.** My brother and me think that most people have the
A
ability to decide how they want to behave toward
B C
others. No error
D E

Chapter Review

B. Identifying Nouns

Read each item below, and label the nouns. Write *C* above common nouns and *P* above proper nouns.

1. When the supermarket [C] doesn't have my cereal [C], I get StartUp Cereal Bars [P] instead.

2. Last week [C], I brought some treats [C] to school [C] and shared them with my classmates [C].

3. Maya [P] says she likes sweet snacks [C] more than salty treats [C].

4. My teacher [C], Mr. Yin [P], warned me that sugary cereals [C], such as Cinnamon Puffs [P], are unhealthy.

5. I need to try to eat more eggs [C], yogurt [C], or fresh fruit [C] in the morning [C].

C. Fixing Pronoun Errors

Circle the pronoun that correctly completes each sentence.

1. When my brother was twelve, (he, him) asked for a surfboard.

2. My mom and dad said (them, they) would think about it.

3. Neither rushed (his or her, their) decision.

4. Everyone thought (they, he or she) would hear my parents say no.

5. The most surprised ones were my little brother and (I, me).

6. Either my dad or uncle would drive (their, his) car to the surf shop.

7. My brother and (me, I) went to the surf shop, too.

8. My parents encouraged (him and me, he and I) to get a surfboard for beginners.

9. (Him and me, He and I) asked the salesperson for help.

10. My family watches my brother surf whenever (they, them) can.

D. Revising a How-to Essay

Read this part of an early draft of a how-to essay. On a separate sheet of paper, rewrite the draft according to the directions below.

Students' revised essays will vary. See sample answer in Answer Key at www.grammarforwriting.com.

1. Circle and move the sentence that is out of order.

2. Add transitions where necessary to show the order.

3. Revise sentences to improve clarity.

4. Fix any errors in pronoun usage.

5. Proofread for mistakes in capitalization and punctuation.

[1]If you're about to pack for vacation, the first thing we need to do is think about the climate in the place where you'll be going. [2]If someone were traveling to Alaska, they would pack a very different suitcase from the one that someone going to hawaii would. [3]That's why it's important to check the weather in their destination before you begin packing. [4]On the Internet, you'll find Web sites that list temperatures for locations around the World.

[5]Once you've found out the weather, make a packing list. [6]Complete the list, and it's time to get packing! [7]Remember to pack your suitcase neatly. [8]You may not think a list is necessary, but us seasoned travelers know it can be a lifesaver. [9]Last but not least, all Travelers should make sure them have important items like tickets and passports.

Chapter Review

CHAPTER 8

Verbs

LESSON 8.1

Verbs

In a sentence, the **verb** expresses an action or a state of being.

Verbs that tell what the subject does or did are called **action verbs.** The action may or may not be one that you can see.

Mrs. Jones **painted** her front door today.

I **wonder** about the red color.

Linking verbs do not express action. They connect the subject to a word that renames or describes it. (See Lesson 6.6 for more about linking verbs.)

Red **is** a bright color for a door.
[The verb *is* connects the subject *red* with a word that renames it—*color*.]

The door **looks** beautiful.
[The verb *looks* connects the subject *door* with a word that describes it—*beautiful*.]

A **verb phrase** has a helping verb and a main verb. The **helping verb** forms tenses and helps the **main verb,** which is the most important verb. Helping verbs are almost always used in questions.

Verb phrase = helping verb + main verb

Was Mr. Jones **consulted** about the red door?
HELPING VERB (Was) — MAIN VERB (consulted)

He **must have agreed.**
HELPING VERBS (must, have) — MAIN VERB (agreed)

Remember: The helping verb in one sentence may be the main verb in another.

She **has taken** painting classes. [helping verb]

She **has** interesting paintings. [main verb]

Some Linking Verbs

am	look
appear	seem
are	smell
become	sound
feel	taste
grow	was
is	were

Some Helping Verbs

am	has
are	have
be	is
been	may
being	might
can	must
could	shall
did	should
do	was
does	were
had	will

ONLINE PRACTICE
www.grammarforwriting.com

Exercise 1 Finding Verbs

Underline every verb and verb phrase in the following article. The first one is done for you.

[1]A monster may be living in a deep lake in Scotland. [2]The creature is called the Loch Ness Monster. [3]Carvings of an unknown animal have been found. [4]Were they made 1,500 years ago? [5]No one knows for sure. [6]The first modern sighting of the monster was reported in 1933. [7]The next year a photograph was taken of a large creature, but it is very fuzzy. [8]To this day, rumors of a monster or animal in the lake persist.

Working Together

Exercise 2 Using Verbs in Sentences

Work with a partner. Choose a topic from the list below. Write five sentences on that topic, using the directions below. Underline the verbs in your sentences.

Answers will vary. Point out that labeling the verbs will help students check to make sure they have followed the directions in writing their sentences. Sample answers are shown.

monsters	legends	dragons
mysteries at sea	unusual animals	dinosaurs

1. a sentence with two action verbs
   People talk and share legends about Big Foot.
2. a sentence with a linking verb
   Big Foot is a legendary apelike creature.
3. a sentence with a verb for an action you can't see
   Many people believe in Big Foot.
4. a sentence with a two-word verb phrase
   I have read two books about this legend.
5. a question with a helping verb
   What do you think about this legend?

TEST-TAKING TIP

On a standardized test, you may be asked to identify parts of speech. When you identify a verb, remember to include all of the words in a verb phrase.

Write What You Think

On a separate piece of paper, write at least five sentences that discuss the question below. Underline the verbs, including helping verbs.

Why do you think every culture has myths about fantastic creatures and animals with special powers? Give reasons and examples.

Answers will vary. Suggest that students consider why stories about make-believe creatures and places are so popular across cultures. See sample answer in Answer Key at www.grammarforwriting.com.

LESSON 8.2

Verb Forms and Regular Verbs

Verbs show action or a state of being. They have four main forms. These forms are called **principal parts.**

A **regular verb** forms its past and past participle by adding *-d* or *-ed* to the present.

Principal Parts of Regular Verbs

Present	Present Participle (Use with *am, is, are, was, were.*)	Past	Past Participle (Use with *has, had, have.*)
play	(is) playing	played	(had) played
talk	(is) talking	talked	(had) talked
wash	(is) washing	washed	(had) washed

See **Lesson 8.4** for more information about verb tense.

1. The **present** shows an action happening in the present time.

   Jaime **follows** instructions.

2. The **present participle** form is used with *am, is, are, was,* or *were.*

   Jaime **is following** in his father's footsteps.

3. The **past** shows an action that has already happened.

   Jaime **followed** me into the store.

4. The **past participle** form is used with *has, had,* or *have.*

   Jaime **has followed** every rule except one.

Remember

To add *-ed* or *-ing* to one-syllable words that end in a single vowel + consonant, double the consonant.

plan → pla**nn**ed → pla**nn**ing

For more help with spelling rules, see **Lesson 12.4.**

Exercise 1 Identifying Verb Forms

Underline the verb in each section below. On the line, identify the form of each verb.

EXAMPLE __present__ Many people wear contact lenses.

__present participle__ **1.** Oscar is reading a report on contact lenses.

ONLINE PRACTICE
www.grammarforwriting.com

past 2. The first true contact lens appeared in 1888.

past 3. Makers studied how to develop better lenses.

past participle 4. Plastic lenses have replaced glass lenses.

present 5. Millions of people today use contact lenses.

Exercise 2 Using the Past Form

Write the past form of each regular verb in parentheses. Use a dictionary if you are unsure of the spelling.

1. Sophia (walk) to the library and back yesterday. walked
2. That was a total of three miles, but she only (stop) once to rest. stopped
3. On the way back, she (carry) three books about inventions. carried
4. One book (slip) from her hand, and she had to go back for it. slipped
5. She (rely) on her trusty wristwatch. relied
6. Unfortunately, she (arrive) late for dinner. arrived
7. Her parents (ask) for an explanation. asked
8. They (encourage) her to call and check in next time. encouraged
9. Luckily, her brother (save) a slice of pizza for her. saved
10. Sophia (vow) never to be late again. vowed

Exercise 3 Writing a Magazine Article

Choose one interesting or important invention in history.

1. On a separate piece of paper, write a short article for a history magazine.
2. Describe the invention, and explain why you chose it.
3. Underline the past and past participle forms of regular verbs.

Answers will vary. Remind students to use as many past tense verbs as they can and to check their spelling of past tense verbs that end in a single vowel and a consonant. See sample answer in Answer Key at www.grammarforwriting.com.

Irregular Verbs

Irregular verbs form their past and past participles in a way other than by adding *-d* or *-ed* to the present form. They can cause problems because they do not form the past or past participle form in predictable ways.

	Present	Past	Past Participle
Regular Verb	wait	waited	waited
Irregular Verb	know	knew	known

The verb *to be* is the most common of all the irregular verbs. Notice its many different forms.

Present	Past	Past Participle
am, are, is	was, were	been

Remember

The best way to learn the parts of irregular verbs is to memorize them. If you're not sure how to spell an irregular verb, use a dictionary.

Common Irregular Verbs

Present	Present Participle (Use with *am, is, are, was, were.*)	Past	Present Participle (Use with *has, had, have.*)
begin	(is) beginning	began	(had) begun
break	(is) breaking	broke	(had) broken
bring	(is) bringing	brought	(had) brought
do	(is) doing	did	(had) done
drive	(is) driving	drove	(had) driven
fall	(is) falling	fell	(had) fallen
feel	(is) feeling	felt	(had) felt
go	(is) going	went	(had) gone
put	(is) putting	put	(had) put
see	(is) seeing	saw	(had) seen
sing	(is) singing	sang	(had) sung
wear	(is) wearing	wore	(had) worn

ONLINE PRACTICE
www.grammarforwriting.com

TEST-TAKING TIP

Standardized tests often include sections on irregular verbs. You can get ready for tests by reviewing a chart of common irregular verbs. Many Web sites include these charts. Search for "irregular verbs."

Exercise 1 Recognizing Irregular Verbs

Underline five irregular verbs in the following paragraph.

[1]Conservation efforts began as early as the seventeenth century. [2]In the English colony of Pennsylvania, William Penn set limits on the amount of land available for settlement. [3]He made sure that one acre of forest was preserved for every five acres. [4]During the nineteenth century, Britain sent a strong message to industries. [5]New laws protected the environment against types of air pollution. [6]In the early twentieth century, countries felt that animals, such as migratory birds, needed protection under the law.

HINT

Two sentences include helping verbs. Remember to use the past participle form in those sentences. Use the chart on the previous page or a dictionary to check irregular verb forms.

Exercise 2 Revising Sentences

Rewrite the sentences, and use the past or past participle form of the verb in parentheses.

1. Last summer, Dad (drive) us through the Everglades. drove
2. My brother and I (think) the drive was boring. thought
3. My dad (keep) to the main road. kept
4. At the rest area, there (is) an alligator! was
5. My brother (tear) his jeans on a tree trying to get closer. tore
6. He had (go) right up to the edge of the water. gone
7. If he (fall) in, he was in trouble. fell
8. Luckily, he (take) a good photograph of the alligator. took
9. Then the alligator slowly (swim) away. swam
10. I have (write) a story about that alligator. written

Verb Tense

LESSON 8.4

The **tense** of the verb shows if an action is happening right now, happened in the past, or will happen in the future.

The three **simple tenses** are **present, past,** and **future.**

Tense	What It Shows	Example
Present Tense	action happening in the present	Amy **performs** well.
Past Tense	action that happened in the past	Amy **performed** last night.
Future (*will* or *shall* and the present tense)	action that will happen in the future	Amy **will perform** tomorrow.

Verbs also have three **perfect tenses.** These tenses use the present participle and past participle verb forms with one or more helping verbs.

Tense	What It Shows	Example
Present Perfect (*has* or *have* and past participle)	action that happened in the past and may still be happening	Amy **has performed** well for years.
Past Perfect (*had* and past participle)	action that happened before another past action or time	Her sister **had performed** the same piece last year.
Future Perfect (*will have* and past participle)	action that will happen before another future action or time	By next spring, she **will have performed** many times on stage.

WRITING HINT

Using consistent verb tenses will help your readers follow your writing. Avoid making unnecessary changes in tense.

INCORRECT For years, Kevin **played** piano and **enjoys** singing.

CORRECT For years, Kevin **played** piano and **enjoyed** singing.

See **Lessons 8.2** and **8.3** to review forming the principal parts of regular and irregular verbs.

Exercise 1 Identifying Tense

Underline the verb in parentheses that correctly completes each sentence. On the line, label the verb tense.

EXAMPLE past In the fifteenth century, Joan of Arc (ride, rode) into battle with the soldiers.

ONLINE PRACTICE
www.grammarforwriting.com

Joan of Arc

present 1. Today, Joan of Arc (remains, remained) a heroine in France.

future 2. People (honored, will honor) her memory years from now.

past 3. During the Hundred Years' War, Joan (leads, led) an army.

past perfect 4. She never (had fought, fight) in a war before.

present perfect 5. I (have been learning, will learn) new facts about her since last year.

Exercise 2 Keeping Tenses Consistent

Rewrite the paragraph so that all verbs are in the past tense. You should change five verbs. Underline them.

> 1 Pompeii was once an ancient city in Italy. 2 In A.D. 63, an earthquake damages (damaged) the port and popular resort city. 3 Then Mt. Vesuvius is erupting (erupted) and buried the city. 4 The cinders and ashes from the volcano preserved Pompeii. 5 Hundreds of years later, archaeologists find (found) the people exactly as they were when Mt. Vesuvius flares (flared) up and poured ashes over the city. 6 The eruption actually protects (protected) art, household goods, and jewelry.

Exercise 3 Writing a Response

Write an essay in response to the question below.

Answers will vary. See sample answer in Answer Key at www.grammarforwriting.com. Remind students to use future tense verbs with the word *will*.

Do you think teenagers today have an easier life than teenagers did fifty years ago? Give reasons and examples.

1. Use present tense verbs for things as they are now.
2. Use past tense verbs to describe anything that happened in the past.
3. Use future tense verbs to show what will happen.

TEST-TAKING TIP

When you respond to an essay question, restate the question in your answer.

QUESTION Should schools ban cell phones?

ANSWER **Schools should** not **ban cell phones** for several reasons.

Verbals

Verbals are words that are made from verbs, but they don't function as verbs. A verbal may look like a verb, but it acts like a **noun,** an **adverb,** or an **adjective** in the sentence.

Verbal	Form	How It Acts	Examples
Gerund	verb + *-ing*	acts like a noun and may be a subject, a predicate nominative, or an object	**Running** develops muscles. José won a competition in **swimming.**
Participle	verb + *-ing* or *-ed*	acts like an adjective and is formed from a present or past participle	The **winning** gymnast was happy. **Relieved,** he hugged his mother.
Infinitive	*to* + present tense of verb	acts like a noun, an adjective, or an adverb	**To be** in the competition was fun. They began **to cheer.**

Remember

Sometimes a participle is used with a helping verb in a verb phrase. A participle in a verb phrase is part of the verb.

VERB PHRASE My team **was losing.**

A participle by itself is used as an adjective.

ADJECTIVE The **losing** team sat quietly.

Writers use verbals to add details, combine sentences, and create sentence variety. Notice the use of verbals in the paragraph below.

Literary Model

[1]Ming continued <u>to play</u> for China's Junior Men's teams in competitions throughout Asia that summer. [2]He learned a lot. [3]He was really beginning <u>to understand</u> the importance of <u>playing</u> defense, how a <u>blocked</u> shot was just as important as a basket <u>made</u>. [4]He understood that personal statistics were only important if they helped your team win, and that you could help your team win without <u>dominating</u> the score sheet. [5]He was improving, one step at a time.

—Excerpt from *Yao Ming: Gentle Giant of Basketball* by Richard Krawiec

Infinitive

Infinitive

Gerund, Participle

Participle

Gerund

ONLINE PRACTICE
www.grammarforwriting.com

EXERCISE 1 Identifying Gerunds

Underline the gerunds in the following sentences.

EXAMPLE Succeeding was important for Walter Payton.

1. Playing for the Chicago Bears made Walter Payton famous.

2. He quit singing in a jazz-rock band at sixteen.

3. Walter thought about attending Jackson State University.

4. He got the nickname "Sweetness" for his smooth running.

5. Payton loved winning and led his team to championships.

EXERCISE 2 Finding Participles and Infinitives

Moses Malone

Underline the participles and infinitives in the following sentences. On the line, write *P* for participle or *I* for infinitive.

EXAMPLE I It is hard to choose the best basketball player.

I **1.** Moses Malone wanted to excel.

P **2.** Surprised teammates never thought he would be great.

P **3.** Malone, named the Most Valuable Player (MVP) four times, played on eight NBA teams.

P **4.** His playing skills never let him down.

I **5.** Malone wanted to be on a championship team.

EXERCISE 3 Writing with Verbals

Working Together

Work with a partner to create five headlines about sports figures or events. Each headline should have at least one gerund, participle, or infinitive. Try to use a variety of verbals, and underline the verbals you used. Not all headlines should be complete sentences. Answers will vary. Students should use at least one gerund, participle, or infinitive in each headline. Sample answers are shown.

EXAMPLE Struggling Coach to Resign

Damaged Stadium Gets a Makeover
Losing Baseball Team to Fire Coach
Exciting Win for Gainesville Gators
Garcia New Hot Shot in Skating
Plainfield Pirates to Trade Baxter

Summary

When you read a book's back cover or a movie synopsis on the Internet, you are reading a **summary.** Summaries retell the main idea and key details of an event, a narrative, or a piece of nonfiction. They focus only on the most important information, such as the kind you would collect in a 5 W's and H Organizer.

5 W's and H Organizer

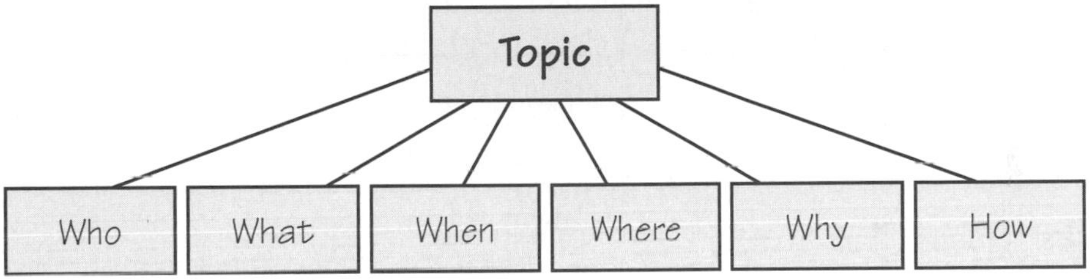

When you write your summary, remember to include the following.

Key Features

- main idea and key details
- accurate information
- your own words and only a few key words from the original
- concise language
- shorter length than the original

ASSIGNMENT

TASK: Write a **summary** of a nonfiction article you've read.

GOAL: to briefly retell the key ideas

TARGET: your teacher and classmates

SPECIAL INSTRUCTIONS: Make your summary about one-third of the original's length.

Plan It Out First, reread the article you want to summarize. List the main idea and key details in Summary Notes.

Summary Notes

Topic	polar bears
Main Idea	Most polar bears will disappear because of global warming.
Details	1. Two-thirds of polar bear population will be wiped out by shrinking summer sea ice. 2. Bears will be confined to Arctic regions and will disappear from Alaska. 3. Even if greenhouse gases are drastically reduced, Arctic ice cap will shrink, destroying most of the bears' habitat.

WRITING HINT

You may quote a few words or a sentence from the original. Make sure to avoid **plagiarism,** or presenting other people's words and ideas as if they are your own. Enclose any original words in quotation marks. See **Lesson 11.5** for more about using quotation marks.

Focus on What's Important Because summaries are short, include only key information. Use a 5 W's and H Organizer like the one on the previous page to track important details.

Leave In	Leave Out
• main ideas	• long explanations and descriptions
• key points	• series of examples and facts
• author's name	• most of the words used in the original
• title of work	• your personal opinions

INCORRECT I was shocked that government scientists held a conference call with reporters at which they stated that the disappearance of sea ice is now unavoidable.

CORRECT Government scientists stated that the disappearance of sea ice is now unavoidable.

Be Concise and Correct Say what you need to say in as few words as possible.

WORDY The whole world's polar bear population is going to be disappearing because of global warming, which is causing Arctic ice to shrink.

CONCISE The world's polar bear population is disappearing as Arctic ice shrinks from global warming.

Be careful not to delete details that end up making your summary inaccurate. Make sure you have accurately summarized the main idea and key details. Check that your facts are correct.

INCORRECT Polar bears will be wiped out by sea ice.

CORRECT Two-thirds of the polar bear population will be wiped out as the sea ice on which they hunt disappears.

Use Your Own Words Check that your summary consists mostly of your own words. Underline key words that appear in both the summary and the article. If your summary includes many words from the original (especially in the same order), rewrite your summary, using your own words and style.

ORIGINAL Polar bears are now thinner compared to bears of twenty years ago. Bears used to feed abundantly on seals they caught on ice, but melting ice diminishes the number of seals they catch.

WEAK Polar bears are thinner compared to previous bears. They used to feed plentifully on seals they caught on ice, but melting ice reduces the number of seals they catch.

GOOD Compared to bears of twenty years ago, polar bears today are thinner. The melting ice is making it difficult for them to catch seals.

CONNECTING Writing & Grammar

Verb tenses indicate when actions took place. See **Lesson 8.4.**

PAST TENSE Scientists **felt** that bears are in danger.

PRESENT TENSE Scientists **feel** that bears are in danger.

Use a consistent verb tense throughout your summary.

Check Your Summary Use this checklist to review your summary. The model below shows one writer's summary.

WRITING CHECKLIST

Did you...

- ✔ accurately and clearly restate the main idea and include only the most important details?
- ✔ use mostly your own words and use concise language?
- ✔ make your summary one-third or less of the original's length?
- ✔ check that your writing is free of grammar and spelling errors?

Writing Model

Title of work
Authors' names
Main idea

[1]According to the article "Warming Is Seen as Wiping Out Most Polar Bears," by John M. Broder and Andrew C. Revkin, the world's polar bear population will decrease by two-thirds over the next forty years due to global warming. [2]As the earth warms, Artic sea ice disappears. [3]Polar bears rely on the sea ice for hunting. [4]While some have adapted by learning to eat new things, such as garbage, most have not.

Key points

[5]Scientists have predicted that the population decline will cause polar bears to disappear entirely from Alaska and remain only in Greenland and the Canadian Arctic. [6]Scientists have also predicted that a drastic reduction in greenhouse gases will have no effect on the shrinking ice cap for at least fifty years. [7]The government has recently decided that polar bears are an endangered species.

Chapter Review

A. Practice Test

Read each sentence below carefully. Decide which answer choice best replaces the underlined part, and fill in the circle of the correct letter. If you think the underlined part is correct, fill in the circle for choice *A*.

EXAMPLE

Ⓐ Ⓑ Ⓒ ● In 2003 in Hawaii, Bethany Hamilton is surfing when she was attacking by a shark.

(A) is surfing when she was attacking
(B) is surfing when she was attacked
(C) was surfing when she attacked
(D) was surfing when she was attacked

Ⓐ Ⓑ ● Ⓓ **1.** Bethany was floated in the water when the shark swum by and bited her left arm.

(A) was floated in the water when the shark swum by and bited
(B) has floated in the water when the shark swum by and bit
(C) was floating in the water when the shark swam by and bit
(D) was floating in the water when the shark swam by and has bitten

Ⓐ Ⓑ ● Ⓓ **2.** One reason Bethany survive was that she was a trained athlete in top condition.

(A) survive was that
(B) survives was that
(C) survived was that
(D) will have survived is that

TEST-TAKING TIP

Before you choose an answer, read the sentence with *each* answer choice in place.

Ⓐ Ⓑ ● Ⓓ **3.** Just months after Bethany losed her left arm, she is gotten back on her surfboard.
(A) losed her left arm, she is gotten
(B) lost her left arm, she is got
(C) lost her left arm, she got
(D) losed her left arm, she got

Ⓐ Ⓑ Ⓒ ● **4.** That same year she will compete in the National Surfing Championships and even won a place on the U.S. National Surfing Team.
(A) will compete in the National Surfing Championships and even won
(B) was to compete in the National Surfing Championships and even winned
(C) has competed in the National Surfing Championships and even won
(D) competed in the National Surfing Championships and even won

Ⓐ Ⓑ ● Ⓓ **5.** Her courage has maked her a hero to admire by people all over the world.
(A) has maked her a hero to admire
(B) has made her a hero to admired
(C) has made her a hero to admire
(D) has maked her a hero admired

B. Identifying Verbals

Read each sentence. On the line, label each underlined verbal as a gerund, an infinitive, or a participle.

gerund, infinitive **1.** Laughing can actually be a very effective way to improve your health.

participle, infinitive **2.** Telling silly jokes, my sister tries to make me laugh whenever she can.

participle **3.** Her jokes are always spoiled by the ruined punch line.

infinitive, participle **4.** She wants to work as a comedian, performing in clubs and on TV.

participle, gerund **5.** Frustrated by her lack of success, she keeps on dreaming of a career in comedy.

C. Choosing the Correct Verb

Read the paragraph below. Choose the verb in parentheses that correctly completes each sentence.

[1]Since 2003, people (have been sending, will have sent) billions of text messages a year in the United States alone. [2]The new cell phone feature first (appeared, had appeared) in 2001. [3]In 2001, 30 million messages (had sent, were sent) worldwide.

[4]While text messaging is convenient, it (is, will have been) difficult to send long text messages. [5]Most people (used, use) abbreviations to write messages. [6]Popular abbreviations (include, have include) BTW for "by the way." [7]Some teachers (worry, worrying) that text messaging is damaging students' ability to spell and write well. [8]Other teachers (will been, are) more concerned with students who use text messaging to cheat on tests.

D. Writing a Summary

Read the article below. On a separate sheet of paper, write a summary of it. Use no more than fifty words.

Answers will vary. See sample answer in Answer Key at www.grammarforwriting.com.

[1]The film *Freaky Friday* takes a comical, endearing look at the strained relationship between a teenage girl named Anna Coleman and her mother, Tess. [2]One night, they have dinner at a Chinese restaurant. [3]Their constant bickering is apparent even to the owner of the restaurant. [4]The owner slyly gives them magic fortune cookies. [5]Anna and Tess wake up the next morning to find that the cookies made them switch bodies.

[6]Anna and Tess are forced to spend the entire day pretending to be each other. [7]Both experience each other's problems firsthand and discover that life is not as easy for the other as they previously believed. [8]Tess realizes that she unfairly blamed Anna for the problems Anna was having at school. [9]Anna discovered the high level of stress that accompanied her mother's job. [10]By the end, their perspective and respect for each other completely change.

CHAPTER 9

Adjectives, Adverbs, and Other Parts of Speech

Adjectives and Adverbs

LESSON 9.1

Modifiers, like adjectives and adverbs, make the meaning of another word or word group more specific.

Adjectives describe, or **modify,** a noun or pronoun. Adjectives answer questions like the ones below.

What kind?	Which one?	How many?	How much?
red book	**this** year	**three** meals	**less** money
difficult book	**best** year	**several** meals	**fewer** coins

Adjectives may come before or after the noun they modify. More than one adjective may modify the same noun.

The **blue** waters are **choppy** and **cold.**

Proper adjectives are adjectives formed from proper nouns. They are always capitalized.

Mexican food   **E**uropean country

Adverbs modify verbs, adjectives, and other adverbs. They tell *when, where, how,* and *to what extent.* Adverbs can come before or after the word they modify.

When?	Ben arrived **yesterday. Now** he is asleep.
Where?	He sailed **here.** Ben took the sails **down.**
How?	He crossed the lake **quickly.**
To what extent?	A **very** strong wind pushed the boat **quite** fast.

If you're not sure whether you need to use an adjective or an adverb, first identify the word you need to modify.

1. If you need to modify a noun or pronoun, use an adjective.

   The ship was **swift.**

2. If you need to modify a verb, adjective, or another adverb, use an adverb.

   The ship moved **swiftly.**

WRITING HINT

Use adjectives and adverbs to help readers visualize what you are describing.

ORIGINAL Soup was served.

REVISED Smooth **and creamy tomato** soup was served **promptly.**

However, don't overdo it. Too many adjectives in a row will make your writing sound awkward and unnatural.

ONLINE PRACTICE
www.grammarforwriting.com

Remember

Remember that a participle is a verb form that functions as an adjective (such as "*smiling* boy").

HINT

Many adverbs end in *-ly*.

angrily extremely
badly freely

Some common adverbs don't end in *-ly*.

here there
then tomorrow

EXERCISE 1 Identifying Modifiers

Circle five adjectives, and underline two adverbs in the passage below.

Literary Model

[1]There was a footstep on the stairs, and the beam from the flashlight danced crazily along the peeling wallpaper. [2]Greg held his breath. [3]There was another step and a loud crashing noise as the man banged the pipe against the wooden banister. [4]Greg could feel his temples throb as the man slowly neared them.

—Excerpt from "The Treasure of Lemon Brown" by Walter Dean Myers

EXERCISE 2 Choosing the Correct Modifier

Underline the modifier—adjective or adverb—that correctly completes each sentence.

1. The actors (excited, excitedly) performed their parts.
2. The audience seemed to be (real, really) interested.
3. When the show ended, they applauded (loud, loudly).
4. They clapped an (incredibly, incredible) long time.
5. After the show, the actors seemed (happy, happily).

Working Together

EXERCISE 3 Writing with Modifiers

Work with a partner to rewrite the passage below. Add adjectives and adverbs to make the writing more descriptive. Include one proper adjective. Add three more sentences. Answers will vary. See sample answer in Answer Key at www.grammarforwriting.com.

[1]The rain has stopped, and a crowd sits under the sun on the October day. [2]The players from England are slipping on the field. [3]One minute is left in the game.

LESSON 9.2

Making Comparisons

Adjectives and adverbs used in comparisons take three different forms. The different forms are called **degrees of comparison (positive, comparative,** and **superlative).**

POSITIVE	My English class is **small.**
COMPARATIVE	I think my science class is **smaller.**
SUPERLATIVE	This math class is the **smallest.**

➡ To compare two people or things, use the **comparative degree.**

ADJECTIVE	My math notes are **neater** than my English notes. Math is **harder** than science.
ADVERB	I write **more neatly** in math than in English. I work **harder** on math than on science.

➡ To compare three or more people or things, use the **superlative degree.**

ADJECTIVE	She gave the **clearest** answer of all. My teacher said that I am the **most confident** student in class.
ADVERB	She answered that question the **most clearly** of all. Of all my friends, I speak the **most confidently.**

Forming Comparative and Superlative Degrees

Modifiers	How to Form	Examples
One Syllable	Add *-er* or *-est.*	fast, fast**er,** fast**est** soon, soon**er,** soon**est**
Two Syllables	Add *-er* or *-est* or use *more* or *most.*	quiet, quiet**er,** quiet**est** careful, **more** careful, **most** careful fairly, **more** fairly, **most** fairly
Three or More Syllables	Add *more* or *most.*	intelligent, **more** intelligent, **most** intelligent intelligently, **more** intelligently, **most** intelligently

Remember

Below are spelling rules for adding *-er* and *-est.*

1. When the word ends in *e*, drop the *e*.

nice nic**er** nic**est**

2. When a final consonant is preceded by a vowel, double the consonant.

thin thin**ner** thin**nest**

3. When the word ends in *y* preceded by a consonant, change the *y* to *i*.

silly sill**ier** sill**iest**

ONLINE PRACTICE
www.grammarforwriting.com

EXERCISE 1 Completing the Sentence

Write the correct comparative or superlative form of the word in parentheses to complete each sentence.
Answers may be opposite (i.e., *more quickly/less quickly*) of those given below.

EXAMPLE Mopping the floor is my _____ chore. (favorite)

Mopping the floor is my least favorite chore.

1. Leon is the youngest member of my family. (young)
2. Babysitting is easier than mowing lawns. (easy)
3. The most positive experience I've had this month was teaching Leon to tie his shoelaces. (positive)
4. I am more confident in my ability to be a good older brother than I was at first. (confident)
5. I can run more quickly than Lisa. (quickly)
6. She competes more seriously than I do. (seriously)
7. That is the most unusual game I have ever played. (unusual)
8. Carla and Lisa were more excited than Leon. (excited)
9. Lisa made the smartest move of all. (smart)
10. This game was more interesting than the old one. (interesting)

HINT

When you compare things that are less rather than more, use *less* for the comparative and *least* for the superlative.

Barry is **less** generous than Evan.

Ava speaks the **least** quickly of any person I know.

EXERCISE 2 Revising a Paragraph

Rewrite this paragraph, fixing any incorrect uses of comparative and superlative adjectives and adverbs. Then add at least three new sentences. Use modifiers with *-er, -est, more, most, less,* or *least.*
New sentences will vary. See sample answer in Answer Key at www.grammarforwriting.com.

[1]The ~~smarter~~ smartest rule at our school is that all students must wear a uniform. [2]Now, no one dresses ~~most~~ more fashionably than anyone else. [3]I might have been the ~~happy~~ happiest of all the students when our school changed to uniforms. [4]Now I can get dressed more efficiently in the morning than before, and I always get to school on time.

Irregular Comparisons

Some adjectives and adverbs have **irregular degrees of comparison.** They do not follow the regular rules for forming the comparative and superlative degrees.

Common Irregular Adjectives and Adverbs

	Positive	Comparative	Superlative
Adjectives	many	more	most
	little	less	least
	good	better	best
	bad	worse	worst
Adverbs	badly	worse	worst
	much	more	most
	well	better	best

Some irregular forms can be used as both adjectives and adverbs.

Tyler has a **worse** cold than his brother does.

In this case, *worse* is an adjective that modifies *cold*. The kind of cold Tyler has is compared to the cold his brother has.

Tyler's brother played **worse** in the game than Tyler did.

In the example above, *worse* is an adverb that modifies the verb *played*.

Avoid **double comparisons.** Use either *more* (or *most*) or *-er* (or *-est*), but never use both together.

INCORRECT Jo's idea was **more better** than mine was.

CORRECT Jo's idea was **better** than mine was.

Avoid the common mistake of adding *-er* or *-est* to all forms of the words *good* and *worse*.

INCORRECT Danielle did a **worser** job than I did.

CORRECT Danielle did a **worse** job than I did.

ONLINE PRACTICE
www.grammarforwriting.com

Remember

Good is always an adjective. *Well* is usually an adverb. When *well* means "in good health," it acts as an adjective.

I have a **good dog.**

The poster looks **good.**

I sang **well.**

Despite my broken finger, I feel **well.**

Exercise 1 Choosing the Correct Form

Underline the correct comparative or superlative form of the adjective or adverb in parentheses. Use the chart for help.

EXAMPLE Ron won (more, most) games than I did.

1. I have the (worse, worst) handwriting ever.
2. Jada got the (bestest, best) grade in class.
3. She wants to help me study so that I do (better, more better) than last time.
4. We plan to spend (more, most) time on verbs than on nouns.
5. Jada says I should spend (less, lesser) time watching television.

Exercise 2 Revising Comparisons

Rewrite the newspaper review below. Correct five comparative and superlative forms that need to be revised.

See the Answer Key at www.grammarforwriting.com.

Robbie's Wins Again

[1]For the second year in a row, people in Detroit have voted Robbie's Pizza the better pizza restaurant in Detroit. [2]The 12,000 people who sent in ballots rated Robbie's well than John's Pizza Place by a margin of 2 to 1.

[3]"John's pizzas are more better than Sally's pizzas," wrote one customer, "but Robbie's pizzas are best of all."

[4]Another customer wrote, "Sally's pizzas are least flavorful than John's pizzas, but Robbie's pizzas are the more deliciouser of the three pizzas I tasted."

Write What You Think

On a separate piece of paper, write a brief expository paragraph to explain your answer to the following question. Use at least three irregular comparative or superlative forms. Check that each comparative and superlative adjective or adverb is correct.

What has been your biggest accomplishment in the last year? Why?

Answers will vary. Students should use at least three irregular comparative and superlative forms in their paragraphs. See sample answer in Answer Key at www.grammarforwriting.com.

LESSON 9.4

Prepositions and Prepositional Phrases

A **preposition** is a word that shows direction, location, or a relationship between things. Notice how the meaning of the sentence changes with different prepositions.

Jared looked **on** the shelf. He looked **above** the shelf.

He looked **by** the shelf. He looked **under** the shelf.

A preposition is always part of a **prepositional phrase,** a group of words that begins with a preposition and ends with the object of the preposition. The **object of a preposition** is the noun or pronoun that follows the preposition.

PREP OBJ PREP OBJ

Trey visited his aunt **for** two **weeks** **in** **July.**

A preposition may have a **compound** (more than one) **object.**

PREP OBJ OBJ

Trey was gone **until** last **Tuesday** or **Wednesday.**

A prepositional phrase modifies another word in the sentence. An **adjective phrase** can modify a noun or pronoun by telling *which one* or *what kind,* as an adjective does. An **adverb phrase** can modify a verb, an adjective, or another adverb. It tells *how, when, where,* or to *what extent,* as an adverb does.

ADJECTIVE The suitcase **in the hall** belongs to Trey.

ADVERB He traveled mostly **by plane.**

A prepositional phrase should be placed close to the word it modifies to avoid confusion.

INCORRECT Passengers looked for the book **on the plane** under the seats. [Is the plane under the seats?]

CORRECT Passengers **on the plane** looked for the book under the seats.

Remember

When the object of a preposition is a pronoun, it is always an object pronoun.

Keep this between you and **me.** [not *I*]

Commonly Used Prepositions

about	inside
above	into
against	near
along	of
around	off
at	on
before	out
beside	over
beyond	through
but	to
by	toward
for	up
from	with

ONLINE PRACTICE
www.grammarforwriting.com

HINT

There is often more than one prepositional phrase in a sentence.

Exercise 1 Finding Prepositional Phrases

In the model, underline the prepositional phrases and underline twice the objects in the phrases. The first one is done for you.

Literary Model

[1]I sit on the back porch and write in my journal. [2]Splashes of orange, red, and yellow dazzle the eyes in the mid-October sun. [3]Late-blooming flowers dance the last dance with the wind.

—Excerpt from *A Friendship for Today* by Patricia C. McKissack

Remember

When you write for a formal purpose, such as a school report, avoid ending a sentence with a preposition.

INCORRECT Whom are you talking to?

CORRECT To whom are you talking?

Exercise 2 Adding Prepositional Phrases

Rewrite the sentences below so that they include prepositional phrases. Underline the prepositional phrases you use.
Answers will vary. Sample answers are shown.

EXAMPLE Anya's luggage is here.

Anya's luggage is here in the pile.

1. This was the family's first trip. This was the family's first trip on a train.
2. Anya's brother brought his laptop. Anya's brother brought his laptop with him on the train.
3. He has it. He has it in its black case under the seat.
4. The trip is short. The trip across Texas is short.
5. Her cousins and aunt will meet them. Her cousins and aunt will meet them at the station under the exit sign.
6. They will travel. They will travel to Arizona from there.
7. There is a family reunion. There is a family reunion for the first time in ten years.
8. Her grandparents are going. Her grandparents are going for several days.
9. Anya laughs. During the family games, Anya laughs.
10. The trip was fun. The trip was fun beyond expectation.

Exercise 3 Writing Song Lyrics

On a separate sheet of paper, write lyrics for a song. Describe your favorite season of the year. You can tell how it looks, sounds, feels, and smells. Use at least five prepositional phrases, and underline them. Answers will vary. See sample answer in Answer Key at www.grammarforwriting.com. Remind students that prepositional phrases can follow each other. Encourage them to use a variety of different prepositions.

Conjunctions and Interjections

Conjunctions and interjections are two parts of speech. A **conjunction** is a word that joins a word or a group of words. **Coordinating conjunctions** join words, phrases, and clauses of equal importance. The most common coordinating conjunctions are *and, but, or, for, nor,* and *yet.*

Conjunctions

Where It Is Used	How It Is Used
Compound Subject	Joins two subjects that share the same verb Maia **and** Skye went to the school dance together.
Compound Verb	Joins two verbs that share the same subject Students danced **or** talked to their friends.
Compound Sentence	Joins two or more main clauses The music was great, **but** there wasn't enough food for everyone.
Between Phrases	Joins two or more phrases Students stayed in the gym **and** on the dance floor.

Remember

Always use a comma before a coordinating conjunction in a compound sentence.

Luis went to the pizza party**, but** Roy did not go.

No comma is needed with compound subjects or compound verbs.

Nikki and Charlise went to the pizza party and danced.

An **interjection** is a word that shows emotion. It is set off by an **exclamation point (!)** or by a **comma (,).** Common interjections are *oh, wow, ouch, no, oops,* and *ugh.* Use an exclamation point with words showing strong emotion.

Amazing! Sam is a great dancer.

Use a comma to set off the interjection when no strong emotions are expressed.

Well, I can't believe Mrs. Kahn is dancing, too.

Interjections should be used sparingly and rarely in formal writing, such as research reports or business letters. Use them when you really want to make a point. Writers who overuse them lessen their effect.

ONLINE PRACTICE
www.grammarforwriting.com

Exercise 1 Identifying Conjunctions and Interjections

Circle each conjunction, and underline each interjection in the following sentences.

EXAMPLE Great! My new computer (and) keyboard came today, (and) I know how to use both of them.

1. Wow! To use a search engine, all you have to do is type in a subject (and) click "search."
2. A long list with many Web sites will appear, (but) you must decide which ones may be useful.
3. Teachers (and) students use search engines to find information about almost anything.
4. Grammar practice exercises (or) online encyclopedias are just two sources of help on the Internet.
5. Oh, it's true that kids often know more about the Internet than their parents, (but) their parents are often happy to learn from them.

Exercise 2 Writing a Dialogue

The photo shows two students working on a computer. Write a **dialogue** (conversation) between the two. Use at least two conjunctions and two interjections. Answers will vary. Have partners or groups of three find the conjunctions and interjections in each other's dialogue.

EXAMPLE "Wow! Look at this," Becky said.

Carol replied, "What is it?"

HINT

Dialogue should be set in quotation marks and introduced with speech tags, such as *he asked*. If a speech tag comes in the middle of the sentence, use commas to separate it from the quotation. See **Lesson 11.5.**

"Oh**,**" Diana said**,** "the Internet is down."

Write What You Think

Answers will vary. See sample answer in Answer Key at www.grammarforwriting.com.

On a separate sheet of paper, respond to the question below. Use at least three conjunctions and one interjection.

Why do young people enjoy being on the Internet so much? List two reasons.

ONLINE MODEL
www.grammarforwriting.com

Personal Response to Literature

When you write a **personal response to literature,** you express your thoughts and feelings about a piece of literature. You use examples from the work to explain why you reacted the way you did.

Topics for Personal Response

- overall meaning
- your favorite parts
- literary element, such as plot, characters, or style
- connections to your life

In this workshop, you will learn how to write a personal response to literature. Your response should include these features.

Key Features

- brief summary of the work
- thesis that clearly states your response
- text evidence, or supporting details from the literary work
- clear organization
- three parts of an essay: introduction, body, and conclusion

ASSIGNMENT

TASK: Write a two- to three-page **personal response** to a literary work you've recently read, such as a poem, short story, or novel.

AUDIENCE: people who have read the same work

PURPOSE: to explain your thoughts and feelings about the work

Prewriting

Choose a Literary Work Before you begin writing, you will need to select a literary work. Make a list of short stories, poems, or novels you've read recently. Use the checklist on the left to help you make the best choice.

To refresh your memory of the work, discuss it with others, or reread parts of it. Encourage classmates and friends to share what parts or characters they liked and disliked. What elements left the strongest impression?

Get Started After your discussion, **freewrite** for several minutes about the work.

- Begin with any idea or detail you remember well.
- Focus on getting your ideas down. Avoid worrying about errors when you write your draft. It's okay to jump from topic to topic.
- When you're done, review what you wrote. Select one idea or topic to write about in detail.
- Try to say something new about the work.

TOPIC CHECKLIST

- ✔ I have a strong reaction to the work.
- ✔ I remember the work well or can read it again.
- ✔ I can identify enough details to explain my response.
- ✔ I can summarize accurately the work's important elements.

Writing Model

Avoid obvious or general statements.

Jot down your thoughts about what you liked.

[1]I was really interested in the characters in <u>James and the Giant Peach</u>. [2]~~James was the best character.~~ James is a regular kid who has amazing things happen to him. [3]His insect friends look strange, but I can relate to them. [4]The way they joke around reminds me of my friends.

Prewriting

Craft a Thesis Next, come up with a strong thesis. Your thesis, or **thesis statement,** is the main idea of your essay. It should make clear what you thought or felt about the literary work, or at least one aspect of it. It should be neither too broad nor too narrow. Avoid a thesis that only states a fact.

See **Lesson 5.2** for more about the qualities of a good thesis statement.

TOO NARROW	The description of Aunt Sponge in the first chapter is funny.
TOO BROAD	I liked the characters, the plot, and the humor in the book.
A FACT	James meets many strange creatures inside the peach.
REVISED	Although the plot is filled with weird events, I can personally connect to many characters in *James and the Giant Peach*.

The thesis should express your response or reaction to the literary work. In the rest of your paper, you will use details from the literary work to explain why you responded or reacted in that way.

Summarize the Work Before you start drafting, jot down information to include in your summary. Because your audience has read this work, your summary should be brief and include only the most important details, such as the ones below.

- **The title and author** (Underline the titles of novels, or set them in *italic* type. Titles of poems and short stories should be placed in quotation marks.)
- **Names of main characters**
- **Important events in the plot**
- **Description of the setting** (where and when the story occurs)
- **Theme statement** (the general idea about life that you think the author is trying to express in the work)

Remember

Spend most of the paper explaining your thoughts and feelings about the work, not just summarizing the plot.

Drafting

Include All the Parts As you draft, include all three parts of an essay.

1. The **introduction** should identify the title and author of the work. Include your thesis statement and summary.
2. The **body** of your essay should explain your response. Include at least two key points, each one supported by specific evidence, such as examples or quotations. Explain each point in a separate paragraph.
3. Your **conclusion** should summarize your response and restate your thesis, using different words.

WRITING HINT

Skim the work to find specific details that will help you explain your points. Your teacher may ask you to include a page number in parentheses for quotations or details you use.

Introduction	
Thesis	Although the plot is full of weird events, I can connect to many characters in James and the Giant Peach.
Body	
Point 1	James seems like a normal kid in a strange world.
Evidence	• parents eaten by rhino (p. 1) • gets magic crystals (p. 9) • scared and hopeless at beginning (p. 13) • fights with Cloud-Men (p. 85) • excited at end just the way I would be (p. 117)
Point 2	James's peculiar friends look bizarre and scary, but they are a lot like my friends and me.
Evidence	• different personalities and skills • Glow-worm = gives light, is shy (p. 34) • Earthworm = gloomy (p. 49) • Centipede's jokes and funny song about "smelly jelly" and "mudburgers" (p. 52)
Conclusion	Although what happens to James and his insect friends is extraordinary, they seem like ordinary people to me.

Revising

Use the Revising Questions below to improve your draft. The model shows how one writer began revising the introduction.

As you revise, keep in mind the traits of good writing. See **Lesson 1.3.**

Revising Questions

- ❑ How clear is my overall response to the work?
- ❑ How effective is my summary?
- ❑ Where should I add supporting text evidence?
- ❑ How clearly have I organized my ideas?
- ❑ How effective are the introduction, body, and conclusion?

Writing Model

[1]<u>James and the Giant Peach</u>, by Roald Dahl, is one of my favorite novels. [2]The main character is James Trotter, an orphan who lives in England with his two horrible aunts. [3]~~They are mean and lazy~~. [4]James's life changes when he climbs inside an enormous peach and discovers some huge talking creatures. [5]The book describes their amazing adventures. [6]~~For example, the peach rolls into the ocean, and sharks attack it~~. [7]Although the plot is full of weird events, I can connect to ~~many~~ characters ^like James and his new friends.

Cut details from the summary.

Make the thesis more specific.

CONNECTING Writing & Grammar

Use the present tense when you write about a work of literature.

James **is** a hero.

The author **describes** the scene in detail.

Editing and Proofreading

Next, use the Editing and Proofreading Checklist to help you find errors in grammar, punctuation, mechanics, and spelling.

Editing and Proofreading Checklist

- ❑ Have I left out or run together any words?
- ❑ Did I use the comparative and superlative forms of adjectives and adverbs correctly?
- ❑ Have I correctly used quotation marks or italics for the title of the work?

Make Comparisons Correctly Remember to add *-er* to one-syllable adjectives and adverbs to compare two things (comparative form). Add *-est* to compare three or more things (superlative form). (See Lessons 9.2 and 9.3.)

Positive	Comparative	Superlative
fast	faster	fastest
rough	rougher	roughest

To form the comparative and superlative of some two-syllable words, you can add *-er* and *-est* (*funnier, funniest*). However, for most two-syllable words and all three- or more-syllable words, use the words *more* (*less*) or *most* (*least*).

Positive	Comparative	Superlative
interesting	more (less) interesting	most (least) interesting
happily	more (less) happily	most (least) happily

Remember

When you add *-er* or *-est* to some adjectives, you may need to change the spelling.

big big**ger** big**gest**

easy eas**ier** eas**iest**

Writing Model

¶ [1]James's peculiar friends look bizarre and scary, but they are a lot like my friends and me. [2]The author's descriptions make them seem like ordin~~e~~ ^a ry people. [3]Each one has special talents and ^a unique personality. [4]For instance, Glow-worm provides light and is shy. [5]Earthworm is the ~~more gloomier~~ ^gloomiest of them all. [6]Some, such ^# as Ladybug, are quiet, and some are louder and ~~silly~~ ^sillier than she is. [7]The funny song that Centipede makes up about "smelly jelly" and "fresh mudburgers" reminds me ^of the jokes that my best friend and I enjoy.

Proofreading Symbols

^	Add.
℘	Delete.
#	Add space.
¶	Start a new paragraph.

Publishing and Presenting

Choose one of these ways to share your personal response.

- **Collect it.** With your classmates, create a booklet of responses for the school library.
- **Talk about it.** Turn your paper into an oral presentation for the class or for your family. Include visual aids when appropriate.
- **Add it to your portfolio.** Keep a writing portfolio to track how you've grown as a writer throughout the year. To decide whether to add a piece to your portfolio, ask yourself, "Why is this one of my best pieces of writing?"

Reflect On Your Writing

- If you could begin this assignment again, what would you do differently?
- What did you find easy or hard about summarizing the literary work?

Chapter Review

A. Practice Test

In the passage below, there is a question *for each numbered item.* Read the passage carefully, and circle the best answer to each question.

Tips for Handling Sibling Rivalry

Whenever there is more than one child in a household (1), sibling rivalry, or competition, is likely to arise. Yes (2), some competition is normal, but there are ways to reduce it in order to make for a more calmer (3) home life. One of the more important things you can do to more lessen (4) competition is to focus on doing your personal best. Let's say you have an older sibling who usually gets more gooder grades than you do (5). On your next test, concentrate on beating your own previous score rather than beating your sibling's score.

Remember also that everyone has his or her own special talents. For instance, playing sports might come quite easily to your sibling, while you may be an extremely (6) clever writer. Try to be happy for your sibling when he or she excels. This attitude will make your sibling more likely to do the same for you (7).

1. What is the best replacement for the underlined section?
- **A.** NO CHANGE
- **B.** in a household there is more than one
- **C.** there are many more children in a household
- **D.** the most children are in a household

2. Which of the following best describes the underlined word?
- **A.** verb
- **B.** subject
- **C.** interjection
- **D.** preposition

3. What is the best replacement for the underlined section?
- **A.** NO CHANGE
- **B.** a calmer
- **C.** the more calmer
- **D.** calmier

4. What is the best replacement for the underlined section?
- **A.** NO CHANGE
- **B.** most important things you can do to lessen
- **C.** most important things you can do to least
- **D.** more important things you can do to make more less

Another common issue is the amount of attention (8) siblings get from their parents. Take turns getting your parents' attention. If it's your sibling's birthday, for example, be generouser, and (9) give your sibling time in the spotlight. If you feel that your sibling gets more attention most of the time, talk with your parents, and try to work out the problem together.

Living with siblings can be difficult. But, as hard as this may be to believe, you and your sibling may turn out to be very close in adulthood. No kidding, (10) brothers and sisters who argue constantly as kids may grow up to be the best of friends.

5. What is the best replacement for the underlined section?
A. NO CHANGE
B. gets the best grades
C. gets more better grades
D. gets better grades than you do

6. What parts of speech are *quite* and *extremely* respectively?
A. adverb, adverb
B. adjective, adverb
C. adjective, adjective
D. verb, adverb

7. Which conjunction(s) can join the two underlined sentences?
A. *since* or *but*
B. *and* or *since*
C. *but*
D. *and* or *or*

8. What is *of attention*?
A. a conjunction
B. a prepositional phrase
C. an adjective
D. an interjection

9. What is the best replacement for the underlined section?
A. NO CHANGE
B. be more generouser, and
C. be generous, and
D. Eliminate it.

10. What function does *No kidding* serve?
A. an interjection
B. an adverb
C. an adjective
D. a noun

Chapter Review

B. Using Modifiers and Prepositions

Write a word or phrase to complete each sentence below. Label your word or phrase *ADJ* for adjective, *ADV* for adverb, or *PREP* for prepositional phrase. Answers will vary. Sample answers are shown.

ADJ ______ **1.** Marcy asked me to try on the striped jacket she's been making.

ADV ______ **2.** The entrants' designs need to be ready tomorrow.

ADJ ______ **3.** Jed is working on an outrageous collection of hats.

PREP ______ **4.** My sister is making her dress in our bedroom, and her sewing supplies are everywhere.

ADJ ______ **5.** She is very talented and might become a famous American designer someday.

ADJ ______ **6.** Her favorite things to design are simple dresses.

ADV ______ **7.** She takes sequins and carefully sews them into the dress.

PREP ______ **8.** My sister and Jed worked together on a hat, which I put on my head.

PREP ______ **9.** My mom says my sister's eye for design comes from her.

ADV ______ **10.** Fashion is extremely important to some people, including my sister.

C. Choosing Modifiers and Conjunctions

Read each sentence below. Underline the correct word in parentheses.

1. I think roller coasters are (funner, more fun) than my dad does.

2. He says they make him sick (immediately, immediate) afterward.

3. Of everyone in our family, I am the (daringest, most daring).

4. My mom won't go near a roller coaster, (so, nor) will my brother.

5. That old roller coaster is good, but the new one is (better, more better)!

6. The (more worse, worst) roller coaster was the Flying Eagle.

7. It was (more shakier, shakier) than the Meteor Flash.

8. My family may not like roller coasters, (but, and) they always get excited when I go on one.

9. When my little sister grows (taller, more tall), I'm going to take her on her first roller coaster.

10. I'm sure the moment will be (scarier, more scarier) for me than for her.

D. Reviewing a Response to Literature

Read the draft of the first two paragraphs of a student's response to literature below. Answers will vary. Sample answers are shown.

- Cross out any incorrect adjectives, adverbs, prepositions, or conjunctions. Write any necessary corrections above the word.
- If a word or phrase should be moved, circle it, and draw an arrow to the spot where it should go.
- Evaluate the draft by answering the questions that follow.

1. What, if anything, is missing from the introduction?
   The introduction should include the author's name and a plot summary.
2. How could the thesis be improved? The thesis is simply a broad opinion. The student says he or she loved the book but doesn't give a specific response. The thesis needs to be narrowed by including one or more reasons the student enjoyed the book.
3. What, if anything, is missing from the body?
   The body needs more specific text evidence.

[1]The novel Tuck Everlasting is ~~most~~ absolutely fantastic. [2]My response is that I loved it! [3]It is by far the ~~more great~~ greatest book I've read all year.

[4]The main character, Winnie Foster, faces a ~~tougher~~ tough question: Is the ability to live forever a blessing, ~~and~~ or is it a curse? [5]The author throughout the book addresses this question.

[6]The part that made me the ~~thoughtfulest~~ most thoughtful is the one where Winnie needs to decide if she wants to live forever. [7]The author builds the suspense ~~amazing good~~ amazingly well, ~~or~~ and you don't find out her decision until the end.

CHAPTER 10

Subject-Verb Agreement

Agreement of Subject and Verb

LESSON 10.1

The **subject** of a sentence is the person or thing that performs the action of the sentence. The **verb** is the word that expresses the action.

➡ The subject and verb of a sentence must **agree** in number. Use a singular verb with a singular subject. Use a plural verb with a plural subject.

Singular	Plural
Marty speaks quickly.	**My friends speak** quickly.
I am late for school.	**We are** late for school.
She wants three cats.	**They want** three cats.

➡ In a **verb phrase,** the first helping verb **(HV)** must agree with the subject **(S)**.

Our car (S) **has** (HV) been making strange noises.

We (S) **are** (HV) leaving soon.

My parents (S) **do** (HV) not know any mechanics.

Remember

A **singular** subject names one person, place, thing, or idea. A **plural** subject names more than one.

See **Lesson 8.1** for more about verb phrases.

STEP BY STEP

To decide whether a verb agrees with its subject:

1. Find the verb or verb phrase.
   My grandparents' neighbor collects coins.
   VERB *collects*
2. Ask *Who?* or *What?* before the verb to find the subject.
   WHO COLLECTS? *neighbor*
3. Use a singular verb with a singular subject and a plural verb with a plural subject.

Remember: The verb needs to agree with only the subject, not with any other word in the sentence.

ONLINE PRACTICE
www.grammarforwriting.com

Present Tense Forms of *Be*

Singular
I **am** hungry.
You **are** hungry.
He **is** hungry.

Plural
We **are** hungry.
You **are** hungry.
They **are** hungry.

Exercise 1 Choosing Correct Verbs

Underline the subject of each sentence. Then circle the verb in the parentheses that agrees with the subject.

1. Video-sharing Web sites (have, has) become popular recently.
2. People (are, is) using them to post their own videos.
3. Many users (watch, watches) other people's videos.
4. One popular site now (air, airs) 100 million videos a day.
5. Many new videos (are, is) added each day.
6. No fancy equipment (are, is) needed.
7. My friends (like, likes) to find funny clips.
8. Even my dad (enjoy, enjoys) online videos.
9. The content (range, ranges) from the silly to the serious.
10. My neighbors (have, has) made several videos.

Exercise 2 Editing an Article

As you read the article below, find five errors in subject-verb agreement. Rewrite the paragraph to correct the errors.

[1]DVD players were introduced in 1997. [2]They ~~offers~~ offer high-quality images. [3]This technological breakthrough ~~have~~ has slowly beaten VCRs. [4]Today most American consumers own DVD players. [5]In fact, more people ~~has~~ have DVD players in their homes than they do computers, VCRs, or cable television. [6]New models ~~is~~ are becoming cheaper. [7]High-definition (HD) DVD players ~~produces~~ produce extremely sharp pictures.

Write What You Think

On a separate piece of paper, write at least five sentences that explain your answer to the question below. Check that each verb agrees with its subject. Answers will vary. See sample answers in Answer Key at www.grammarforwriting.com.

Is lying ever the right thing to do?

LESSON
10.2

Phrases Between Subject and Verb

In many sentences, **prepositional phrases** (**P**) come between, or interrupt, the subject (**S**) and verb (**V**).

The plants **in the garden** need water. [S = plants; P = in the garden; V = need]

The subject of a sentence is never in a prepositional phrase. Make sure the verb agrees with the subject and not with the object of the preposition.

INCORRECT The **road** to the mountains **are** bumpy.

CORRECT The **road** to the mountains **is** bumpy. [The subject is *road*, not *mountains*, which is the object of the preposition *to*. *Road* is singular and needs a singular verb.]

INCORRECT The **classes** at the school **begins** at noon.

CORRECT The **classes** at the school **begin** at noon. [The subject is *classes*, not *school*, which is the object of the preposition *at*. *Classes* is plural and needs a plural verb.]

Remember

A prepositional phrase is a group of words that begins with a preposition. It ends with the object of the preposition, which is a noun or a pronoun.

PREPOSITION → *inside* ... OBJECT → **park**

inside the **park**

near the **sand**

For more on prepositional phrases, see **Lesson 9.4.**

Exercise 1 Explaining Agreement

In each sentence below, cross out the prepositional phrase that comes between the subject and the verb. Then write a sentence that identifies the subject and explains the agreement.

EXAMPLE The wings ~~of a monarch butterfly~~ are orange and black.

The verb, are, is plural because the subject, wings, is plural.

1. The stages ~~in a butterfly's life cycle~~ look different.
The verb, *look*, is plural because the subject, *stages*, is plural.
2. The four stages ~~of the cycle~~ are egg, larva, pupa, and adult.
The verb, *are*, is plural because the subject, *stages*, is plural.
3. The eggs ~~of a butterfly~~ are round or oval.
The verb, *are*, is plural because the subject, *eggs*, is plural.
4. A butterfly ~~in the early stages~~ is called a caterpillar.
The verb, *is*, is singular because the subject, *butterfly*, is singular.
5. The colors ~~of a monarch butterfly~~ are orange and black.
The verb, *are*, is plural because the subject, *colors*, is plural.
6. An adult ~~of some species~~ lives only about a month.
The verb, *lives*, is singular because the subject, *adult*, is singular.
7. Insect lovers ~~around the world~~ collect moths and butterflies.
The verb, *collect*, is plural because the subject, *lovers*, is plural.

ONLINE PRACTICE
www.grammarforwriting.com

8. A butterfly, ~~with its bright colors,~~ differs from a moth.
The verb, *differs*, is singular because the subject, *butterfly*, is singular.

9. The wings ~~of a butterfly~~ are covered with scales.
The verb, *are*, is plural because the subject, *wings*, is plural.

10. The cover ~~of our science books~~ shows a butterfly.
The verb, *shows*, is singular because the subject, *cover*, is singular.

Exercise 2 Choosing Correct Verbs

Circle the verb in parentheses that agrees with the subject.

1. Most tarantulas in North America (is, are) found in the South and the Southwest.
2. Tarantulas imported from South America (sell, sells) in pet stores.
3. One kind of tarantulas (come, comes) from Central America.
4. An owner of tarantulas (know, knows) how to provide the right food.
5. That picture of a spider's legs (amaze, amazes) me!

Working Together

Exercise 3 Proofreading a Report

Proofread the report below to find and correct the five errors in subject-verb agreement. Compare your changes with those made by a partner.

[1]Cockroaches are one of the oldest insects. [2]Fossil remains of one cockroach ~~dates~~ date back 200 million years. [3]Several species of cockroach ~~lives~~ live in the United States. [4]The wings of the American cockroach ~~is~~ are reddish-brown. [5]The color of many German cockroaches is light brown with two dark stripes on the back. [6]The body of many cockroaches ~~appear~~ appears flat. [7]The favorite habitats of the cockroach ~~is~~ are warm and muggy places.

Compound Subjects

LESSON
10.3

A **compound subject** is made up of two or more subjects that have the same verb.

➡ When two or more subjects are joined by *and,* use a plural verb.

Snowboarding **and** parasailing **are** exciting sports.

Robert **and** his friends **like** to scuba dive.

➡ When two or more singular subjects are joined by *or* or *nor,* use a singular verb.

On weekends, either Keisha **or** Mary **goes** swimming.

Neither Brad **nor** Kirk **plays** hockey.

➡ When two or more plural subjects are joined by *or* or *nor,* use a plural verb.

Skates **or** helmets **make** a great gift.

Either the Hawks **or** the Lions **are** in first place.

➡ When a singular subject and a plural subject are joined by *or* or *nor,* the verb must agree with the subject closer to it.

Neither the coach **nor** the players **have** the trophy.
[*Players* is closer to the verb, *have*. Because *players* is plural, the verb is plural.]

Neither the players **nor** the coach **has** the trophy.
[*Coach* is closer to the verb, *has*. Because *coach* is singular, the verb is singular.]

For a review of compound subjects and verbs, refer to **Lesson 6.4.**

Exercise 1 Choosing Correct Verbs

Underline the subject(s) in each sentence below. Then circle the verb in parentheses that agrees with the subject.

EXAMPLE Meg and Kelly (are, is) learning about energy in school.

1. Solar panels and sand (contains, contain) silicon.
2. Electricity and batteries (works, work) together.
3. Highway signs and calculators (use, uses) solar panels.

ONLINE PRACTICE
www.grammarforwriting.com

4. Businesses or even a home now (benefits, benefit) from easy-to-install solar panels.

5. Either super-efficient light bulbs or solar panels (is, are) ways to make buildings environmentally friendly.

6. Wind and waves (are, is) both forms of energy.

7. Light and sound (travel, travels) as waves.

8. Neither thunder nor lightning bolts (scares, scare) me.

9. My dog and my cat (do, does) not like lightning.

10. Either Mrs. Smith or Mr. LaRue (is, are) teaching our science class tomorrow.

Working Together

Exercise 2 Writing Sentences

Work with a partner or small group to write three sentences about the graph below and the information in it. You may also write about which science topics interest you and your friends.
Answers will vary. Sample answers are shown.

1. Use present tense verbs, and check for subject-verb agreement in each sentence.

2. Write at least two sentences that contain compound subjects. If you're not sure what to write about, try completing these sentences:

The graph...
The graph lists five subjects.

Most boys and girls...
Most boys and girls chose weather.

Weather and electricity...
Weather and electricity are popular choices.

My friends and I...
My friends and I are interested in volcanoes.

No boys or girls...
No boys or girls chose plants.

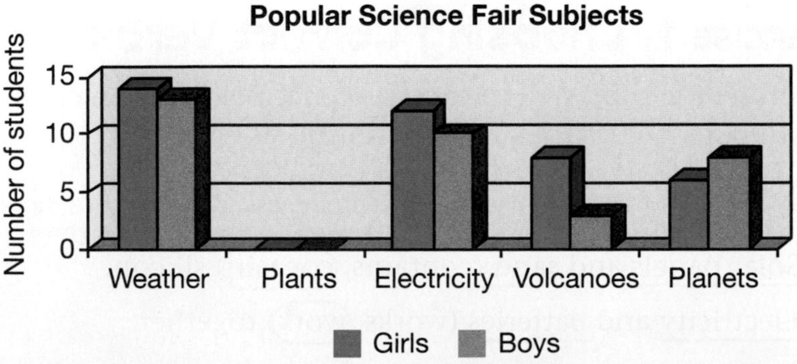

LESSON 10.4

Other Agreement Problems

In many questions and in sentences that begin with *here* or *there*, the subject follows the verb. Remember that *here* and *there* are never the subject of a sentence.

SINGULAR When **is** the **play**?

PLURAL **Were** the **stamps** on the envelopes?

SINGULAR There **is** the **letter** from the school.

PLURAL There **are** many **boxes** in the garage.

Pronouns that do not refer to a specific person, place, thing, or idea are called **indefinite pronouns.** As the lists on the right show, some indefinite pronouns are always singular and need singular verbs. Others are always plural and need plural verbs.

Singular	**Each** of the girls **has** new sunglasses. **Everyone is** surprised.
Plural	**Many know** the author's name. **Few are** still here.

The indefinite pronouns *all, any, most,* and *some* can be singular or plural, depending on their meaning in a sentence. The object of a preposition that follows the pronoun can often help you decide if the pronoun is singular or plural.

Singular	**Most** of the fruit **is** ripe. [*Most* needs a singular verb because *fruit* is singular.]
Plural	**Most** of the apples **are** crisp. [*Most* needs a plural verb because *apples* is plural.]

Some Singular Indefinite Pronouns

anybody	neither
anyone	no one
each	nobody
either	one
everybody	somebody
everyone	someone

Plural Indefinite Pronouns

both	many
few	several

For more on indefinite pronouns, see **Lesson 7.2.**

Exercise 1 Choosing Correct Verbs

Underline the subject of each sentence. Then circle the verb in the parentheses that agrees with the subject.

EXAMPLE Neither of my parents (has, have) a bowling ball.

ONLINE PRACTICE
www.grammarforwriting.com

HINT

Remember that subjects are never in a prepositional phrase. See **Lesson 10.2.**

One of my friends **bowls** every Saturday.

1. There (are, is) many different kinds of bowling balls.
2. Where (are, is) bowling balls sold?
3. No one (like, likes) a ball that is too heavy.
4. There (is, are) many different ways to throw a bowling ball.
5. Some of the beginners (develops, develop) their own style.
6. Here (is, are) an article about the sport's history.
7. (Does, Do) anybody know the date tenpin bowling started?
8. Each of the champions (bowl, bowls) every day.
9. Only one of my cousins (watch, watches) bowling on TV.
10. Neither of the bowling shoes (is, are) comfortable.

Exercise 2 Editing a Paragraph

Edit the following paragraph to correct errors in subject-verb agreement. Not every sentence has an error.

[1]In the last five years, there ~~has~~ have been many championship teams at Bedford Middle School. [2]Several of the teams ~~receives~~ receive lots of media attention. [3]For instance, most of the basketball and football players get their pictures in the local newspaper. [4]However, one of the teams ~~receive~~ receives almost no publicity. [5]Which one of Bedford's teams is ignored? [6]Here ~~are~~ is the answer: the bowling team. [7]~~Does~~ Do any of the bowlers complain? [8]No. [9]Where ~~is~~ are the stories about them? [10]Everyone on a championship team deserves some recognition.

WRITING APPLICATION

Business E-mail

Because they can be instantly sent and received, e-mails have become a common way to communicate. In fact, e-mail is used for both casual messages to friends and for more formal writing in the workplace. **Business e-mails** share many of the same purposes as business letters.

Purposes of Business E-mails

- apply for a job
- seek information
- make a complaint
- make a request

When you write your e-mail, include the features below.

Key Features

- a clearly stated request
- a greeting and closing
- a single purpose and only essential information
- concise and formal language
- correct spelling, punctuation, grammar, and capitalization

© Joseph Farris, www.CartoonStock.com

ASSIGNMENT

TASK: Write a one-page **business e-mail.**

GOAL: to request information

TARGET: a business, such as a music school

SPECIAL INSTRUCTIONS: Be polite, and avoid poor e-mail habits, such as using all capital letters.

Keep It Short As you draft your e-mail, use these tips to maintain your focus:

1. State your purpose right away, and focus on one main idea.
2. Include only necessary information. Ask yourself, "What details does the person who reads the e-mail absolutely need to know?"
3. Make sure your sentences are concise. Take out any **wordiness,** or unnecessary language.

Writing Model

[1]~~Ever since I was a little kid I wanted to play guitar.~~ [2]I am writing to request information about guitar classes at Edge Music School this fall. [3]~~I was given one hundred dollars for my birthday to spend on lessons.~~ [4]Also, I would like to know ~~the amount that is~~ the cost of each class.

WRITING HINT

If you are sending a business e-mail to make a request of someone you do not know, be courteous, and use **formal language.** Avoid slang.

ORIGINAL What's the deal about how much this costs?

REVISED Could you please tell me the cost of each class?

Remember Your Audience Abbreviations and fragments may have a place in messages to friends, but avoid them in business e-mails. Follow the tips below.

1. **all lowercase or ALL CAPITAL LETTERS** Using no capital letters can be confusing, and capitalizing every word makes it seem as if you are shouting. Be professional, and stick to the rules of capitalization.
2. **:) >:) ;)** Symbols like these, called emoticons, are fun for friends, but unprofessional in business e-mails. Use words, not faces, to express yourself.
3. **"Utilize the interface."** Keep your use of **jargon,** or technical terms your audience may not know, to a minimum.
4. **"Like, I could've gone, you know?"** Avoid contractions and meaningless filler words, such as *like, well,* and *you know*.

Check Your E-mail Use the checklist to review your e-mail. The model shows one writer's e-mail.

WRITING CHECKLIST

Did you...

- ✔ state your request clearly?
- ✔ eliminate all wordiness and unnecessary details and use polite, formal language?
- ✔ include a greeting and a closing and avoid poor e-mail habits?

CONNECTING Writing & Grammar

Remember to check that all verbs agree with their subjects, not with words that come between.

The **cost** of the classes **is** unclear.

See **Lesson 10.2** for more examples.

Writing Model

To:	M.Ruiz@school.com
From:	E.Zikowski@school.com
Subject:	Questions about guitar classes

Dear Mrs. Ruiz: *(Greeting)*

[1]I am writing to request information about guitar classes at Edge Music School this fall. [2]I am especially interested in the schedule for beginner classes on the weekends. [3]Do you offer classical guitar classes? *(Purpose and specific requests)*

[4]Also, I would appreciate information about the cost of each class and the deadlines for registration. [5]I look forward to hearing from you. [6]Thank you for your help. *(Formal language)*

Sincerely, *(Closing)*

Emma Zikowski

Chapter Review

A. Practice Test

Read each sentence below carefully. Decide which answer choice best replaces the underlined part, and fill in the circle with the corresponding letter. If you think the underlined part is correct, fill in the circle for choice *A*.

EXAMPLE:

Ⓐ Ⓑ Ⓒ Ⓓ Melissa and her best friend have dance class on Saturdays.
(A) Melissa and her best friend have
(B) Melissa and her best friend has
(C) Melissa or her best friend have
(D) Melissa and her best friends has

Ⓐ ● Ⓒ Ⓓ **1.** Dance involve using the body to express music.
(A) Dance involve
(B) Dance involves
(C) Dances involves
(D) Dances involving

Ⓐ Ⓑ ● Ⓓ **2.** Each style of dance have a unique history.
(A) of dance have
(B) of dancing have
(C) of dance has
(D) dance have

Ⓐ ● Ⓒ Ⓓ **3.** Tap dance, for example, consist of African, Scottish, English, and Irish influences.
(A) Tap dance, for example, consist of
(B) Tap dance, for example, consists of
(C) Tap dances, for example, consists of
(D) Tap dance consisting of

Ⓐ Ⓑ Ⓒ ● **4.** In addition to graceful dance techniques, music, costumes, and scenery makes up ballet, a dance form from France.
(A) music, costumes, and scenery makes
(B) costumes, scenery, and music makes
(C) music, costumes, or scenery make
(D) music, costumes, and scenery make

Ⓐ Ⓑ Ⓒ ● **5.** Both salsa and rhumba has Afro-Cuban roots.
(A) has Afro-Cuban roots.
(B) has roots that are African and Cuban.
(C) has roots in Africa and Cuba.
(D) have Afro-Cuban roots.

● Ⓑ Ⓒ Ⓓ **6.** Some dances from the 1930s regain popularity after decades pass.
(A) Some dances from the 1930s regain
(B) Some dances from the 1930s regains
(C) Some dance from the 1930s regain
(D) Dances from the 1930s regains

Ⓐ ● Ⓒ Ⓓ **7.** Flexibility and strong muscles is characteristic of a good dancer.
(A) is characteristic of a good dancer.
(B) are characteristic of a good dancer.
(C) is characteristic of good dancers.
(D) is characteristics of a good dancer.

Ⓐ Ⓑ ● Ⓓ **8.** Ballroom dance and tango dance competitions is held each year in Europe and the United States.
(A) Ballroom dance and tango dance competitions is
(B) Ballroom dance or tango dance are
(C) Ballroom dance and tango dance competitions are
(D) Ballroom dance or tango dance competitions is

● Ⓑ Ⓒ Ⓓ **9.** Originating on the streets of Chicago, footworking blends tap, African tribal dance, and break dancing.
(A) Originating on the streets of Chicago, footworking blends
(B) Footworking blend
(C) Originating on the streets of Chicago, footworking blend
(D) Originating on the streets of Chicago, footworkings blends

Ⓐ ● Ⓒ Ⓓ **10.** Is there any new dances you know?
(A) Is there any new dances
(B) Are there any new dances
(C) Are there any new dance
(D) Is there some new dances

Chapter Review

B. Choosing the Correct Verb

Read each sentence below. Underline the verb in parentheses that agrees with the subject.

1. Today's MP3 players (provides, provide) a tremendous number of options for music lovers.
2. If you're always on the go, there (are, is) no better way to carry your music with you.
3. The prices of MP3 players (have, has) come down a great deal in recent years.
4. Some of the inexpensive models (are, is) sold at grocery or toy stores.
5. Almost nobody in my family (uses, use) cassette players anymore.
6. My player, for instance, (stores, store) all the soundtracks of my favorite movies.
7. My friends Ethan and Adina (like, likes) to download and watch movies on the weekend.
8. I think the screen is too small to watch movies, but neither Ethan nor Adina (agrees, agree).
9. (Does, Do) my little sister want a player for her birthday?
10. Both my mother and father (thinks, think) she is old enough to have one.
11. My sister, unlike her friends, (enjoy, enjoys) country music.
12. All of Theo's friends (listens, listen) to hip-hop music when they are riding on the bus.
13. There (are, is) always a new brand of MP3 players on sale.
14. I shouldn't be surprised that each of the brands (has, have) more features than the last.
15. My father (has, have) asked me to teach him how to use new technology.

C. Revising Sentences

Rewrite the sentence below, correcting any errors in subject-verb agreement. Some sentences may have more than one error.

1. My older sister and I are glad to have new twin brothers, even if they is noisy sometimes.
   My older sister and I are glad to have new twin brothers, even if they are noisy sometimes.
2. Our mom or our dad often ask us to babysit.
   Our mom or our dad often asks us to babysit.
3. Neither of my sisters mind babysitting the boys.
   Neither of my sisters minds babysitting the boys.
4. There is times when all of us feels tired, but we say yes.
   There are times when all of us feel tired, but we always say yes.
5. In your family, do everyone help one another?
   In your family, does everyone help one another?

D. Reviewing an E-mail

Carefully read the e-mail below, and then rewrite it on a separate sheet of paper. Correct any errors in subject-verb agreement, and add any information that is missing. Delete any unimportant information.

Students' revisions will vary. Sample answer is shown.

To:	spellingbeegroup@school.com
From:	M.Koslowski@school.com
Subject:	Schedule change

Dear Spelling Bee Competitors:

[1]The spelling bee practice session that was scheduled for this Friday afternoon is being changed. ~~because the debate club members needs the auditorium.~~ ~~[2]Last year the debate club won the division championship.~~ [3]The new practice session ~~are~~ is scheduled for ~~the day of~~ Thursday, October 23, at 4:45 P.M. ~~in the afternoon.~~ [4]Everyone in all grades ~~are~~ is expected to attend.

Thanks,

Matt

Chapter
Review

CHAPTER 11

Punctuation

End Marks

LESSON 11.1

End marks are punctuation marks used at the ends of sentences.

➡ The end mark you use depends on the purpose of the sentence.

1. A **period (.)** ends a **declarative sentence.** Declarative sentences make a statement.

   Ringo is a Maine coon cat.

A period also ends an **imperative sentence,** which gives a command or makes a request.

   Take good care of him while I am gone.

2. A **question mark (?)** ends an **interrogative sentence,** which asks a question.

   Where did you adopt him?

A question mark, however, is not used after an indirect question.

   Tasha asked me where I adopted him.

3. An **exclamation point (!)** ends an **exclamatory sentence,** which is a sentence that expresses a strong feeling.

   He's the cutest cat I've ever seen!

It is also used after an interjection or in a command that expresses a lot of emotion.

   Yikes! Don't let him eat that bug!

➡ A period is also used in many **abbreviations,** which are shortened forms of words.

INITIALS	Juan P. Rodriguez		A.J. Jackson		
TITLES	Mr.	Mrs.	Ms.	Jr.	Dr.
TIMES	A.M.	P.M.	B.C.	Sat.	Oct.
OTHERS	etc.	vs.	Co.	Ave.	

Remember

Abbreviations save time when you take notes or write informal letters. In formal writing, such as essays and business letters, use only common abbreviations, such as initials, titles, and those for time. Spell out everything else.

ONLINE PRACTICE
www.grammarforwriting.com

Exercise 1 Adding End Marks

Remember

When an abbreviation comes at the end of a sentence, use only one period.

The movie won't be over until 7 p.m.

Add the correct punctuation mark at the end of each sentence.

1. The audience gasped when the singer held a lengthy note.
2. Don't talk during the performance.
3. This is the best concert ever!
4. Let's wait in line to get her autograph.
5. Did you bring a camera?

Exercise 2 Using Abbreviations

Correct the abbreviations below. Use each one in a sentence you might write to a friend. Students' sentences will vary. See sample answers in Answer Key at www.grammarforwriting.com.

1. pm (P.M.)	**3.** mrs (Mrs.)	**5.** dr (Dr.)	**7.** us (U.S.)	**9.** aug (Aug.)
2. ave (Ave.)	**4.** lbs (lbs.)	**6.** in (in.)	**8.** ft (ft.)	**10.** etc (etc.)

Working Together

Exercise 3 Improving a Paragraph

Work with a partner to find and correct five errors with end marks. Then write four to five sentences explaining the type of book you would write. Check your use of end marks and any abbreviations. Students' created paragraphs will vary. See sample answer in Answer Key at www.grammarforwriting.com.

Proofreading Symbols

^ Add.

ℓ Delete.

[1]If I were an author, I would write mystery novels? . [2]I like that they are suspenseful and draw the reader into the story. [3]Most people like to read books that grab their attention? . [4]The one thing about mystery novels, however, is that they are often scary. [5]Sometimes they are terrifying? ! [6]I don't think that mysteries have to involve violence or present a frightening situation in order to be thrilling and entertaining? . [7]What do you think. ?

LESSON 11.2

Commas in Compound Sentences and Series

A **comma (,)** is a punctuation mark that signals a slight pause but not a complete stop.

Commas are used before a conjunction in a compound sentence.

I do enjoy cooking**,** but directions can be confusing.

Fantasy football is fun**,** and most of my friends have a team.

Be careful not to confuse a compound subject or compound verb with a compound sentence. Compound subjects and compound verbs do not need a comma.

Sara and I have similar hobbies. We play the guitar and sing.

Commas are also used between items in a series of three or more items. Add a comma after every item except for the last one.

Painting**,** gymnastics**,** and reading are my favorite hobbies.

I love dancing to rap**,** pop**,** and rock.

Remember

A compound sentence has two or more independent clauses joined by a conjunction, such as *and, but, or, nor,* or *yet*. See **Lessons 3.4** and **3.5.**

I went to the theme park**, and** the lines were long.

Exercise 1 Adding Commas

Add the missing commas in the following sentences.

1. The killer whale glides through the water, and the trainer waits on the other side of the pool.
2. The whales live in theme parks in California, Florida, and Ohio.
3. Scientists want to understand whales' behavior, so they study the sounds killer whales make.
4. The killer whales at theme parks live in huge pools, and people can see them swim.
5. The killer whales swim, slide, leap, and dive.
6. Fish are their main food source, but they also eat other whales and dolphins.

7. Killer whales are found in oceans all over the world, and they usually swim within five hundred miles of land.
8. Scientists think that shoving, leaping out of the water, and splashing are ways the whales exhibit their strength.
9. Killer whales sound mean, but trained whales can be friendly.
10. Have you read much about whales, or have you ever seen one?

Exercise 2 Editing a Paragraph

Edit the draft below to correct the comma usage. Use the proofreading symbols to add missing commas and eliminate unnecessary ones.

Proofreading Symbols

- ^, Add a comma.
- Delete.

[1]The cheetah is the world's fastest land mammal. [2]It is yellow with a white belly, and black spots cover most of its body. [3]Cheetahs can reach speeds of seventy mph. [4]They have strong hearts, long legs, and keen eyesight. [5]Their bodies are narrow, and strong. [6]The cheetah's long tail helps to balance its body weight.

Write What You Think

Read the question below. Answers will vary. See sample answer in Answer Key at www.grammarforwriting.com.

What is your favorite animal? Why do you like it the best?

1. On a separate sheet of paper, write at least five sentences that answer the question above.
2. Include each type of comma usage twice.
3. Then check your paragraph for comma errors.

LESSON 11.3

Other Comma Uses

Learn these additional rules for using **commas.**

	Rule	Example
Direct Address	Use a comma to set off a noun of direct address (the name of the person being spoken to).	David**,** I want to finish our science project.
Introductory Phrases or Words	Use a comma to set off an introductory phrase or words such as *well*, *yes*, and *no* that begin a sentence.	After weeks of work**,** I'm still not sure we can finish on time.
Interrupters	Interrupters are unnecessary words that comment on or add information to a sentence. When an interrupter comes in the middle of a sentence, use two commas.	You know**,** of course**,** that Mrs. Yang is counting on us.
Date and Year	Use a comma to separate the date and year. Add a comma after the year if the date comes in the middle of a sentence.	My article is due on February 21**,** 2010**,** which is also my birthday.
Direct Quotation	Insert a comma to separate a direct quotation from the rest of a sentence.	Her teacher said**,** "Let's review your homework."

Remember

Interrupters are words and phrases that interrupt the main thought of a sentence. They include common transitions and parenthetical expressions such as these:

as a result
for example
for instance
furthermore
however
in fact
nevertheless
of course

Exercise 1 Using Commas

Read the following sentences. Add commas where needed. If the sentence is correct as is, write *C*.

1. Charles Lindbergh was born on February 4,1902.

2. Lindbergh,of course,is an aviation hero.

3. In fact, he gained international fame as the first pilot to fly solo across the Atlantic Ocean on May 21, 1927. C

4. Yes,Lindbergh learned to drive when he was eleven.

ONLINE PRACTICE
www.grammarforwriting.com

Charles Lindbergh

5. In his teen years, Lindbergh was a dedicated student.
6. He spent hours, for example, studying aspects of flying.
7. Excited by the journey ahead, he took off May 20, 1927, in a plane named the *Spirit of St. Louis.*
8. President Calvin Coolidge awarded him the Distinguished Flying Cross on June 11, 1927. C
9. He is best known for being the first person to fly solo across the Atlantic. C
10. On June 13, 1927, New York City honored Lindbergh with a huge parade.

Working Together

EXERCISE 2 Writing Sentences

Review the chart on the previous page. For each rule, write one example sentence on a separate sheet of paper. Exchange papers with a partner, and check each other's use of commas. Discuss any rules you used incorrectly. Answers will vary. See sample answers in Answer Key at www.grammarforwriting.com.

Remember

A **speech tag** is the group of words that identifies the speaker, such as *she said.*

1. If a tag appears before the quotation, place a comma at the end of a tag.

Mom said**,** "Please get ready."

Note that a period always appears inside the end quotation mark.

2. If a tag appears after a quotation, place a comma inside the end quotation mark.

"Get ready**,**" said Mom.

EXERCISE 3 Using Commas with Quotations

Now write sentences with direct quotations.
Answers will vary. See sample answers in Answer Key at www.grammarforwriting.com.

1. Imagine that you are on a train, bus, or plane.
2. Write at least five statements with direct quotations. You may use one or more of the quotations below. Use commas to separate the rest of the sentence from the quotation.

EXAMPLE "I love to fly."

"I love to fly," said the excited young girl.

- "We'll be flying over the ocean today."
- "I'm excited about this trip."
- "This is the bumpiest flight I have ever taken."

LESSON 11.4

Semicolons and Colons

Semicolons (;) and **colons (:)** are punctuation marks that signal a pause. Sometimes people confuse colons and semicolons, but these punctuation marks do very different jobs.

➡ Use a semicolon in place of a comma and a conjunction to join independent clauses in a **compound sentence.** Only use a semicolon if the sentences are very closely related.

Felix likes the summer**;** Kim likes the winter.

➡ Follow these guidelines for using a colon.

Purpose	Example
To introduce a list of items at the end of a complete sentence	My backpack contains the following**:** two books, three pencils, a ruler, and my lunch.
To separate the hour and minutes	I have to be in class at 7**:**15 on the dot.
To punctuate a greeting in a business letter or an e-mail	Dear Mr. Wang**:**

For a review of compound sentences and independent clauses, refer to **Lessons 3.3** and **3.4.**

Exercise 1 Using Semicolons

On a separate sheet of paper, rewrite the following compound sentences so that each sentence includes a semicolon.

EXAMPLE Frida Kahlo is Mexico's most famous female artist, and this honor is well earned.

Frida Kahlo is Mexico's most famous female artist; this honor is well earned.

1. Kahlo had three sisters, but she was her father's favorite.
Kahlo had three sisters; she was her father's favorite.
2. The family lived near Mexico City, and they lived there during the Mexican Revolution.
The family lived near Mexico City; they lived there during the Mexican Revolution.
3. At eighteen, she was in a bus accident, and her spine was permanently damaged.
At eighteen, she was in a bus accident; her spine was permanently damaged.

WRITING HINT

Do not use a colon between a preposition and its object(s).

INCORRECT Elena went to**:** Oregon, Idaho, and Montana.

CORRECT Elena went to these states**:** Oregon, Idaho, and Montana.

ONLINE PRACTICE
www.grammarforwriting.com

Frida Kahlo

4. Kahlo married muralist Diego Rivera, and he was one of the most famous artists of the time.
Kahlo married muralist Diego Rivera; he was one of the most famous artists of the time.

5. Although her work was praised, she did not have a solo art show until 1938, and it was held in New York.
Although her work was praised by famous artists, Kahlo did not have a solo art show until 1938; it was held in New York.

Exercise 2 Adding Punctuation Marks

Insert the missing colons or semicolons in each sentence. Add no other words or punctuation marks.

HINT

Each sentence needs either a semicolon or a colon, not both.

1. I need the following items: a brush, an easel, and a model.
2. My easel is heavy; it weighs nine pounds.
3. We should begin our projects at 9:00 A.M. and finish no later than noon.
4. Clean the brushes gently; they can be damaged easily.
5. Miss Erst is our teacher; she is very patient.
6. My day goes like this: classes, lunch, classes, homework, and computer games.
7. I ate lunch quickly; we only get fifteen minutes.
8. Lou left class at 11:24 A.M. and never returned.
9. I love these kinds of art: painting, sculpture, and pottery.
10. I like to paint lakes; the scenes seem so peaceful.

Exercise 3 Writing a Business E-mail

Imagine that you want to volunteer at a local art center. On a separate sheet of paper, write a business e-mail to the director. Make up names and details as necessary.

Answers will vary. See sample answer in Answer Key at www.grammarforwriting.com.

1. Include the times of day you are available.
2. Add a sentence with a colon that lists reasons that you're right for the job.
3. Use a semicolon in at least one sentence.

Include a greeting and a closing in your business e-mail. For tips on writing a business e-mail, see the workshop in **Chapter 10.**

LESSON 11.5

Quotation Marks

Quotation marks (" ") are used to enclose the exact words of a speaker and to set off certain titles.

See **Lesson 11.3** for more about using commas with quotations.

➡ Use quotation marks at the beginning and end of a **direct quotation.** A directly quoted sentence begins with a capital letter. If a **speech tag,** such as *she said,* interrupts a quoted sentence, begin the second part with a lowercase letter.

Alyssa grumbled**, "W**e are so hungry."

"Be patient**,"** Max responded**, "w**hile I finish the project."
[Use commas to set off the direct quotation from the rest of the sentence.]

➡ Periods and commas always go inside, not outside, closing quotation marks.

Alyssa said**,** "The movie was boring**.**"

"I liked the ending**,**" Max replied.

See the rules on the right about where to place other punctuation marks.

➡ Use quotation marks to enclose the titles of short works.

POEMS	"Dreams"
ARTICLES	"America Remembers"
SONGS	"Hound Dog"
SHORT STORIES	"Thank You, Ma'am"
BOOK CHAPTERS	"Maple Sugar Time"
SINGLE TV PROGRAMS	"Time After Time"

Remember

When the quotation is a question or an exclamation, place the question mark or the exclamation point inside the closing quotation mark.

The announcer yelled, "We won**!"**

When the whole sentence (<u>not</u> the quotation) is a question or an exclamation, place the end mark outside the closing quotation mark.

Who said, "Less is more**"?**

Exercise 1 Using Quotation Marks

Add quotation marks and commas in each sentence.

EXAMPLE "I have a new bike**,"** said Claire.

1. Claire's brother exclaimed, "Wow! I like the design!"

2. "Mom, can I ride my bike to the park?" Claire asked.
3. Claire's mother suggested, "I think we should go over some safety rules."
4. "Oh, I know how to use a bike," sighed Claire.
5. "Sure, but did you know many teens have accidents because they don't wear helmets?" asked Claire's mother.
6. "Okay," said Claire, "and I will always remember to wear my helmet."
7. "You need a map of the local bike path," her brother said, "or you won't know where you're going."
8. Their mother responded, "Let's make a list of safety gear you should put on your bike, such as a reflector."
9. "I want to ride the bike soon," replied Claire.
10. "You can be safe and have fun at the same time," explained Mrs. Bronsky.

Exercise 2 Punctuating Titles

Put quotation marks around titles where they are needed. One sentence is correct as is. Mark it *C*.

1. Jack wrote his report on a book about the history of the White House. C
2. "Poor" is a poem that touches your emotions.
3. The teacher read an article called "Gas Prices Soar."
4. His favorite chapter is "Scrambling for Answers."
5. They read O. Henry's story "The Gift of the Magi."

Exercise 3 Writing a Paragraph

On a separate sheet of paper, write about a short story you've recently read. Include the title, and make sure to use at least two pairs of quotation marks. Read over your paragraph to check for grammar and quotation mistakes. Answers will vary. See sample answer in Answer Key at www.grammarforwriting.com.

LESSON 11.6

Apostrophes

Apostrophes (') are used to show **possession** or **ownership.**

Bertha**'**s coat—the coat that belongs to Bertha

the girls**'** clothes—the clothes that belong to the girls

Follow these rules for forming **possessive nouns.**

Possessives	Rule	Examples
Singular nouns	Add an apostrophe and *s*.	brother**'s** cat Jess**'s** book
Plural nouns that end in -*s*	Add an apostrophe.	babies' bibs the Smiths' house
Plural nouns that do not end in -*s*	Add an apostrophe and *s*.	women**'s** names children**'s** toys

Remember

Possessive pronouns like *hers, his, yours,* and *theirs* never have apostrophes. Avoid this error in your writing.

The cat licked ~~it's~~ its paw.

Is this pen ~~yours'~~ yours?

Apostrophes also indicate where letters have been left out in contractions. A **contraction** is a shortened form of a word, numeral, or group of words.

we**'**re (we are)	I**'**ll (I will)	I**'**m (I am)
he**'**s (he is)	it**'**s (it is)	they**'**re (they are)

The word *not* can be shortened to *n't* and added to a verb.

isn**'**t (is not) hadn**'**t (had not) don**'**t (do not)

EXERCISE 1 Forming Possessives

Read the sentences below. In the blank, write the possessive form of the word in parentheses. Identify the word as singular (*S*) or plural (*P*).

EXAMPLE The kaleidoscope's colors are beautiful. (kaleidoscope) S

1. Many babies' rooms have pictures. (babies) P

2. The picture's main color is green. (picture) S

3. My parents' hobbies include painting. (parents) P

ONLINE PRACTICE
www.grammarforwriting.com

4. One of the world's most famous artists is Alexander Calder. (world) s

5. Many of Calder's works are large enough to take up a museum's lobby. (museum) s

Exercise 2 Using Contractions

Students' sentences will vary. See sample answers in Answer Key at www.grammarforwriting.com.

Combine each pair of words below by making a contraction. Then on a separate sheet of paper, write a sentence using each one.

1. did not — didn't
2. should not — shouldn't
3. could not — couldn't
4. will not — won't
5. were not — weren't
6. they are — they're
7. does not — doesn't
8. it is — it's
9. what is — what's
10. he will — he'll

Working Together

Exercise 3 Editing a Paragraph

Work with a partner to find the errors in apostrophe usage or missing apostrophes in the following paragraph.

Vincent Van Gogh

[1]Vincent Van Gogh was a great painter. [2]Van Goghs [Gogh's] best work was painted in under three years, but he ~~was'nt~~ [wasn't] initially successful as an artist. [3]His paintings' [paintings] werent [weren't] well received while he was living. [4]People ~~didnt~~ [didn't] think his paintings were anything out of the ordinary. [5]Unfortunately, he didnt [didn't] live to see his great success in the art world. [6]Only after his death did people begin to appreciate and collect the artists [artist's] work.

Other Marks of Punctuation

Other marks of punctuation include the **hyphen (-)** and the **dash (–).**

➡ The hyphen is used in many ways, as indicated in the chart below.

Hyphen Uses	Example
To divide a word at the end of a line, if necessary	Every time it rains, puddles gradu-ally form in the basement.
In numbers from twenty-one to ninety-nine	There are twenty-four children who live on this street.
To spell out a fraction	The apartment building takes up one-third of the block.
To divide some compound words	The half-price sales sign caused a real mix-up.

➡ The dash is used to indicate a sudden break or change in thought.

Every night—or maybe once a week—a car alarm goes off.

Remember

Divide words only between syllables. If you're not sure how to hyphenate a word, use a dictionary to check where to break it. Also use a dictionary to check if a compound word should be hyphenated.

Exercise 1 Using Dashes and Hyphens

Read the sentences below. Decide whether the sentence is missing a dash or a hyphen, and insert it where necessary.

1. I read a newspaper‸—or perhaps a magazine‸—every day.
2. About one‸-third of my books are about sports.
3. My great‸-grandmother never watches sports.
4. There are at least fifty‸-one different sports channels.
5. That interview‸—the one with the coach‸—was too short.

HiNT

You may need to add more than one dash or hyphen to a sentence.

ONLINE PRACTICE
www.grammarforwriting.com

Exercise 2 Adding Hyphens

Add hyphens where needed in the paragraph below.

[1]How much fat should be in a child's diet? [2]Chil-dren between nine and twelve should eat about seventy-five grams per day. [3]Babies need more; adults and children older than two should be careful to get no more than one-third of their calories from fat.

Exercise 3 Adding Dashes

Add dashes in the following sentences.

1. Lou Gehrig played baseball for fifteen seasons—about 2,130 games—before his retirement.
2. Gehrig was known as the "Iron Horse"—an appropriate name—and was widely respected for his strength.
3. His grand slam record—I forget the exact number—is still unbroken.
4. He joined the Yankees in the 1923 season—I think as a pinch hitter—but played very little at first.
5. Gehrig's accomplishments on the field—it needs to be said—are still recognized today.

Exercise 4 Writing Instructions

On a separate sheet of paper, write brief instructions for a healthy snack you know how to make.

Answers will vary. Sample answers are shown.

1. Include at least three steps.
   Slice two stalks of celery in half.
2. Give one measurement that uses a hyphen.
   Fill each stalk with one-quarter cup of peanut butter.
3. In one of your steps, include a sentence interruption that requires the use of a dash.
   Sprinkle raisins—or peanuts, if you prefer—on top of the peanut butter filling.

ONLINE MODEL
www.grammarforwriting.com

Research Report

How often do you go online to check the weather, find out sports scores, or look up somebody's name? Though you might not think of it this way, you are researching.

In this workshop, you will learn how to write a **research report.** A research report presents information gathered from multiple sources about a single topic.

Some Purposes of a Research Report

- tell the story of someone's life
- explain an aspect of nature
- describe a period in history
- analyze a process
- evaluate an idea
- analyze current events
- compare and contrast two historical figures

Your research report should have the features below.

Key Features

- strong, clear thesis
- variety of supporting evidence
- Works Cited list
- strong introduction, body, and conclusion
- formal language
- a combination of primary and secondary sources

ASSIGNMENT

TASK: Write a three- to four-page **research report** that answers a question you have always wondered about. Use at least three sources.

AUDIENCE: your teacher and classmates

PURPOSE: to explain

WRITING HINT

Think of a research report as a chance to find the answer(s) to a question you are curious about. To choose a topic, ask *Who? What? Where? When? Why?* and *How?* questions about subjects that interest you.

Prewriting

Narrow the Field Every good research paper begins with a good topic. Choose a topic that you and your readers want to know more about.

1. Start by brainstorming topics in different subject areas. Do some preliminary research to decide on a specific focus. Ask an interesting question that you'd like to answer.

environment ⟶ loss of rainforests ⟶ When rainforests disappear, what happens to the animals that live there?

2. Next, make your topic fit the length. Ask yourself, "Will I be able to write about this topic in just three pages?" If you don't think you can, try narrowing it even more by creating a list of subtopics. For example, "rainforests" is too broad, but the subtopic "shrinking rainforests" is narrow enough.

WRITING HINT

When you write a research report, use **formal language.** Formal language is free of contractions, such as *didn't*, and **slang,** such as *cool*.

Think About Your Point Now that you've chosen your topic, write the first draft of your **thesis.**

- Your thesis is your essay's main idea. Think of your thesis as the answer to a question that you want to explore.
- It should appear in the introductory paragraph.
- The thesis is more than just a fact or a restatement of your topic. It should reflect your opinion about the topic.

INCORRECT	Rainforests are getting way too small, which isn't cool.
CORRECT	Shrinking rainforests will damage the world by causing countless extinctions.

As you research your topic and learn more about it, you'll likely revise your thesis along the way.

Prewriting

Dig into the Topic Use the steps below as a guide as you gather information and begin to organize your ideas.

1. **Make a list of questions about your topic.** For example, ask, "What kinds of animals and plants live in rainforests?"
2. **Use the Internet carefully.** Only trust Web sites from reliable sources, such as library, university, encyclopedia, and government sites. Check that the sites you use are free of errors, are regularly updated, and describe the subject fairly.
3. **Visit the library.** Use the online library catalog to collect a variety of primary and secondary sources. **Primary sources** are firsthand accounts, while **secondary sources** are descriptions or explanations of primary sources.

Primary	Secondary
• journals • eyewitness accounts and interviews • scientific data • literature and works of art	• interpretations of data • analyses of literature • descriptions of photos and works of art • news stories and encyclopedia articles • textbooks

4. **Find a variety of sources.** Collect a variety of evidence, including facts, statistics, dates, examples, anecdotes, and quotations that address your question.
5. **Jot down notes on note cards.** Always keep track of your sources. You'll need this information later when you create your Works Cited list, which includes all the sources you used for your paper. Tracking sources will help you avoid **plagiarism,** which is presenting others' ideas and exact words as your own. Plagiarism will result in a failing grade.
6. **Make an outline.** Organize your note cards by grouping similar information into main points. List the points in the order you will present them.

Remember

Addresses for government Web sites end in *.gov*. Addresses for university Web sites end in *.edu*.

Drafting

Use an Outline An outline for a paper is like a blueprint for a house. It maps out where everything goes so you can more easily build your paper. As you draft, refer to the outline you made during the prewriting stage. You may decide to revise it as you write.

Review this part of one writer's outline.

Thesis: Shrinking rainforests will damage the world by causing countless extinctions of plant and animal life.

1. Species of plants are threatened.
   A. Nearly half of the world's species of plants will be destroyed if the Amazon rainforest keeps shrinking.
   B. About one-third of a square mile of land in the Amazon rainforest holds 90,000 tons of plants.

Write a Complete Draft Draft an introduction, a body, and a conclusion.

1. Capture your readers' attention with an interesting **introduction.** Keep their interest throughout by including little-known and surprising information. Make sure to include your thesis in the introduction.
2. In the **body,** present the information that supports your thesis. Write at least one paragraph for each main point in your outline. Include supporting information for each point. If you don't have enough information to develop a paragraph, either revise your outline, or do additional research.
3. Finish your report with a strong **conclusion.** Summarize the main points, and restate your thesis. You can also leave your readers with a question or thought to ponder.

Revising

Now that you have finished drafting, slowly reread your work. Use the Revising Questions below to guide your revision.

Revising Questions

- ❏ How clear and strong is my thesis?
- ❏ How effective are my introduction, body, and conclusion?
- ❏ How varied is my supporting evidence?
- ❏ How well did I use formal language?
- ❏ How well did I use both primary and secondary sources?

As you revise, keep in mind the traits of good writing. See **Lesson 1.3.**

Get Feedback After you have answered all of the Revising Questions, exchange papers with a classmate. When a classmate reviews your work and offers suggestions, you are participating in a **peer review.**

Remember

Peer reviewers should give specific comments, both for identifying what works and what doesn't. Comments such as "good job" or "work on this" are too vague to be helpful.

Have your classmate ask these questions as he or she reads your paper:

- How interesting does the topic seem to me? Do I think others will be interested in it?
- How well did the introduction grab and hold my attention?
- How interested does the writer seem in his or her topic?
- How strong is the evidence? Do I find it convincing?
- Which part of the paper did I find most interesting?
- Which parts of the paper did I have trouble following?

Editing and Proofreading

Use the checklist to edit and proofread your paper.

Editing and Proofreading Checklist

- ❑ Have I capitalized the first word of every sentence?
- ❑ Did I correctly use commas in a series of three or more things?
- ❑ Did I end each sentence with the correct end mark?
- ❑ Did I include a Works Cited list at the end of my report?

Proofreading Symbols

- ℣ Delete.
- ^ Add.
- ⊙ Add a period.
- / Make lowercase.
- ≡ Capitalize.
- ^, Add a comma.

Scientists

[1]~~Sceintists~~ believe that 50 to 90 percent of the world's plant and animal species live in tropical rainforests. [2]Therefore, countless species of birds^, fish^, mammals^, and plants are threatened by the loss of rainforests. [3]Many of these species are still unknown to scientists^; their disappearance will prevent many discoveries from occurring. [4]In fact, many medical breakthroughs are directly linked to plant and animal research. [5]For example^, one of the most effective cancer drugs is made from a kind of periwinkle flower found in rainforests⊙

Proofread Your Works Cited List Follow these tips:

- Alphabetize the list using the authors' last names.
- Separate last and first names with a comma. Place middle names or initials after first names.
- Place periods between the main parts of each entry and at the end of each entry.
- Indent all lines, except for the first line, of every entry.
- Double-space throughout.

Ask your teacher which format to use for listing sources. One common format is as follows:

Book
Last Name, First Name. *Title*. Place of Publication: Publisher, Year Published.

Magazine
Last Name, First Name. "Title." *Title of Publication* Date: Page Numbers.

Williams, Michael. *Understanding Rainforests*. Chicago: University of Chicago Press, 2002.

Youst, Allen Q. "Tropical Rainforests." *Earth Today Magazine* April 2007: 13–14.

Publishing and Presenting

Choose one of these ways to share your report.

- **Create a binder.** Group your class's reports into categories. Insert them in a binder, and give the binder a title, such as "The Environment."
- **Post it.** Publish your report on a Web site about your topic.

CONNECTING Writing & Grammar

When you create your Works Cited list, remember to use quotation marks for the titles of articles. See **Lesson 11.5.**

"Rainforests in Danger"

Reflect On Your Writing

- Which part of the process did you like better: researching or writing? Why?
- What have you learned about researching?

CHAPTER 11

Chapter Review

A. Practice Test

Read each sentence below. Decide which answer choice best replaces the underlined part, and fill in the circle of the corresponding letter. If you think the underlined part is correct, fill in the circle for choice *A*.

EXAMPLE

Ⓐ●ⒸⒹ Anne Frank was born on June 12 1929 in Frankfurt, Germany.
(A) June 12 1929 in Frankfurt,
(B) June 12, 1929, in Frankfurt,
(C) June 12, 1929 in Frankfurt,
(D) June 12: 1929, in Frankfurt,

ⒶⒷⒸ● **1.** When Hitler came to power in Germany—an event that many had hoped would never come to pass; the Franks moved to Amsterdam!
(A) Germany—an event that many had hoped would never come to pass; the Franks moved to Amsterdam!
(B) Germany; an event that many had hoped would never come to pass; the Franks moved to Amsterdam.
(C) Germany—an event that many had hoped would never come to pass, the Franks moved to Amsterdam!
(D) Germany—an event that many had hoped would never come to pass—the Franks moved to Amsterdam.

ⒶⒷ●Ⓓ **2.** However Hitlers power soon spread and Amsterdams Jewish citizens were forced to wear yellow stars.
(A) However Hitlers power soon spread and Amsterdams Jewish citizens
(B) However, Hitler's power soon spread and Amsterdams Jewish citizens
(C) However, Hitler's power soon spread, and Amsterdam's Jewish citizens
(D) However, Hitler's power soon spread, and, Amsterdams' Jewish citizens

● Ⓑ Ⓒ Ⓓ **3.** In July 1942, Anne Frank went into hiding with her father, mother, and sister.

(A) In July 1942, Anne Frank went into hiding with her father, mother,
(B) In July, 1942 Anne Frank went into hiding with her father, and mother,
(C) In July, 1942, Anne Frank went into hiding with her father, mother
(D) In July, 1942, Anne Frank went into hiding with her father mother,

Ⓐ Ⓑ ● Ⓓ **4.** After two years in the attic the family was discovered and arrested, they were then taken to a concentration camp.

(A) After two years in the attic the family was discovered and arrested, they
(B) After two years in the attic, the family was discovered and arrested, they
(C) After two years in the attic, the family was discovered and arrested; they
(D) After, two years in the attic the family was discovered and arrested; they

Ⓐ Ⓑ Ⓒ ● **5.** In one of her last diary entries, Anne Frank wrote: I still believe, in spite of everything, that people are truly good at heart."

(A) I still believe, in spite of everything, that people are truly good at heart."
(B) I still believe, in spite of everything, that people are truly good at heart.
(C) "I still believe, in spite of everything, that people are truly good at heart.
(D) "I still believe, in spite of everything, that people are truly good at heart."

B. Using Commas and End Marks Correctly

In each sentence below, add any missing commas and end marks.

1. Do you always do what your friends say, or do you stand up to them when you disagree with them?

2. Peer pressure is something many students have to deal with, and it can involve serious issues.

3. Some issues include cutting class, stealing, and cheating.

4. Giving in to peer pressure can make you do something wrong, and it can get you in trouble with your teachers or parents.

5. Imagine getting grounded for a month!

6. Peer pressure is not worth it.

7. Pick friends who listen to you, care about you, and like you for yourself.

8. You should always be yourself, of course, and you should choose friends who support you.

9. After all, you can always just walk away.

10. Yes, you can do it. *or* !

C. Matching Punctuation Marks

Match each punctuation mark in the left column with its correct use, listed in the right column. Write your choice in the space provided.

d **1.** apostrophe

a **2.** hyphen

e **3.** quotation marks

b **4.** semicolon

c **5.** colon

a. in a fraction

b. to form a compound sentence without using a conjunction

c. to introduce a list

d. to show ownership

e. around the title of a poem

D. Writing Quotations

Choose one topic of conversation below. Students' sentences will vary but should be punctuated correctly. See sample answer in Answer Key at www.grammarforwriting.com.

- a movie you want to see this weekend
- a poem or article you read recently
- a song or TV show you like

1. Imagine a conversation about the topic between you and a friend. On a separate sheet of paper, write five sentences. In each one, include a direct quotation that you or your friend might say.
2. Use a variety of speech tags. Check your sentences for correct use of punctuation.

E. Reviewing Thesis Statements

Read each thesis statement below.

Revised thesis statements will vary. See sample answers in Answer Key at www.grammarforwriting.com.

1. Use proofreading symbols to correct any errors in punctuation.
2. On a separate sheet of paper, explain how effective each thesis statement is for a four-page research report.
3. Rewrite one weak thesis statement.

Proofreading Symbols

Delete.	Add a comma.
Add.	Add a period.

- China has contributed many great pieces of art to the world!
- Sometime after his death in 210 B.C. the Chinese emperor was buried with over 6,000 clay soldiers' to protect him. Called the terra-cotta army and composed of life-size figures, it wasn't discovered until 1974?
- Because of increased industrialization after 1990 China made several important advances in aerospace manufacturing.
- China has the world's largest population.
- As China has increased its' manufacturing of red toy cars, it has become a world economic leader.

CHAPTER 12

Capitalization and Spelling

LESSON 12.1

Proper Nouns and Proper Adjectives

Proper nouns, which name a specific person, place, thing, or idea, must be capitalized. (See Lesson 7.1.) **Proper adjectives,** which are formed from proper nouns, should be capitalized, too. (See Lesson 9.1.)

Rule	Examples	
Capitalize the names of specific people, places, holidays, and calendar terms.	**Z**ora **N**. **H**urston **E**urope **L**abor **D**ay	**M**r. **R**uiz **N**ew **Y**ork **A**pril
Capitalize proper adjectives.	**E**nglish **S**panish **S**hakespearean	**P**ersian **A**sian **V**ictorian
Capitalize names of specific languages, peoples, races, and religions.	**J**apanese **C**herokee **C**atholic	**I**roquois **C**anadian **B**uddhism

Remember

The names of school subjects are not capitalized, except for proper nouns, adjectives, and particular course names.

math	**L**atin
science	**B**iology 1

Exercise 1 Fixing Capitalization

Read the sentences below. Add a proofreading symbol (≡) under all proper nouns and proper adjectives that should be capitalized.

EXAMPLE south africa was a segregated country for more than forty years.

1. nelson mandela is an important south african leader.
2. Our history class learned about him in november.
3. He studied law at the university of witwatersrand.
4. After becoming a lawyer, he joined the african national congress and focused on ending segregation.
5. He was arrested for treason, or crimes against the state, and spent a total of twenty-eight years in a prison near cape town, south africa.
6. In february of 1990, mandela was released from prison.

ONLINE PRACTICE
www.grammarforwriting.com

7. mandela went on to become the first democratically elected leader of south africa.
8. In 1993, he received the nobel peace prize.
9. Have you heard of the nelson mandela children's fund?
10. I hope to study more about african history in social studies next year.

Exercise 2 Editing an Article

As you read the article below, correct the capitalization errors.

[1]rosa parks, a civil rights activist, died monday, October 24, 2005, in detroit, michigan. [2]She was ninety-two. [3]In the city of Montgomery in Alabama, american-born parks refused to give up her bus seat to a white man in 1955. [4]Her arrest triggered a bus boycott organized by martin Luther king and many african-american followers. [5]The boycott led to a court ruling that allowed all people to ride and sit where they please on montgomery buses.

Write What You Think

On a separate sheet of paper, answer the question below.

Which twentieth-century hero or heroine do you believe will always be remembered? Why?

1. Write at least five sentences.
2. Include at least two proper nouns and one proper adjective.

Answers will vary. Review the rules for capitalizing proper nouns and proper adjectives. See sample answer in Answer Key at www.grammarforwriting.com.

LESSON 12.2

First Words and Titles

➡ Always capitalize the first word in every sentence.

Adults in America now live an average of seventy-eight years.

➡ Capitalize the first word in a direct quotation if the quotation is a complete sentence. If a quotation is interrupted, begin the second part with a lowercase letter.

My mother said, "**M**y neighbor hopes to live to be 100."

"Well," I added, "**t**hat is a great goal."

➡ Capitalize the first and last words and other important words in titles of works.

__H__oot *__J__ulie of the __W__olves* *__B__ook of __T__hree*

Do not capitalize short and unimportant words, such as *a, an, the, at, up,* or *for,* unless they begin or end the title.

"**O**ver the **R**ainbow" "**T**he **S**tar-**S**pangled **B**anner"

__T__he __A__ll-__A__merican __S__lurp *__A__ __W__rinkle in __T__ime*

__T__he __L__ion, the __W__itch, and the __W__ardrobe

Remember

Avoid using quotation marks for an indirect quotation.

DIRECT **"**What time is it?**"** she asked.

INDIRECT She asked me what time it was.

EXERCISE 1 Using Capital Letters

Use the rules above and the proofreading symbols to the right to correct capitalization mistakes in the sentences below.

Proofreading Symbols

≡ Capitalize.

/ Make lowercase.

EXAMPLE we like to study Weather.

1. el Niño is a climate Pattern.
2. my teacher explained that El Niño causes The water in the Pacific Ocean to get hotter than usual.
3. "it affects weather patterns around the world," she stated.
4. the climate pattern can change the weather in the United States, according to the book *Climate patterns*.
5. warm ocean currents come farther north.
6. Did you see the show, "wonders Of nature"?

ONLINE PRACTICE
www.grammarforwriting.com

7. She told me, "la Niña is sort of the opposite of El Niño."
8. "during La Niña," she said, "Water temperatures drop."
9. Ms. Gomez said, "this climate pattern affects weather around the globe and in the United States."
10. scientists say That la niña generally creates a more active hurricane season in the Atlantic Ocean.

Exercise 2 Capitalizing Titles

Use the proofreading symbol (≡) to fix capitalization errors in the titles below.

1. *killer whales and their environment*
2. "introduction to insects"
3. *storm chasers*
4. "pollution and wildlife"
5. *earth's mightiest storms*
6. *life in a rotten log*
7. "the dying sea"
8. *eye of the storm*
9. *storms of the sea*
10. "forces of nature"

Working Together

Exercise 3 Capitalizing Direct Quotations

Work with a partner to add the necessary capital letters to direct quotations in this paragraph. Then, write three more sentences. Include one direct quotation, and use correct capitalization.

Answers will vary. Sample answers are shown. She said it is important to be calm and follow all directions. "A tornado is a scary thing, but if you know what to do, you will be okay," she told us. Ms. Katz is good in emergencies.

For help with punctuating quotations, refer to **Lesson 11.5.**

1"if there is a tornado warning," said Ms. Katz, "line up and move quickly to the basement." 2Ms. Katz then told us to get away from any windows and ordered, "go to the hallway." 3She said that we should crouch down in front of the lockers. 4"it's important," she warned, "to use your arms to protect your head and neck."

LESSON 12.3

Other Capitalization Rules

Read each of the capitalization rules below.

Rule	Examples	
Capitalize names of places, including countries, cities, states, streets, highways, and monuments.	**C**hicago **M**ain **S**treet **H**ighway 75	**N**orway **F**ifth **A**venue **L**incoln **M**emorial
Capitalize names of bodies of water, geographical features, and sections of a country.	**L**ake **E**rie **M**ississippi **R**iver **S**ahara **D**esert	**H**udson **B**ay **M**t. **E**verest **N**ew **E**ngland
Capitalize historical periods, events, and documents.	**R**enaissance **B**oston **T**ea **P**arty	**I**ce **A**ge **B**ill of **R**ights
Capitalize names of organizations, institutions, and businesses.	**P**olk **S**chool **U**nited **N**ations **H**abitat for **H**umanity	**G**irl **S**couts **A**pex **B**akery
Capitalize a title or family relationship that comes before a name.	**P**resident Lincoln **M**rs. Bixby **U**ncle Anthony	

Exercise 1 Adding Capital Letters

Add the necessary capital letters in the sentences below. Refer to the rules above to decide which words need to be capitalized.

EXAMPLE The cape of good hope was originally called the cape of storms.

1. The missouri river travels west to east.
2. Before the civil war, the state now known as missouri was acquired through the louisiana purchase.
3. Because of the homestead act of 1862, the government gave free land to people who chose to settle on the frontier.
4. The u.s. constitution contains the bill of rights.
5. The mississippi river runs between iowa and illinois.

6. During the mexican-american war, mexico lost over half of its territory.

7. Through the treaty of guadalupe hidalgo, the united states gained a lot of land in the southwest.

8. The war happened during president Polk's term in office.

9. After Polk, whig party member Zachary Taylor became the twelfth president.

10. Taylor was from virginia, where my aunt and uncle were also born.

Exercise 2 Proofreading a Travel Ad

Find and correct the capitalization errors in the travel ad below.

[1]If you want to see penguins, make sure to visit port elizabeth, south africa. [2]Not only is this port beautiful, but it lies on the indian ocean. [3]Its location has attracted colonies of african penguins. [4]Tourists travel from around the world to catch a glimpse of these penguins. [5]You can see african penguins eat small fish, such as sardines and anchovies. [6]African penguins are so friendly that they allow visitors to take close-up pictures. [7]Be sure to visit the islands around port elizabeth, such as dyer island. [8]This island boasts a large colony of penguins. [9]Organizations such as the international fund for animal welfare help to ensure the survival and safety of penguins.

Exercise 3 Writing a Travel Ad

On a separate sheet of paper, write a travel ad for an exciting place you have visited or would like to visit. Write at least five sentences. Include specific details about the place and its features. Then review your ad for correct capitalization.

Answers will vary. See sample answer in Answer Key at www.grammarforwriting.com.

LESSON 12.4

Spelling Rules

Follow the spelling rules below, and use a dictionary whenever you are not sure how to spell a word.

Rule	Examples	Some Exceptions
Put *i* before *e* except after *c*, or when it sounds like a long *a* as in *neighbor* and *weigh*.	bel**ie**ve, f**ie**ld, p**ie**ce rec**ei**ve, perc**ei**ve, c**ei**ling **ei**ght, fr**ei**ght, v**ei**n	weird either neither science
Drop a word's final silent -*e*, before adding a suffix that begins with a vowel.	nice + -*est* = nic**est** write + -*ing* = writ**ing** like + -*able* = lik**able**	mileage courageous outrageous
Keep the final silent -*e* if the suffix begins with a consonant.	like + -*ly* = like**ly** care + -*ful* = care**ful** hope + -*less* = hope**less**	truly argument wisdom
For a one-syllable word that ends with a single vowel followed by a consonant, double the consonant before adding a suffix that starts with a vowel.	drag + -*ed* = dra**gged** hop + -*ing* = ho**pping** hot + -*er* = ho**tter** swim + -*ing* = swi**mming**	rowing employer
To add a suffix to words ending in a consonant + -*y*, change the -*y* to *i*.	mercy + -*less* = merc**iless** heavy + -*er* = heav**ier** happy + -*ness* = happ**iness**	flying trying shyness
To add a suffix to words ending in a vowel + -*y*, keep the -*y*.	play + -*er* = play**er** joy + -*ful* = joy**ful**	daily

Real-World Writing

Consider this author's thoughts on spelling and punctuation.

"Spelling and punctuation are part of a writer's basic tools. To write without attending to them is like trying to play the piano without learning the notes."

—Marion Dane Bauer

Exercise 1 Applying Spelling Rules

Circle the misspelled word in each group, and spell it correctly. Then use the word in a sentence.

ONLINE PRACTICE
www.grammarforwriting.com

"I won the spell-check bee."

CartoonBank/ © 2003 The New Yorker Collection from cartoonbank.com. All Rights Reserved.

Answers will vary. See sample answers in Answer Key at www.grammarforwriting.com.

1. niece, piece, (wierd)
   weird
2. noisy, raising, (dareing)
   daring
3. (braging), dropping, shopping
   bragging
4. brief, their, (sliegh)
   sleigh
5. (scarey), daring, flaring
   scary
6. (tryied), easier, denied
   tried
7. timeless, truly, (arguement)
   argument
8. eight, (recieve), vein
   receive
9. babyish, easier, (dryed)
   dried
10. (decieve), perceive, conceive
    deceive
11. placing, (wavey), priceless
    wavy
12. funny, (buny), frying
    bunny
13. (saveing), wasteful, voicing
    saving
14. sipping, robbing, (poping)
    popping
15. funniest, cheesier, (heavyest)
    heaviest
16. relieving, (sceince), either
    science
17. hairiest, (crazyer), lazier
    crazier
18. (careing), hating, wasting
    caring
19. robbed, bidding, (riping)
    ripping
20. finest, (takeing), basing
    taking

EXERCISE 2 Proofreading an Editorial

Correct the ten misspelled words in the editorial below.

[1]I ~~beleive~~ believe in ~~recycleing~~ recycling. [2]I've ~~braged~~ bragged about what I do to help our planet, and I'm ~~braging~~ bragging again. [3]The earth is not ~~timless~~ timeless. [4]When I recycle, I begin by ~~separateing~~ separating cans and bottles and ~~puting~~ putting them into bins. [5]By ~~recycleing~~ recycling and buying recycled products, I can really make a difference. [6]I'm ~~helpping~~ helping to save energy by ~~conserveing~~ conserving our natural resources.

EXERCISE 3 Writing an Editorial

Imagine that your community has received a $50,000 grant. How do you think that money should be spent? On a separate sheet of paper, write an editorial for your local newspaper.

Answers will vary. See sample answer in Answer Key at www.grammarforwriting.com.

1. State your opinion clearly, and back it up with at least two strong reasons.
2. Write six to seven sentences. Be sure to check your spelling.

Plural Nouns

LESSON 12.5

Plural nouns name more than one person, place, thing, or idea. Below are rules for forming plural nouns.

Rule	Examples
Add *-s* to most singular nouns.	bell + *-s* = bell**s** book + *-s* = book**s**
Add *-es* to nouns that end in *-s, -sh, -ch, -x,* and *-z.*	lunch + *-es* = lunch**es** dish + *-es* = dish**es**
For nouns ending in a consonant + *-y,* change the *-y* to *i,* and add *-es.*	baby + *-ies* = bab**ies** penny + *-ies* = penn**ies** candy + *-ies* = cand**ies**
For nouns ending in a vowel + *-y,* add *-s.*	boy + *-s* = boy**s** monkey + *-s* = monkey**s**
For most nouns ending in *-f* or *-fe,* change the *-f* to *v,* and add *-es* or *-s.*	leaf + *-es* = lea**ves** loaf + *-es* = loa**ves** life + *-s* = li**ves**
Watch out for irregular plurals that follow no rules. You'll need to memorize the plural form of these words.	child → children mouse → mice foot → feet tooth → teeth woman → women man → men

Remember

Some nouns have the same singular and plural forms. Some can be spelled in more than one way.

deer → deer

sheep → sheep

fish → fish *or* fishes

Exercise 1 Writing with Plurals

Form the plurals of the nouns below. Then use each word in a sentence on a separate sheet of paper.

Sentences will vary. See sample answers in Answer Key at www.grammarforwriting.com.

EXAMPLE bus The school buses arrived on time.

1. age
ages
2. hobby
hobbies
3. enemy
enemies
4. piece
pieces
5. foot
feet
6. child
children
7. treasure
treasures
8. jewel
jewels
9. lunch
lunches
10. story
stories
11. Monday
Mondays
12. box
boxes
13. mouse
mice
14. thief
thieves
15. tie
ties

ONLINE PRACTICE
www.grammarforwriting.com

Exercise 2 Editing an Advice Column

Read the following advice column from a student newspaper. Find the misspelled words. Correct and rewrite the article on a separate piece of paper.

Bullies
[1]~~Bullys~~ are mean kids who hurt the lives ~~lifes~~ and feelings of others–usually for no reason. [2]They tend to pick on kids smaller or younger than themselves ~~themselfs~~. [3]That way they can feel like big shots. [4]They are like wolves ~~wolfs~~ tracking their prey. [5]My advice is either to stop a bully in action or to report the actions to a teacher or parent.

Exercise 3 Writing from a Model

Read the passage below from *Becoming Naomi León.* Answers are shown.

1. Underline the plural nouns in the passage. On a separate sheet of paper, write the rule each plural noun follows.
2. Then use the passage as a model for your own writing. Fill in the blanks to complete two sentences of your own.

Literary Model

[1]Mrs. Maloney was eighty-eight and lived in the double-wide next door. [2]She came out every afternoon to water her <u>cactuses</u>, <u>rocks</u>, and cement <u>bunnies</u>, and only then did she ever come over for a visit.

—Excerpt from *Becoming Naomi León* by Pam Muñoz Ryan

cactuses: Add *-es* to nouns that end in *-s*. rocks: Add *-s* to most singular nouns.
bunnies: For nouns ending in a consonant + *-y*, change the *-y* to *i* and add *-es*.

________ (NAME) was ________ (AGE) and lived in a ________ (NOUN). ________ (HE/SHE) came out every afternoon to ________ (VERB) ________ (HIS/HER) ________ (PLURAL NOUN), ________ (PLURAL NOUN), and ________ (ADJECTIVE) ________ (PLURAL NOUN), and only then did she ever come over for a visit.

Students' sentences will vary. See sample answer in Answer Key at www.grammarforwriting.com.

Essay Question Response

In school, you will often come across essay questions on tests. They require you to craft a thoughtful response based on a task.

Task	What You Must Do
Analyze a passage from a literary work.	Discuss a piece of literature, supporting your claims with evidence from the text.
Explain a topic.	Provide relevant information about a topic.
Interpret a quotation or passage.	Explain the meaning of a passage.
Argue a point.	Take a position on an issue and provide strong reasons and evidence to support your opinion.

When you write your **response,** include the features below.

Key Features

- key words from the essay question
- clear and complete answer to the question
- supporting details, such as facts, quotations, and examples
- correct grammar and spelling

"Your thesis on 'how to keep warm in winter'? Interesting."

ASSIGNMENT

TASK: Write a one- to two-page **essay question response.**

GOAL: to provide a complete answer to a prompt

TARGET: your teacher

SPECIAL INSTRUCTIONS: Include at least two supporting reasons.

Understand the Question The first step is to understand the essay question or prompt.

1. **Read the question twice.** Note key words, such as *respond* or *persuade*, which describe the purpose of the essay. Other key words identify requirements, such as length.
2. **Identify the form.** Ask yourself, "What should I write? A story? A persuasive paragraph? An expository paragraph?"
3. **Identify the purpose.** Are you being asked to entertain, describe, explain, or persuade?

Purpose: to persuade

Requirements

PROMPT: In a letter, President John Adams wrote: "The Revolution was in the minds and hearts of the people.... This radical change in the principles, opinions, sentiments, and affections of the people, was the real American Revolution." Do you agree or disagree? In a two-page essay, support it with strong reasons.

WRITING HINT

Keep track of the amount of time you have. Be sure to save two to three minutes at the end to reread and proofread your writing.

Make a Plan Once you fully understand the question, plan your response. Outline your major points. Remember to include three parts.

1. **Introduction** Your introductory paragraph includes your thesis statement. In your thesis, restate the question, and state your opinion clearly.

   I **agree** completely with **President Adams** that the real American **"Revolution was in the minds and hearts of the people."**

2. **Body** State the reasons that support your opinion. Write one paragraph for each reason. Support each reason with evidence, such as facts or examples. Put the most important reason first, and end with the least important one.
3. **Conclusion** Your final paragraph should restate your thesis in different words and sum up all of your main points.

Check Your Work Use the Writing Checklist to improve your writing. Below is part of one writer's response.

WRITING CHECKLIST

Did you...

- ✔ include key words from the essay question?
- ✔ give a clear and complete answer to the question and include at least two supporting reasons?
- ✔ proofread for errors in grammar, punctuation, and spelling?

To review spelling and capitalization rules, see **Lessons 12.1** through **12.4.**

Writing Model

[1]I agree completely with President Adams that the real American "Revolution was in the minds and hearts of the people." [2]History shows that the American people had formed their own nation before the revolution legalized their separation from Great Britain. — *Clear thesis*

[3]First, many colonists thought that it was unfair that they were taxed by Britain without having any voice in their own government. [4]For example, the Sons of Liberty protested against British taxes for more than ten years before the revolution began and famously dumped tea into the Boston Harbor in 1774. — *First reason; Transition; Evidence (example)*

[5]Second, colonists began forming their own local government. [6]For instance, in 1772 they began forming Committees of Correspondence in several colonies. — *Second reason; Transition; Evidence (example)*

Chapter Review

A. Practice Test

Read the draft and questions below carefully. The questions ask you to choose the best revision for sentences or parts of the draft. Fill in the corresponding circle for your answer choice.

(1) Amy tan was born on february 19, 1952, in california. **(2)** Her parents were both Chinese immigrants. **(3)** As a Chinese-American author, Tan is known for writing moving stories about mother-daughter relationships. **(4)** *The joy luck club*, published in 1989, was tan's first novel. **(5)** The book is made up of sixteen storys told by chinese women and their american daughters. **(6)** It was on the *new york Times* best-seller list for nine monthes. **(7)** tan has also written books for children, including *the chinese siamese cat*.

TEST-TAKING TIP

Beware of tricky test-makers! Some choices are only partially correct.

Ⓐ Ⓑ Ⓒ ● Ⓔ **1.** Which is the best version of sentence 1?

(A) Amy Tan was born on february 19, 1952, in california.
(B) Amy tan was born on February 19, 1952, in california.
(C) Amy Tan was born on february 19, 1952, in California.
(D) Amy Tan was born on February 19, 1952, in California.
(E) amy tan was born on february 19, 1952, in California.

Ⓐ●ⒸⒹⒺ **2.** What is the best version of sentence 4?

(A) *The Joy Luck Club,* published in 1989, was tan's first novel.

(B) *The Joy Luck Club,* published in 1989, was Tan's first novel.

(C) *The Joy Luck Club,* published in 1989, was Tan's first Novel.

(D) *The joy Luck Club,* published in 1989, was tan's first novel.

(E) *the Joy Luck Club,* published in 1989, was Tan's first novel.

ⒶⒷⒸⒹ● **3.** Which is the best version of sentence 5?

(A) The Book is made up of sixteen stories told by Chinese women and their American daughters.

(B) The book is made up of sixteen stories told by Chinese women and their american daughters.

(C) The book is made up of sixteen stories told by Chinese Women and their American daughters.

(D) The book is made up of sixteen storys told by Chinese women and their American daughters.

(E) The book is made up of sixteen stories told by Chinese women and their American daughters.

●ⒷⒸⒹⒺ **4.** Which best describes the errors in sentence 6?

(A) publication title capitalized incorrectly, plural spelled incorrectly

(B) place name not capitalized

(C) misuse of *i* before *e* spelling rule

(D) *i* not changed to *y* before adding suffix

(E) publication title capitalized incorrectly, consonant not doubled before adding suffix

ⒶⒷ●ⒹⒺ **5.** Which of the following should <u>not</u> be done to correct sentence 7?

(A) Capitalize the first letter in *chinese.*

(B) Capitalize the first letter in *siamese.*

(C) Capitalize the first letter in *children.*

(D) Capitalize the first letter in *cat.*

(E) Capitalize the first letter in *tan.*

Chapter Review

B. Editing Sentences

Read the sentences below. Then rewrite each sentence on a separate sheet of paper to correct any capitalization or spelling errors.

1. people celebrate birthdayes in different ways around the World.
   People celebrate birthdays in different ways around the world.
2. In argentina, Italy, and Brazil, the birthday child gets one gentle pull on the earlobe for each Year.
   In Argentina, Italy, and Brazil, the birthday child gets one gentle pull on the earlobe for each year.
3. In vietnam, everyone's birthday is celebrated on the same day. Tet, the vietnamese equivalent of new year's Day, is considered the vietnamese people's Universal Birthday. In Vietnam, everyone's birthday is celebrated on the same day. Tet, the Vietnamese equivalent of New Year's Day, is considered the Vietnamese people's universal birthday.
4. In Hong kong, noodles are a special birthday dish. The long noodles symbolize long lifes.
   In Hong Kong, noodles are a special birthday dish. The long noodles symbolize long lives.
5. on canadian children's birthdays, their noses are greased with butter! The idea is that they will be too slipery for bad luck to catch them. On Canadian children's birthdays, their noses are greased with butter! The idea is that they will be too slippery for bad luck to catch them.
6. In the united states, people eat cake or have a birthday Party.
   In the United States, people eat cake or have a party.
7. Cuban familes celebrate in a way similar to families in the United states, But the partys are generally larger, and they always have piñatas. Cuban families celebrate in a way similar to families in the United States, but the parties are generally larger, and they always have piñatas.
8. at Fifteen, a girl in ecuador wears a pink dress, and her Father presents her with high Heels. At fifteen, a girl in Ecuador wears a pink dress, and her father presents her with high heels.
9. In korea, *Paegil* is a celebration of a child's 100th day.
   In Korea, *Paegil* is a celebration of a child's 100th day.
10. people generally don't celebrate Birthdays in Saudi arabia, but they do celebrate weddings and religious Holidays. People generally don't celebrate birthdays in Saudi Arabia, but they do celebrate weddings and religious holidays.

C. Proofreading and Evaluating an Essay Response

Read the following essay question and one student's response to it. Evaluate the response by answering the questions below.
Answers will vary. Sample answers are shown.

1. Use proofreading symbols to correct any errors in capitalization, punctuation, and spelling.
2. What is the strongest part of the essay? Why? The strongest part of the essay is the conclusion. It restates the thesis while leaving the reader with something to think about.
3. What is the weakest part of the essay? How could it be improved?
   The weakest part of the essay is the body. There are many errors in spelling and capitalization to correct. Also, the examples should be more detailed.

ESSAY QUESTION: To what extent do you agree with the following statement? *The most important thing about a job is the money earned from doing it.* Support your answer with specific reasons and examples.

Proofreading Symbols

Delete.	Switch order.
Add a period.	Add.
Make lowercase.	Capitalize.

1People say Money makes the world go around, but this is not true. 2you can get much more out of a job than the salary. 3Enjoying your job is more important than money

4For example, my Uncle ted is a music teicher, and I know he likies his job a lot. 5He can play many different instruments, like the piano, trumpet, and french horn. 6He's an amazeing musician. 7He always says, "every instrument is worth practicing." 8For another example, my Mom is a bank teller. 9She says that It's exciteing because of all the people you meet.

10when you're choosing a career, You have to think about more than money. 11after all, many americans spend their lifes on the Job. 12People should choose jobs that will bring joy to their lifes

Chapter Review

Frequently Misspelled Words

abbreviate
accidentally
achievement
all right
analyze
anonymous
answer
apologize
appearance
appreciate
appropriate
argument
athlete
attendance
awkward
beautiful
because
beginning
believe
bicycle
brief
bulletin
business
cafeteria
calendar
campaign
cancel
candidate
canoe
cemetery
certain
changeable
characteristic
chorus
clothing
colonel
column
committee
courageous
criticize
curiosity
decision
definite
dependent
description
desirable
despair
development
dictionary
different
disappear
disappoint
discipline
dissatisfied
eighth
eligible
embarrass
enthusiastic
environment
especially
exaggerate
exceed
existence
experience
familiar
fascinating
favorite
February
foreign
forty
fragile
generally
genius
government
grammar
guarantee
height
humorous
immediately
independent

jewelry
judgment
knowledge
laboratory
leisure
library
license
lightning
literature
loneliness
mathematics
minimum
mischievous
misspell
muscle
necessary
neighbor
nickel
niece
ninety
noticeable
nuclear
nuisance
obstacle
occasionally
opinion
opportunity
original
outrageous
parallel
particularly
people
permanent
persuade
pneumonia
possess
possibility
prejudice
privilege
probably
psychology
realize
receipt
receive
recognize
recommend
repetition
restaurant
rhythm
ridiculous
sandwich
schedule
scissors
separate
similar
sincerely
souvenir
specifically
success
surprise
syllable
sympathy
symptom
temperature
thorough
throughout
tomorrow
traffic
tragedy
truly
Tuesday
unnecessary
usable
usually
vacuum
variety
various
vicinity
Wednesday
weird

Commonly Confused Words

accept, except *Accept,* a verb, means "to receive" or "to agree to something." *Except,* a preposition, means "but."

We **accept** the invitation.

Everyone went to the party **except** Julia.

affect, effect *Affect,* typically a verb, means "to influence." As a noun, *effect* means "the result of an action."

Flowers **affect** my allergies.

The **effects** are itchy eyes and a runny nose.

all ready, already *All ready,* a phrase, means "completely ready." *Already,* an adverb, means "before now."

The class is **all ready** for the field trip.

They **already** visited the science museum last year.

borrow, lend *Borrow* and *lend* have opposite meanings. *Borrow* means "to take something temporarily for later return." *Lend* means "to give something temporarily."

May I **borrow** your dictionary?

I will **lend** you my dictionary until tomorrow.

bring, take Use *bring* to refer to an action toward or with the speaker. Use *take* to refer to an action away from the speaker.

Maria will **bring** a camera.

Please **take** the photo album to Mr. James.

desert, dessert As a noun, *desert* is a hot, dry area of land. *Dessert* is a sweet treat.

A lizard rested on a rock in the **desert**.

For **dessert**, we had sliced pineapple and strawberries.

fewer, less Use *fewer* to refer to nouns that can be counted. Use *less* to refer to nouns that can't be counted.

Fewer students performed in this year's talent show.

The committee spent **less** time recruiting acts.

good, well *Good* is always an adjective. *Well* can be an adjective or an adverb. As an adjective, *well* refers to health. As an adverb, *well* means "done in a satisfactory way."

Mr. Yang has a **good** trainer.

On the day of the competition, he felt **well**.

He performed **well** and earned a medal.

it's, its *It's* is a contraction for "it is." *Its* is a possessive pronoun.

We should hurry because **it's** getting late.

Take the dog for **its** daily walk.

lay, lie *Lay* means "to place." *Lie* means "to recline."

Lay the guitar on the table.

If you feel sick, **lie** down and rest.

loose, lose *Loose* means "free or not tied up." *Lose* means "to misplace."

Brave officers captured the **loose** bulls.

They carefully avoided **losing** sight of them.

passed, past *Passed,* a verb, means "went by" or "succeeded." As an adjective, *past* means "of a previous time." As a noun, *past* means "a previous time."

Ramiro **passed** Jake in the hall.

We were happy because we **passed** the test.

Our **past** exams were easier. We had longer study periods in the **past**.

peace, piece *Peace* means "a state of calm or stillness." *Piece* means "a part of something."

We enjoyed the **peace** of the forest.

A small **piece** of rock fell from the mountainside.

their, there, they're *Their* is a possessive pronoun. *There* is a pronoun used to introduce a sentence. *They're* is a contraction for "they are."

Students will showcase **their** best paintings.

There are several students with remarkable talent.

They're the likely winners.

to, too, two *To,* a preposition, means "in the direction of." *Too,* an adverb, means "also" or "very." *Two* is the number 2.

At the concert, Derrick sat **to** the left of Gina.

Lisa joined them, **too.** However, the music was **too** loud for her.

They took **two** photos with the band.

whose, who's *Whose* is an interrogative pronoun. *Who's* is a contraction for "who is."

Whose jacket is this?

Who's missing a jacket?

your, you're *Your* is a possessive pronoun. *You're* is a contraction for "you are."

Your mom is on the phone.

I hope **you're** not in trouble.

Index

U

V

W

Y